Magic Mushrooms

in Religion and Alchemy

Clark Heinrich

Park Street Press
Rochester, Vermont

*For Carolyn, Anandi, and Rama, who have lovingly
and often patiently endured my fevered pursuits.*

Park Street Press
One Park Street
Rochester, Vermont 05767
www.InnerTraditions.com

Park Street Press is a division of Inner Traditions International

LIBRARY OF CONGRESS CATALOGING-IN-PUBLICATION DATA

Heinrich, Clark, 1945-
[Strange fruit]
Magic mushrooms in religion and alchemy / Clark Heinrich.
p. cm.
Includes bibliographical references and index.
ISBN 0-89281-997-9
1. Amanita muscaria—Religious aspects. 2. Christianity and other religions.
3. Religions—History. 4. Elixir of life. I. Title.
BL65.D7 H45 2002
291.3'7—dc21
2002010399

Printed and bound in the United States at Capital City Press

10 9 8 7 6 5 4 3 2 1

This book was typeset in Appoline with Oxalis as the display typeface
Text design by Cynthia Coad
Text layout by Virginia Scott Bowman

Contents

	ACKNOWLEDGMENTS	iv
	A BRIEF EXPLANATION OF AN UNUSUAL BOOK	v
1	BEATING AROUND THE BURNING BUSH	1
2	THE SOMA DRINKERS	8
3	THE FLY AGARIC	13
4	CURIOUS EVIDENCE	19
5	THE DWARF SUN-GOD	28
6	THE RED-EYED HOWLER	38
7	THE SECRETS OF EDEN	64
8	THE PROPHETS OF ANCIENT ISRAEL	71
9	LIVING WATER AND THE BREAD OF LIFE: THE STORY OF JESUS	105
10	THE KNOWERS OF GOD	135
11	THE MYSTERIOUS GRAIL	154
12	ELIXIR: THE SECRET STONE OF ALCHEMY	165
13	AN ARTISTIC CONSPIRACY?	198
14	HEAVEN AND HELL	200
	LAST WORD	206
	APPENDIX: THE LEGEND OF MISKWEDO	209
	NOTES	213
	ILLUSTRATIONS	217
	INDEX	219

Acknowledgments

I WISH TO THANK SEVERAL PEOPLE for their direct or indirect help, support, and encouragement in this project, especially my wife, Carolyn, and daughters, Anandi and Rama, all of whom may be hoping never to hear the word "mushroom" again as long as they live. Thanks for your love and for not locking me out of the house. Thanks to my parents, Ken and Helen, and my three brothers, Jeff, Greg, and Ken, for not being afraid to join me on uncertain journeys. Thanks to Robert Forte for invaluable aid and comfort. I am very grateful to Huston Smith and Frank Barron, two fine and gentle men whose wisdom shines in their eyes. Thank you for having perfected the arts of listening and encouragement and for your pioneering work in the entheogenic realms.

Thanks to Ron Lau and Michael Kilpatrick for unflagging and enthusiastic support. Thanks to Loran Gayton for research assistance on the Grail myths and to Demetrie Tyler for graphics help.

Thanks also to Spalding Gray, who helped me understand that history often depends on who is relating it.

I hope we all meet someday in paradise. I've been there, it's nice.

A Brief Explanation
of an Unusual Book

No one ascends into the heaven which ye seek, unless he who descends
from the heaven which ye do not seek, enlighten him.

Dorn, *Philosophia speculativa*

HISTORY IS NEVER AN ACCURATE portrayal of what has gone before. Based as it is on the interpretation of whatever data might be available, even the best historical record fails at its task of reconstructing the past. Usually the more recent the past event, the closer its reconstruction will be to reality; yet even events that happened only yesterday cannot be recreated perfectly in the present, even with the aid of television or motion pictures. The event is forever gone; what remains as memory is a different thing, however much it may resemble the past. And the more time that passes between an event and its retelling, the less the retelling is likely to resemble what actually happened, especially those events that transpired before the advent of the photographic plate and the audio recording device. Which is another way of saying that our knowledge of world history is sometimes little more than a patchwork of facts and assumptions made by consenting individuals.

All retellings of history that go beyond a mere listing of events, names, and dates are somewhat speculative in nature, but it is religious history that often pushes the art of speculation over the line into fantasy, given the fact that many of the claims of religion are not only unprovable but incredible.

The very nature of religious histories makes them especially vulnerable to interpretation, interpolation and, perhaps especially, exaggeration. "Selective memory" and "invention" have long been the bywords of redactors everywhere whether political or religious, and it's a toss-up if we try to determine which category changes history the most to suit its purposes. We know now that what has come to be regarded as the "truth" within a religious system is really a temporary consensus-reality based on centuries of interpretation and interpolation and is not necessarily factual or accurate (all metaphysics aside). There is ample room for dispute and reinterpretation in every religious and spiritual system, regardless of the current consensus.

It is easy for religions to lose their focus. Rather than remaining, as they began, the means to an end, they often become the end itself. Emphasis switches almost imperceptibly from saving souls to saving and perpetuating the institution and its putative savior, sometimes at any cost.

Suppose the leaders of such an institution discovered an embarrassing or damaging fact from their religion's own history. They could reveal the truth and take the consequences or simply destroy the evidence. Which would they do? If, for example, it were known only by the Vatican that the body of Jesus had in reality been spirited away from its tomb and secretly buried, could anyone seriously entertain the notion that the information would be released? Not for a moment. With that foundation block removed the entire structure of Christianity would collapse like a house of cards, the papacy included.

A given religion does whatever it can to protect and build on the status quo. Scholars working from within a religion—that is, believers—generally aren't looking for anything new in their research; they are seeking confirmation of the official positions. Those doing research from the outside of a system may criticize or reinterpret doctrine, dispute historicity, or, as in the case of the Nag Hammadi texts and the Dead Sea scrolls, work with other scholars to translate and reveal to the world recently discovered documents. Those with an antipathy toward religion might seek to undermine or destroy the credibility of a religious institution, while others, regarding religion as a bothersome anachronism based in fantasy, might simply choose to view the whole field as irrelevant.

What is seldom done by scholars and researchers of any persuasion, however, is to look at religious writings for evidence of secret information that may be encoded within the texts. This is because there are very few to whom the idea even occurs, and also because such secrets, should they exist, would be not only very difficult to detect but also difficult or impossible to verify after so long a time. If today's religions and myths hold dark secrets from their respective beginnings they must have been entombed better than Jesus was.

Yet if such encoding were found to exist it could, depending on the content, force an immediate reevaluation of everything concerned with the given religion or system of belief. It is clear today that some early religions did have secret teachings, even though their contents are not readily traceable in existing texts. We know, for example, that the teachings of Jesus are filled with references to his duplicitous method of teaching "those who have not" (the general public) only by reciting obscure parables of slight spiritual value, while privately giving "those who have" (his inner circle) secret teachings reserved for them alone. We know he did it but we don't know why. What would this breakaway cult have had to hide?

Considering what we know about drug use and group sexual activities in certain early religious cults, there may have been quite a bit to hide. I believe that a number of the writings that have come down to us from ancient religious movements do contain secret *double entendres,* the alternative meanings of which, quite intentionally, are not apparent in a casual reading of the text. Many of these writings contain curious sayings and references that have never been adequately explained or understood; they are seemingly designed to remain forever hidden unless the ruse could be revealed and the passwords made known. I believe I have discovered some of the passwords.

The theme of religious symbolism has been worked to near exhaustion over the course of centuries, but I am speaking of a different kind of symbolism altogether, one that truly throws the two halves of the coin together, in the original sense of the word "symbol," to reveal a secret message and allow entry into the *sanctum sanctorum* of the cult.

I have given new readings to some well known spiritual stories as well as to a number of lesser known and sometimes exceedingly bizarre tales, many of which deal with the use of magical foods and drinks. This is a subject usually given short shrift by scholars and exegetes, an apparent lack of interest I find rather odd given the strange and wonderful things that were said to have happened to the characters who did the eating and drinking.

Some of these stories have assumed the form of myth, while others are still actively promoted as being accurate and true accounts of real events, even to the point of inerrancy. I know it is considered impolite and sometimes dangerous to look critically at religion, but not to do so is to help speed freedom of religion (which includes the freedom not to espouse any religion) on its way to becoming just another revised memory.

Often a religion will claim to own the only (or best) truth in the universe. In giving alternative readings for these various "truths" I am not making any such claim for myself or this book, although I do believe that everything I am proposing is plausible, however unlikely it may seem at first. I also happen to believe it may be true, but belief doesn't prove anything. It's simply belief. Even though my interpretations can't be proved, they can be compared to the accepted or standard interpretations, and this is what I have done, making good use of Occam's Razor in the process.

Carving away at the complicated, irrational, and unnatural explanations offered by theologians for the strange or "miraculous" events recounted in the stories, I didn't stop until all that remained were simple, rational, and natural explanations. Or so they seem to me; some people may feel otherwise. There is already too much religious "truth" being rammed down people's throats for my taste; my ideas are suggestions, not demands.

I call the work a speculative history, though others, after reading it, may prefer to call it a historical fiction. Some will consider much of the material to be blasphemous, shocking, scandalous, or utterly ridiculous, but that is to be expected, even though most religious doctrine is less believable than what you are about to read. "True religion" will withstand the tests of both blasphemy and scrutiny; if none of my speculations ring true they will quickly be forgotten.

More than anything else this is a book of correspondences, a book of parallels. The longer I researched my subject the more astonished I became at the parallels I was finding. After a while, speculating as to the meaning of these parallels became the natural thing to do; therefore, this is also a book of speculations. Quantum physics speaks of possible parallel universes existing alongside the one we know; this book can be thought of as a parallel history. These things may have happened as I am presenting them or they may not have, but one thing is certain: namely, that I have discovered a definite pattern of related symbols in story after story, even stories from different traditions and different parts of the world. As disparate as these stories are they all have in common distinct correspondences to one and the same thing: the beautiful and intoxicating *Amanita muscaria* mushroom, commonly known in English as the fly agaric.

Already I have been accused of being a monomaniac who sees mushrooms everywhere and I understand this accusation, but the truth is I don't see mushrooms everywhere; I just see them in some places where others haven't, and this book shares with the reader my many years of mushroom-sightings. I don't expect that everyone will see what I see. In some stories and artwork it will be easy to find the hidden mushrooms; in others it will be more difficult. The key to my findings is the fly agaric itself and the knowledge of its appearance, life cycle, and effects, all of which will be described in some detail; the many original and unusual color photographs of the mushroom included in the book will greatly help the reader in this regard.

I wanted to see how many locks the fly agaric key might fit and possibly open, and I was amazed at the number of times it appears to do both. This "unlocking" of secrets will unfold throughout the book; I urge the reader not to form premature judgements. One speculation may seem right on the mark, while the next may appear to be nonsense; I freely admit that some assertions are more tenable than others. The continuity of the material will become apparent only when the whole work has been examined: the stories, the parallels, the photographs, and the artwork.

The correspondences contained in the succeeding chapters are too numerous to assign to mere chance or an overactive imagination, although some will do just that. If it is simply a matter of imagination I invite anyone to take any other single plant or fungus (real, not imaginary), or anything else for that matter, and make it fit these stories and works of art as easily as the fly agaric does. The futility of the exercise should become apparent very quickly.

Magic Mushrooms in Religion and Alchemy was originally published in England under the title *Strange Fruit: Alchemy, Religion, and Magical Foods*. This first North American edition, released in a new expanded format, includes ten new illustrations, one of which presents the first archaeological evidence that psychoactive mushrooms were being used in the religions of ancient India. The book is the fruit of many years of research, fieldwork, intuitional reasoning, and what I can only call revelation. I am not a scholar in the traditional sense, and the book does not pretend to be a model of high scholarship; I am, however, a poet and natural philosopher, well used to expressing myself without worrying overmuch about what others will think. As such I am free to speculate where many scholars and academics would not for fear of jeopardizing their reputations. ("But, after all," writes Robert Graves, "what is a scholar? One who may not break bounds under pain of expulsion from the academy of which he is a member.") Is this then a case of the fool rushing in where academics fear to tread? That is for the reader to decide.

Many years ago I decided that I could no longer allow any religion, person, or government to make certain decisions for me, to determine what is best for me or what is true and what is not. Why should I, or any mature person, take another's word, without question, concerning the most important things in life? I don't think we should, and we certainly don't have to. Those who want a real education have to obtain it on their own, sometimes outside the officially sanctioned realms. This can be a lonely or even frightening undertaking, but I believe as the alchemists did that we should investigate nature and experiment when necessary, plumbing the depths of our nascent consciousness and comparing all the versions of reality that we can find or dream up, until ultimately we distill the truth in ourselves. We should seek out the available data, ask the right questions and make up our own minds. Or at least open them.

> Let him who seeks continue seeking until he finds. When he finds, he will become troubled. When he becomes troubled, he will be astonished, and he will rule over the all.
>
> **Jesus, *The Gospel of Thomas***

Good hunting.

1

Beating Around the Burning Bush

There are birds in here
Fire-birds
Phoenixes for excesses
A remedy for ills
Big birds and little birds
and not a few sheep as well
and certainly a scapegoat
Flush them out
and they will flush you out
like they did to Moses
on the mountain
A fruit
A drink
A cup
An altar
A sheep
A bull
A bird
A wheel
The penis of God
The holy cross
The serpent's head bruised by a heel
All are aflame
and all the same
The crown is yours
if you guess their name

THIS BOOK DOES NOT, like Moses, beat around the bush. On the contrary, it cuts to the heart of a number of troubling questions and unsolved mysteries of religious history and mythology, and the solutions it offers may be more troubling than the questions. Any book that attempts to reinterpret a given religious episode or myth will meet with intense scrutiny and skepticism; add drugs and sex to the retelling and scrutiny can turn quickly into outright condemnation. To borrow a phrase, there is something in this book to offend just about everyone, though this certainly is not its purpose.

In order fully to appreciate a play it is necessary for the audience to suspend its disbelief until the play is over; not to do so is to thwart the audience's own intention in seeing the play as well as the author's in writing it. A similar suspension of disbelief is requested from the reader of this book. I have discovered that some people readily accept certain parts of my hypothesis but balk at others, usually those parts that cause them to examine their own religious beliefs. A few of these balkers became so indignant at some of my contentions that further discussion was rendered impossible; hence no further evidence could be brought to bear. If the reader perseveres through the portions of this work that he or she may find unseemly or unacceptable, rather than skipping over them or putting the book down, the troubling parts will at least be understood in the context of the whole work. They still may not be agreeable, but they will be understandable.

I have been interested in religion for as long as I can remember, and not all my memories about the subject are pleasant. There was the time, for example, that my Christian minister uncle came into my room at night and made me ask Jesus to come and live in my heart. I must have been all of five or six years old, but I will never forget the sheer terror that possessed me when I thought that there was really going to be someone else living in my body. I couldn't imagine anything more dreadful or that I wanted less, but still, sobbing and choking, I did what I was told; my uncle had made it very clear what fate awaited me in hell if I had "chosen" not to do so. I imagined hell to be something even worse than the torment I was in at the moment, so I went along with it just to get him out of there. I may have asked Jesus to come into my heart that night, but I don't think the door was open.

I was happy when I later realized that I was still the only one inhabiting my body, but the horrifying experience had left its mark: I became distrustful and nervous anytime religion was mentioned, or, God forbid, when I had to go to church or Sunday school (which has to be one of the more inhumane punishments ever foisted on children). I have a vivid picture in my mind even now of a huge and sour-faced God sitting in heaven with an enormous Black Book on his lap (God was male, of course); he did nothing all day long but watch poor benighted humans make one mistake after another, which he would immediately and with disgust note in his book by putting black marks next to their names, all made with indelible ink. I envisioned a whole chapter devoted to me and my black marks. I was always a nervous kid, but religion had made me nervous long before the nightmare-producing visit of my uncle.

In my earliest memories I lie in bed after saying goodnight to my parents. It was the same every night: the door closed and suddenly I was adrift in a great void, a blackness so deep it frightened me more tangibly than anything revealed in light. At a time when most children my age were not even aware of the word, I was terrified of death. I would quickly say my prayers to prevent imminent disaster and then implore God to bless my family and make me a good little boy, though I knew if by chance I *were* made good it was already too late: I had my own chapter in the Black Book. But hope wells eternal and I would add, "May we all be together in heaven for this many years after we die: one, two, three, four, five . . ." And so I would continue every night, often counting well into the thousands, until I fell asleep. It was a dodge, a way of magically conquering death. It was a child's version of eternity.

This unchildish fear and the desire to be fearless, all somehow mixed with religion, became a preoccupation that I have carried with me all my life, but it has become more than a morbid fear of losing everything and everyone. Instead it has manifested as a deep curiosity about the whole mystery of human life and how we humans react to it, especially to the reality of death and the concept of God. With so many versions of the "truth" to choose from and such a short life to live, it soon became apparent that I had to find my own truth. Who would leave such important work to others? I developed a need to find out what is really going on here; at least as much as I possibly could. I needed to make sense out of a seemingly chaotic and hostile universe so I wouldn't be swamped by the feelings of ennui and despair I had carried for so many years.

Like many others before me, I was driven by these tendencies to a deeper study of religion and philosophy, yet the more I read, the more I realized that something was missing at the core. It was some time before I discovered what it was.

After a while it dawned on me; sometimes the most obvious things are the hardest to see. What I was having trouble finding is the one thing that should never be missing from religion: the personal experience of God in the here and now. Much of philosophy seemed to be too abstract for its own good, while much of what religion offered was pie-in-the-sky schemes of deferred bliss in after-death-only heavens, which is a lot to take on faith. Every religious system has its mystics, of course, those who claim to have made the celestial connection, but they represent only a small fraction of the whole and usually are regarded as a fringe element, a little crazed. Nearly everyone else in religion is dealing with dogmas and rituals handed down from times and cultures much different from their own, the relevance of which ranges from questionable to nonexistent. All of this made me wonder not only what could be sustaining these religious systems today but what may have inspired and created them in the first place. I had an inescapable feeling that in a number of religions "then" and "now" represented two completely different worlds of both thought and practice, far removed from each other.

In the early days of Hinduism, Judaism, and Christianity certain people were always talking with some god or demon or other; it was almost commonplace. Today it is also commonplace, but now we have a name for people who talk to God and the devil: schizophrenic. Were all such stories from the past meant to be taken metaphorically? Do they represent conversations with the gods or the rantings of madmen? What do all the accounts of heavenly discourse really mean? As far as I have been able to determine, there is a major shortage of prophets, saints, and messiahs walking and talking with God in our time, though there is certainly no shortage of pretenders. Are we so much worse than our brothers and sisters of long ago that God no longer deigns to give us even the time of day, not to mention pithy prophecies or unspeakable bliss? And if we *are* that much worse isn't that all the more reason for God to start talking? After all, doesn't God *love* sinners? Simple logic dictates that if it could happen then it can happen now. Or God could be dead, of course, which would explain everything.

Short of the death of God there had to be something that was different in the past, perhaps something in the religious practices themselves, unless people today are having the same kinds of experiences but not recognizing them as such. Because of some decidedly mystical states I had experienced I believed that both alternatives were true. And because of the cause of most of these experiences, I suspected that mind-altering plants may have played a central role in some of those ancient conversations with divinity. If a person of the modern era, with the aid of psychoactive plants, could gain access to the heavenly realms without years and years of practice, then it must have been a method for someone in the past to do the same thing. In any case, personal intervention by a capricious deity seemed the least likely scenario of all. I began reading books that dealt with the beginnings of religions, especially the Judeo-Christian and Hindu-related varieties with which I was most familiar, to see if I could pick up any type of drug-related trail or tale. If the ancients were on to something (or *on* something) I wanted to know about it.

I had been studying for some time with a woman in her nineties who was a mystic and teacher. She taught a loose version of Christianity which I assumed must be more like the original than modern Christianity, for which I had little affinity if not outright antipathy. "Be still and know" was her byword and a quick summation of her teaching. She stressed the need to search the scriptures to find what was hidden there, always stressing the word *search*, which I was already doing. Studying with her reexposed me to the Bible, which I'd never really read when I was raised a nominal Christian. In fact I never read it at all when I was young, not one word, and who can blame me? I wanted no part of this Jesus fellow, this invader of bodies and possessor of souls. To me he didn't seem much different from the demons who supposedly lurked around every corner, also waiting to invade me if I had a weak moment. But now I was interested, so I read and reread the Bible and other related works with an eye toward discerning their mystical contents and secret teachings.

I sensed a lot going on beneath the surface in both the Jewish and Christian Bibles, but all the so-called miracles made the more believable parts hard to accept. There is also a great deal of secrecy evident and what seems like purposeful obfuscation, so much so that it seemed clear to me that if Jesus, for instance, was teaching a system for contacting God, he was deliberately disguising it. Or his redactors were.

At the same time I was studying yoga theory and practice with a Himalayan yogi who hadn't spoken for quite a number of years. The nonspeaking was not because he had nothing to say but because he believed that speaking wasted *prana,* or life force. By not speaking one would conserve prana and thereby have more energy, live longer, and never be at a loss for words. He communicated by writing on a smallish chalkboard. He wrote a *lot.* I studied intimately with him for over twelve years and learned a great deal about Indian religious systems. I became proficient in yoga, both theory and practice, and taught both for many years. I was instructed in the performance of Vedic fire ceremonies, esoteric Himalayan healing rituals, and elaborate Tantra practices. Jnana Yoga, Mantra Yoga, Bhakti Yoga, Karma Yoga, Tantra Yoga, Laya Yoga, Raja Yoga—I learned and practiced all of them. For years I would rise at four in the morning and do four hours of practices to begin my day. I read the Vedas, the Brahmanas, the Upanishads, the Samhitas, the Puranas, the Yoga Sutras, the Epics, and the Commentaries. I was obsessed with "finding God," as though God were hidden somewhere in a box.

The Yoga Sutras in particular present a system for temporarily shutting down the thought processes of the mind and entering states of superconsciousness called *samadhi,* which roughly translates as "with complete higher consciousness and knowledge." I recognized many of the states described in the sutras and in mystical Christianity from my own experiences with psychedelics. The simultaneous study of Indian philosophy and esoteric Christianity served me well in my new line of research.

The idea of drug use in religion is a very controversial subject. It is also a subject about which many people are rather sensitive, preferring to consider such usage as an aberration of the distant past; yet it remains a topic that ignorance will not make disappear. In a time when wars are being waged against drug use and all illegal drugs are lumped together as the enemy, it is more important than ever to speak openly and rationally about drugs, especially those that serve a useful and relatively benign purpose.

It is known that certain religions of antiquity did use drugs, though which drugs they employed remains a matter of speculation and debate. Yet many people both in and out of the field consider such ancient drug use to be largely irrelevant to the study of religion today, and would rather not discuss it, a position I don't quite understand. It seems to me that this information should make an enormous difference in our understanding of a given religion, but very few take the subject seriously.

I knew that certain plants and drugs were capable of imparting feelings of spiritual rapture and bliss, but this seemed to happen almost in spite of religion. Virtually all religions today eschew and condemn the use of drugs, regarding them at best as obstacles on the path to salvation, and at worst as the devil's tools of enslavement. Yet I found references to drug use scattered throughout the scriptures of India, especially within Vedism and Tantra. This is not condoned by the mainstream practitioners of today, of course, nor is it discussed very much.

In Vedic India a drug called *Soma* was drunk, but the plant from which it was made has been a mystery for over two thousand years. Soma's identity has been hotly debated by scholars for well over a century, yet the only thing we can ascertain from this debate is that Soma could not possibly be any of the plants suggested by these same scholars. The plants put forward, Sarcostemma, Ephedra, and others, simply do not produce any effects which even come close to the experiences described by the Soma-drinking poets of the Rig Veda. Why was the identity of Soma lost? The most common explanation is that it was harvested out of existence, which in today's world of disappearing species is not an unreasonable assumption.

Later Tantric rituals called for the use of a drink called *panchamrita*, five nectars, which originally included Soma among the five. *Amrita*, which means "non-death," was a synonym for Soma, the drink that conferred immortality on the imbiber. (*Amrita* is cognate with the Greek *ambrosia*, the immortality-bestowing food of the Greek gods.) Surrogates for Soma such as marijuana and datura, a devastatingly powerful hallucinogen, were employed after Soma became unavailable, and are still used to this day among the "Left-hand," or impure, Tantric sects.

Yoga philosophy mentions drug plants as one of the valid means of attaining *siddhi*, or supernormal power resulting from the practice of samadhi, but fails to mention which plants they might be. The use of drugs for this purpose is frowned upon by modern yoga teachers. The only readily accessible remnant of India's ancient drug use that can be found today is among the many wandering ascetics known as *sadhus*, who spend a good portion of each day preparing and smoking large pipefuls of a varying mixture of hashish, marijuana, tobacco, and sometimes datura.

So my research into religious drug use had barely begun when I came upon actual drug use in Hinduism and its antecedents, a fact long known to scholars but generally unknown in the West. It appeared to be something Indian religion of today would just as soon forget, as though it had been merely a phase, much the way modern parents might regard their teenager's marijuana smoking; but still the fact remains that centuries ago gods and humans alike drank the divine Soma and danced together on the stage of life. Why, I wondered, would they have given it up?

If the great religious systems of India had their beginnings in the cups of the Soma priests, it no longer seemed unreasonable to assume that their Hebrew counterparts and contemporaries may have been doing the same thing, perhaps with the same drug, whatever it was. But my initial enthusiasm soon gave way to disappointment as I read through the Bible. Judaism and Christianity appeared to be strangely lacking in even the mention of drugs, unless I was overlooking some less-than-obvious clues. After all, even if Jews and Christians *had* engaged in the use of sacred drugs it wouldn't necessarily have been incorporated into the state religion as it had been with the Vedic Aryans. The Jewish priests and prophets wielded extraordinary power on the basis of their "special" relationship with Yahweh. If they had used drugs to gain and keep that relationship, as the Vedic priests did, it is quite likely that they kept it a secret among themselves.

As I thought about this I realized that in both the Jewish and Christian Bibles there are a number of significant episodes involving eating and drinking which led to, or at least preceded, a dramatic change in the consciousness of the person or persons involved. People raised within a given religious system, as I had been, tend not to question what is regarded as scripture or the Word of God. These things just happened as written and that's that. If a particular passage is problematic it can be explained away as metaphor. And most importantly, "miracles" and conversation with God happened then but don't happen now, which is one line I could never swallow. A few well-aimed questions, I found, opened up a rather large can of worms.

What, for instance, was the all-important fruit eaten by Eve and Adam in the Garden of Eden? It gave them knowledge yet it didn't kill them as God had told them it would. What was the mysterious flame-colored god-plant encountered by Moses on the Mountain of God that gave him amazing power, courage, and tricks enough to defeat Pharaoh's magicians? What was the "cake" that an angel gave to Elijah when he too was on his way to the Mountain of God and which gave him the endurance to walk, on the strength of that food alone, for forty days? What was the curious "scroll" that an angel gave Ezekiel to eat that lifted him up to heaven? Or the similar scroll eaten by John on Patmos so that he could prophesy? Or the sacred meals of the Essenes and the Gnostics; what were these and why were they secret? And what about Jesus, himself the bread of life and the human dispenser of living waters, whose very flesh and blood were eaten in a ceremony of ritual cannibalism? A can of worms indeed, and they were crawling all over the Bible.

If a drug had been used by the biblical prophets, what could it have been? There was no science of chemistry then, so it had to have been some kind of plant, a plant that could be ingested both as a solid and as a liquid. And it had to have been a powerful psychedelic in order to convince people that they were being lifted up to heaven for conversations with God. What desert plant could fit the bill? Peyote could, but it isn't found in the Middle East, at least not today. Perhaps it had been harvested out of existence there as Soma supposedly had been in India. Maybe those itinerant drug peddlers, the Magi, had introduced some dried nonnative species from the East into the region. Maybe it wasn't a desert plant but a mountain plant. Maybe, maybe, maybe. This was going to take some detective work. And as luck would have it someone else was already on the case.

2

The Soma Drinkers

Try to grab the restless Soma and he breaks away
and overpowers everything.

Rig Veda 8.79.1

R. GORDON WASSON WAS as unlikely a gumshoe as I could imagine. A successful investment banker until his retirement, he was conservative in his thinking and patrician in his bearing. His avocation surprised everyone: he was an expert amateur mycologist, and his speciality was the psychoactive fungi, especially the psilocybin-related species. He was the first to document, in 1957, the existence of a still-functioning mushroom cult among the Mazatec Indians in the mountains of Mexico. His experiences with psilocybin mushrooms and the *curandero* María Sabina were recorded that year in a *Life* magazine photoessay. He later published a full account of his research in a book, *María Sabina and Her Mushroom Velada,* which included recordings of the songs and prayers she used during her ceremonies. What interested me even more than this was a book Wasson published in 1968 entitled *Soma, the Divine Mushroom of Immortality.* In this book Wasson presented the radical hypothesis that the Soma drink of the Vedic Aryans was made from the red and white *Amanita muscaria* mushroom, known in English as the fly agaric. The only significant problem with this theory was that Wasson was unable to verify personally the effects of fly agaric consumption.

This is not to say Wasson didn't consume the mushroom and experience effects; he did. But the effects he experienced were something less than spectacular and certainly not of the kind so glowingly reported in the Vedas. One member of his original fly agaric research team, a Japanese man, did report a euphoric episode after toasting his mushrooms over an open fire, but Wasson was unable to duplicate the results himself. Because of his failure in this regard and the fact that most people (at least in the West) who eat the mushroom rarely experience anything more gratifying than slightly lucid dreams, copious perspiration, and nausea, Wasson's conclusion that Soma was the fly agaric has been doubted by some researers who are otherwise convinced by the preponderance of textual and photographic evidence he produced. Wasson was so sure that he was correct in his identification of Soma, and so frustrated and perplexed at not being able to find a Westerner who had gained access to Soma's considerable gifts, that toward the end of his life he postulated that perhaps Caucasians were genetically unable to process the drug.

Even if this were so, why should this lack of experiential evidence deter us from accepting his proposition? What *should* we experience if we were to drink the true Soma? The Rig Veda gives us the answer in no uncertain terms. A brief but representative sample of the huge corpus of verses tells the story:

> The white goblet overflowing with cow's milk, the finest honey, the clear [Soma] juice offered by the priests—now let the generous Indra raise it to drink until ecstatic with Soma; let the hero raise it to drink until ecstatic with Soma.[1]

> Where the high priest speaks rhythmic words, O Purifier, holding the pressing stones, feeling that he has become great with Soma, giving birth to joy through the Soma, O drop of Soma flow for Indra.

> Where the inextinguishable light shines, the world where the sun was placed, in that immortal world, unfading world, O Purifier, place me. O drop of Soma, flow for Indra.

> Where they move as they will, in the triple dome, in the third heaven of heaven, where the worlds are made of light, there make me immortal. O drop of Soma, flow for Indra.

> Where there are joys and pleasures, gladness and delight, where the desires of desire are fulfilled, there make me immortal. O drop of Soma, flow for Indra.[2]

> I have tasted the sweet drink of life, knowing that it inspires good thoughts and joyous expansiveness to the extreme, that all the gods and mortals seek it together, calling it honey [Soma].

> When you penetrate inside, you will know no limits, and you will avert the wrath of the gods . . .

> We have drunk the Soma; we have become immortal; we have gone to the light; we have found the gods. What can hatred and the malice of a mortal do to us now, O immortal one?

The glorious drops that I have drunk set me free in wide space . . .

Inflame me like a fire kindled by friction; make us see far; make us richer, better. For when I am intoxicated with you, Soma, I think myself rich . . .

Weakness and diseases have gone; the forces of darkness have fled in terror. Soma has climbed up in us, expanding . . .

The drop we have drunk has entered our hearts, an immortal inside mortals. O fathers, let us serve that Soma with the oblations and abide in his mercy and kindness.

Soma, you give us the force of life on every side. Enter into us, finding the sunlight, watching over men. O drop of Soma, summon your helpers and protect us before and after.[3]

A few verses like this and we quickly grasp the reason that the Soma plant was made a god, for what are these flights of rhetoric if not divinely inspired? The Soma plant was condensed God. And those who pressed out its intoxicating blood and drank it felt the god come to life within them and were lifted up in spirit to the heavenly realms of endless light. Naturally Wasson's critics were looking for evidence that the fly agaric could produce similar effects and for the most part such evidence was sorely lacking. Certain critics who ate the mushroom themselves only to have rather mundane or sickening experiences became even more convinced that the Soma mystery remained unsolved. They began putting forth their own candidates, some of which (in their effects) approached the level of bliss described in the Rig Veda, yet none of which matched all the other characteristics of Soma in the way that the fly agaric does.

What does all this talk of Soma and the fly agaric mushroom have to do with the magical foods and drinks of the Bible? The first clues lie in Wasson's discussion of the ancient legends from various cultures concerning the Tree of Life. He mentions the biblical Tree of Life and Tree of Knowledge, both which were said to grow in the Garden of Eden, and argues convincingly that these two trees were probably one and the same and refer to the birch tree, regarded in the countries of the northern latitudes as both a literal and figurative tree of life.

The birch is a literal tree of life because it is host to a particular type of shelf fungus that grows on the trunk. The top of the fungus is extremely hard and impervious to water; the underside is completely dry and is commonly used as tinder. Our word "punk" in its sense of tinder comes from the name of this fungus among the Uralic peoples. A person caught in a snowy forest would regard the source of good tinder as a true tree of life—his own. This same birch is also a tree of knowledge because it is one of the favored host trees of the fly agaric, used since time immemorial by the northern peoples for attaining the knowledge of the gods. It is still used today by some Siberian tribes.

Wasson thought that the devilish knowledge-giving fruit eaten by Eve and Adam was this same mushroom, though at the time *Soma* was written he thought the Garden of Eden story was a retelling of an older northern myth and didn't represent mushroom use by ancient Jews. In his last book, *Persephone's Quest,* Wasson rethought the matter and says the story does represent ancient Jewish mushroom use, the holy trees of Eden representing the cedar, fir, and other conifers that grow in the Middle East, rather than the birch. I offer my own interpretation of the story in the chapter on Judaism.

I took to heart Wasson's hints about the fruit of Eden. The experiences described in the Rig Veda seemed, on first analysis, to have much in common with the cosmic eating and drinking episodes of the Bible. I needed to examine the biblical texts more carefully in the light of the Vedas to see if there really was a correspondence. I knew there was a plethora of prophesying and nay-saying in the Bible, but what about bliss and light? Did these have a place in the Judeo-Christian purview? It seems they did, as these verses testify:

Who will give us sight of happiness, many say. Show us the light of your face, turned toward us. Yahweh, you have given more joy to my heart than others ever knew, for all their corn and wine.[4]

Yahweh is my light, my salvation, whom need I fear?[5]

. . . how precious, God, your love . . . [Men] feast on the bounty of your house, you give them drink from your river of pleasure; yes, with you is the fountain of life, by your light we see the light.[6]

Light dawns for the virtuous, and joy for upright hearts.[7]

Yahweh, my god, how great you are! Clothed in majesty and glory, wrapped in a robe of light![8]

For the upright he rises like a lamp in the dark, he is merciful, tender-hearted, virtuous.[9]

As your word unfolds it gives light, and the simple understand.[10]

The people that walked in darkness have seen a great light; on those who live in a land of deep shadow a light has shone. You have made their gladness greater, you have made their joy increase . . .[11]

. . . and that life was the light of men, a light that shines in the dark, a light that darkness could not overpower.[12]

You were darkness once, but now you are light in the lord; be like children of light, for the effects of the light are seen in complete goodness and right living and truth.[13]

. . . it is all that is good, everything that is perfect, which is given us from above; it comes down from the Father of the lights . . .[14]

. . . [it was] God who called you out of darkness into his wonderful light.[15]

God is light; there is no darkness in him at all. [16]

The Vedic poets sang of their personal experience of light and joy; so, apparently, did their Jewish and Christian counterparts. Now my task was threefold. First, for my own satisfaction, I needed to determine whether or not the fly agaric was capable of producing such experiences. Wasson's proofs in this regard were not entirely convincing. Truly speaking, the only way I could ever be sure was to eat the mushroom myself, though with its less-than-desirable reputation I found myself wishing Wasson's data were stronger. (I did subsequently try the mushroom and after much trial and error was supremely successful in my attempt to have experiences such as those described above; these experiences are described in detail in chapter 14.) Second, I needed to review the Rig Veda to see if I could find other verses which described fly agaric. If this mushroom had actually played such a prominent role in the formation of Indian religions then it should be found in other Indian scriptures and myths as well, so I would not confine my search to the Rig Veda alone. Third, I would take the fly agaric key to see what locks it opened in the Bible and elsewhere, especially in those places where profound spiritual experiences seemed out of place or out of character, such as in the Grail myths or among the alchemists.

But first things first: what is it about the fly agaric that caused Wasson to suspect that it was the ancient and long-lost Soma?

3

The Fly Agaric

This work comes about as suddenly as the clouds
come from heaven.

Theatrum chemicum

THE FIRST SIGHT OF THE FLY AGARIC growing in the wild can be a little disconcerting. With its base and stalk of the purest white and its perfectly formed cap a fiery blood-red set about with flecks of white, this mushroom is no shrinking violet. It is a presence, a rapidly appearing and expanding force come seemingly from out of nowhere, self-generating yet the spawn of thunderstorms, breaking open the earth to reveal its power and glory to the world. "Here I am," it says.

The mushroom lives for the most part underneath the ground as a mass of white, threadlike tubes called a mycelium. Fly agaric mycelia will grow only in mycorrhizal (symbiotic) association with the rootlets of certain trees, chiefly birch, pine, fir, and oak, although fly agaric has been found growing under a number of other trees as well, including a number of other conifers and eucalyptus. Apart from the favored hosts, what is important to note is that *the fly agaric will never be found growing where there are no trees.* This fact figures prominently in its mythology.

When the first major rains of the season (which season depends on the locale) seep down to the mycelium it begins to send up toward the surface individual specialized threads that will become the fruiting bodies above the ground, what we commonly know as mushrooms. The mushroom first takes form just below the surface, where it creates an egg-shaped mass. The "egg" is a pure and brilliant white at this stage as it is covered with what is called the universal veil. This veil is differentiated into pointed cells in the portion that covers the red cap. Contiguous at first, these pointed cells help to break up the soil or leaves that cover the mushroom in its infancy. When the cap expands to a certain point the egg shape changes to a figure eight shape. It looks like two spheres stacked one on top of the other. As the cap expands so does the stalk, hidden from view until such time as the cap breaks apart from the base. When this happens the stalk is revealed, and the mushroom now resembles a dumbbell set on end.

The expanding cap causes the cells of the universal veil to separate, allowing the blood-red color of the cap to show through. At the same time the cap begins to pull away from the stalk and turn upwards, like an umbrella. As it does so it stretches out a new veil, called the annulus, which hides the gills from view. It is attached to the stalk and to the outer circumference of the cap, stretching taut as the cap expands and finally tearing away from the cap to hang skirtlike on the stalk. When the annulus drops, the mushroom's spore producers, the gills, are exposed on the underside of the cap. They are pure white, and somewhat resemble feathers. The gills are extremely efficient, producing literally millions of microscopic spores during the mushroom's short life. The spores, also white, fall to the ground below the mushroom and are also blown virtually all around the world. Each spore is capable, under the proper conditions, of establishing a new mycelium under any compatible tree.

In the process of expanding, the cap will turn itself inside out, creating a cup shape. The white gills then form the convex side of the cup while the red portion of the cap forms the concave inside. If flies lay eggs on the mushroom, a common occurrence, the resulting worms will usually destroy the mushroom before it gets to this stage. If rains persist during growth the mushroom could rot at any point in its cycle. If sunshine and breezes hold sway the mushroom can dry while standing, which produces specimens that are highly prized by Siberian users. The outer edge of the drying cap then curls back under and the whole cap can take on a metallic sheen ranging in color from red-orange to golden or bronze. The whole process, from egg to cup, can take from five to ten days, possibly more. Fly agaric mycelia generally fruit only once each year for a period averaging four to six weeks.

The size of each mushroom is extremely variable due mainly to differences in soil and weather. I have seen mature specimens scarcely one inch tall and even less than that across the cap, and I have seen specimens a foot tall and a foot across that looked more like small tables than mushrooms.

What I have described thus far is common knowledge among mycologists; it is when the effects of consuming the mushroom are described that opinions vary, and vary widely. I will describe effects that I have personally experienced as well as those I have heard about. The effects vary from mushroom to mushroom and it is not possible to tell before-hand what sort of effects will be experienced; this has led to the fly agaric being considered an unreliable intoxicant, which generally speaking is true. To consider it an ineffective intoxicant on the basis of its unreliability, however, is to make a rash assumption and a false one. The Taoist principle that "perseverance furthers" is nowhere truer than with *Amanita muscaria.*

A caveat is in order at this point. I am not encouraging the reader or anyone else to eat the fly agaric or drink its expressed juice. While it can be a literally enlightening experi-ence, it also can be rather harrowing and extremely unpleasant, and there is no way of telling at the outset which it will be. There is also the possibility, however unlikely after viewing the photographs in this book, that someone will mistakenly pick and eat one of the *deadly* species of *Amanita,* resulting in either a liver transplant or, more likely, a horri-ble and painful death.

While there have been a few unsubstantiated reports of persons dying after eating vast quantities of *Amanita muscaria,* there are only two recorded deaths from eating the mush-room (actually one from *Amanita muscaria* and one from *Amanita pantherina*); both of these fatalities involved persons who were elderly and infirm (Ott, 1993). One Siberian tribe believes that eating ten or more dried caps can be fatal, but this again is anecdotal (we should remember that eating too much of *anything* can be fatal). That such deadly rumors about the fly agaric even exist should give pause to the overly eager person.

There will probably be some, however, who choose to ignore these and other warnings and proceed with personal experimentation. To these people, in the interests of safety, I'll make a few recommendations. *Make absolutely sure you know which mushroom you are eating* and eat only thoroughly dried (or cooked), mature specimens. It is my experience that immature and/or fresh specimens are more toxic than mature, dry specimens and much more likely to produce an unpleasant reaction. Dried specimens are also much smaller and lighter, and therefore easier to ingest. *NEVER eat an* Amanita *specimen that is either all white or of a greenish hue:* these may be deadly species. Begin very slowly, consuming no more than one cap, preferably less, over the course of an hour or more, and then assess your condition. Sometimes the full effects are not felt for two hours or more after inges-tion. Proceed with caution, as the dosage is cumulative.

Among experienced users in Siberia three dried caps is considered the average effective dose, though for a novice this could be considerably too much. This problem is com-pounded by the fact that *number* is an unreliable guide in determining dosage, as is size: the active ingredients of *Amanita muscaria* vary considerably from mushroom to mush-room. The age and weight of the consumer should also be taken into account. *Any experi-mentation should be done in safe, protected surroundings with a sitter who is not intoxicated.* The following paragraphs describe some of the effects that users may notice.

Nausea in varying degrees is commonly experienced in the early stages, though some people never feel nauseous. The nausea may pass quickly or may remain as the distinctive feature of the experience. Vomiting is not altogether uncommon either, and usually ends the nausea, but not necessarily; in fact the nausea and vomiting can continue for hours. The nausea of such intense sessions is sometimes abated by passing out, an event that, should it occur, is not at all voluntary. This unconscious state can mimic death to the extent that people have been thought dead when discovered by others. (Sounds like a lot of fun so far, doesn't it?) This dying-that-is-not-dying motif is present throughout the hidden mythology of the fly agaric, as we shall see. Intense perspiration also becomes apparent in the early stages, sometimes in unbelievable amounts. "Rivers of perspiration" is a term I have heard used to describe it.

Vision distortion is another common feature of fly agaric intoxication. Users may find it impossible to focus on anything more than a few feet away, or anything at all, while moving an object close to the eye may bring it into sharp focus, as though it were under a microscope; this condition is known as macropsia. These distortions can be mild or severe, depending on the dosage. This temporary change in vision presents a distinct short-term danger to the user. Driving a car would be a big mistake. Distant objects are not only out of focus when the user is in this condition; they can be unrecognizable. Getting out of the woods might be considerably more difficult than getting in.

The unique nature of this visual condition has led to many of the photographs in this book. By using extension tubes between the camera body and lens I have attempted to recreate some of the visual effects experienced during fly agaric intoxication, especially magnification of objects and very shallow depth of focus. Seeing the fly agaric in this way offers clues to the mushroom's place in history and legend which may not have been apparent otherwise.

Increased saliva flow accompanies all of this. Saliva pools at the back of the throat as though someone had turned on a tap.[17]

Once the nausea goes away, if it does, things start to look up. Sometimes a tremendous vitality is felt, as though the user could conquer the world, or perhaps carry it; Atlas comes to mind. Along with this feeling of tremendous strength some people experience a powerful urge to speak about the godliness and wonderful power they are experiencing. In this state one feels incapable of saying anything that is not true, while what is said is spoken with great conviction, passion and, so it seems at the time, eloquence. Yet sometimes in the midst of all this power comes a contentment that obviates the need for strength. As the Rig Veda poet sang, "What can harm me? I have drunk the Soma!" Depending on the dosage and certain other factors, this feeling of contentment can generalize throughout the body into elation or euphoria.

The Yoga Sutras of Patanjali say that when one is well practised in samadhi the thoughts of people nearby are revealed; in other words, one-way telepathy takes place automatically. This same phenomenon can occur under the influence of the fly agaric. If two persons are under the influence the telepathy is two-way and actual conversations can take place without a word being spoken. I realize this sounds fantastic if not unbelievable, and at this point I have no proof to offer other than my own testimony and that of a friend, although the phenomenon should be possible to test. I describe my own attempts at testing telepathy in chapter 14.

The elation and euphoria, if they are attained, can amplify to the point of what can best be described as bliss. I would use the term "ecstasy" except that its real meaning is "standing outside," that is, being beside oneself. The bliss experienced with fly agaric *is* oneself; the body is fully involved. It is as if every pore of the body were a sexual organ in orgasm, and I am not overstating things.

Alternating with this extremely intense state are others in which it feels as if absolutely nothing is going on; as if the user hadn't consumed anything. The only difference between this state and ordinary reality is that in this state one doesn't *care* that it feels like ordinary reality; one is as content without the bliss as with it.

Often the fly agaric seems to act almost as an anti-hallucinogen. By this I mean that the changes rung by the mushroom, though incredible, often do not include what are ordinarily called hallucinations or visions; and sometimes the "higher" one goes the less appears to be happening, that is if one is expecting something along the lines of LSD or psilocybin visions. One tends to see things just as they are, without a lot of mental overlay, and they shine in their essential thing-ness. This again is a defining feature of samadhi as described by Patanjali in the Yoga Sutras.

While the bliss-state I have described might appear to be the apotheosis of the fly agaric experience, it is not. The contentment earlier referred to is partly due to one of the mushroom's strange side effects. To better explain it I go again to the Yoga Sutras. Sutra number two, which may be the shortest statement of an entire religious philosophy in existence, says, "Yoga is the cessation of thought-waves in the mind." Then, we are told in sutra three, the seer abides in itself. The word *yoga*, usually understood in the West as bodily contortions, means union of the individual with God or the Self. Patanjali is saying that such union is automatically achieved when, and if, one can bring the ceaselessly breaking thought-waves to a halt for a certain length of time.

The usual Western reaction to the idea of stopping the mind is incredulity: why would anyone want to become unconscious? That's a good question but the wrong one, because when this subtlest of mental states is realized quite the opposite of unconsciousness is experienced; rather, there is a tremendous increase in consciousness, as though one's ordinary, mundane mind had been subsumed by the very mind of God. The experience is sublime.

Yet what is extremely simple in concept can prove exceedingly difficult in practice, which is why dozens of additional sutras were appended to the only vital information. Patanjali links thinking with breathing. Breathing can be thought of as a sort of bellows for the coals of thought. An entire and complex branch of Yoga called *pranayama* developed out of this relationship. When one is in a state of bliss the breath, as a matter of course, becomes very calm and sometimes stops for periods of time. Pranayama tries to reverse this process. It seeks to induce the bliss state by first calming or stopping the breath. It takes a great deal of practice.

The mushroom, however, can bring this about as a matter of course. After a certain threshold has been crossed thoughts are reduced when one takes the fly agaric. Whether the mushroom acts first on the mind, calming it and thereby calming the breath, or first calms the breath, which causes the mind to follow suit, I don't know; perhaps it works on both at once. What I do know is that if everything goes right and the mind becomes like a clear pool in which no ripple stirs the surface, light breaks. In the midst of darkness, light visible to the mind's eye breaks above the head and floods the universe and everything in it. If this is not God it is so far above anything else of value that one instantly ceases trying to conceive of anything higher. It is joy incomprehensible; it is peace that passes understanding; yet it is both comprehended and understood in the secret chamber of the mind that stands forever above rational thought. This is the apotheosis of which I spoke; this is the revelation of, the creation of, divinity.

4

Curious Evidence

"Begin at the beginning," the King said, very gravely,
"and go on till you come to the end: then stop."

Lewis Carroll

SOMA WAS A GOD for the Vedic Aryans; he was also a plant and the intoxicating drink made from the plant. An important factor in Wasson's identification of Soma is the curious fact that in the Rig Veda verses composed during the time Soma was still being used, no mention is made of the plant's roots, leaves, blossoms, or seeds; an omission that would, be very unusual unless the plant being described is a mushroom, notably lacking in those attributes.

Soma was always described as growing in the mountains, which in India is the only place the fly agaric is found, growing in pine and birch forests. Soma was red in most descriptions, the color of fire or the rising sun, or golden-yellow, or reddish-brown, and the color was said to be brilliant and lustrous. The Soma plant was so brilliant that the god Soma was often identified with Surya, the sun-god and Agni, the fire-god; but just as often he was called a bull, a bull who was forever sharpening his horns. Some modern researchers have used Soma's "bull" epithet as proof that Soma was not *Amanita muscaria* but a species of the *Psilocybe* genus, some of which will grow only in the dung of ruminants such as cattle. Wasson's explanation was that calling Soma a bull was a reference to the amazing power the fly agaric sometimes exhibits when it bursts through the ground, occasionally splitting rocks or roots as it does so.

This no doubt is part of the answer, but overlooked by both Wasson and his critics is the distinctly "horned" appearance of the young mushroom just after it first makes itself visible (plate 1). A bull sharpens his horns by digging up the ground with them. The Rig Veda poet says that Soma, the terrifying bull, bellows and tears up the ground, sharpening his shining horns. The fly agaric appears to do the same thing as it breaks up the ground with its own shining white "horns" (plate 2). And because bulls are known for their powerful sexuality, the fact that in its early stages the mushroom resembles a large red-tipped penis supplies a third reason to call Soma a bull.

Other common Rig Veda names for Soma are "mainstay of the sky," "navel," "single eye," "pillar of the sky," and "fire," all of which can easily be understood by looking at various photographs of the mushroom. One curious and especially telling name for Soma is "not-born one-foot" *(Aja Ekapada),* a reference to the mushroom's appearing without the benefit of parents, and to the fact that it stands on only one "foot" and one "leg."

A number of references are made to the Soma plant's "head," his "stalk," and his "udder." In fly agaric terms the "head" is the cap and the "stalk" is the stem. "Stalk" in Sanskrit has the alternative meaning of "shoot," which sometimes is used to refer to the whole Soma plant and corresponds to the whole mushroom. The "udder" is again the cap, and refers to the expanded, breast-shaped stage of the mushroom's development, as well as to the dried cap that has been put into water. After soaking for some time the cap absorbs water and expands, reinflating itself; it is then pressed, or "milked" of its juices. Because the mushroom releases its virtues in water, the expressed liquid contains the mushroom's intoxicating chemicals.

One unusual feature of the fly agaric that led Wasson to feel sure he had correctly identified Soma is that its active ingredients pass unmetabolized into the urine of its consumer. While there are a number of Rig Veda verses that speak of Soma's transit through the body, Wasson cites one in particular that speaks of the "swollen" officiants who piss the flowing Soma.[18] Elsewhere in the text the vivifying rains are referred to as showers of urine, an extremely odd metaphor unless urine had its own vivifying properties; the only time it does is when it contains chemicals from the fly agaric. It takes a special kind of dedication and detachment to experiment with drinking one's urine. Its use as a beverage is not something I had considered prior to my knowledge of the fly agaric; yet sometimes in the interest of science one must do the dangerous or difficult thing that no one else wants to do, visceral resistance or no. I believe I am presenting the only first-hand research on the subject.

Two other significant texts are brought in by Wasson to support his urine-drinking hypothesis. The first is from the Persian Zend Avesta,[19] in which Zoroaster asks when practitioners will get rid of the "urine of drunkenness" that the priests have been using to delude the people. He was referring to the cult of *Haoma,* the Persian equivalent of the Soma cult. During the great Aryan migrations of circa 1500 B.C.E., one branch went into what is now India while another went into the Iranian plateau. "Haoma" is the Persian pronunciation of "Soma." Certain priests of the cult apparently were using the Haoma urine in an unscrupulous way (my speculations as to what they were doing appear below).

Whether Zoroaster was opposed to urine-drinking in particular or to the use of the fly agaric in general is unknown, but it *is* known that he received the "drink of omniscience" from Ahura Mazda, and it must not have been Haoma urine. It has recently been proposed that Haoma was not fly agaric but Syrian rue, *Paganum harmala*.[20] The above reference from the Avesta suggests that the fly agaric was the original plant, as in India, but was replaced by a more available plant and one perhaps more predictable in its effects.

The second passage Wasson cites is from the Indian epic the Mahabharata.[21] The god Krishna has offered a boon to the sage Uttanka. Uttanka requests water whenever he wants it, and Krishna agrees. All the sage needs to do is think of Krishna and he will have water. One day he gets thirsty and thinks of Krishna, expecting thereby to get water as promised. Instead he sees a filthy "untouchable,"an outcast, surrounded by dogs. The man is urinating a copious stream and calls out to Uttanka to come and drink. Uttanka is not thrilled by the offer, but the untouchable keeps ordering him to drink. Uttanka refuses and the pissing man vanishes. Then Krishna speaks to Uttanka, telling him that he has been offered water *in the proper form* but was unable to recognize it. Krishna explains that he had ordered Indra, the storm-god, to give *amrita* (Soma) to Uttanka, but Indra protested that mortals should not drink amrita. Krishna insisted and Indra finally relented, saying he would only give the amrita in the form of an untouchable. So the storm god took the form of an outcast and offered Uttanka "amrita" from his penis.

This brief story by itself is almost enough to prove that the fly agaric was once used in India as an intoxicating drink.[22]

Wasson offers further support for his urine hypothesis by citing ancient Chinese accounts of the religion of Mani, a Persian version of Gnosticism than began about a thousand years after Zoroaster and spread to China around 700 C.E. In these documents a Chinese official is listing the "evil" practices of the Manichaeans, among which is that the Manichaeans use urine (the inference is *human* urine) in their rituals and for their ablutions, a strange practice unless urine had been elevated to divine status as it had among the Aryans of India. Wasson completes his suggestion by noting that the modern Parsi religion is a descendant of the Zoroastrian religion; in their rituals they drink token amounts of bull's urine which, Wasson believed, is probably a throwback to the practice of urine-drinking in the ancient Haoma religion of pre-Zoroastrian times.

The veneration of urine is prevalent even today among Hindus in India. The urine of cattle is used as an antiseptic and for ritual bathing. One's own urine is often drunk as a tonic. Why would urine-drinking persist in a scrupulously hygienic group such as the Brahmins unless at one time the drinking of urine carried its own reward? Drinking Soma urine had such a salutary effect that it generalized to urine without Soma, as though drinking it anyway must still have some good effects.

The *guru* system in India remains as a remnant of the time when the guru was a Soma priest and could offer the disciple a true taste of the other world in the Soma cup. We know that the priests drank the expressed juice of the plant; the manner in which it was shared with others is unknown. Another unusual remnant practice may hold at least a partial answer. Among the circles of gurus and their followers the *prasad* of the guru is thought to have special merit, even supernatural power. Prasad means "holy food or drink"; it becomes holy when it is offered to God or touched by the guru. It is a common practice for disciples to eat the leftovers on a guru's plate, for example; these are people who would regard the same practice with someone else's food as unthinkable. I was told by a Himalayan yogi that as a special blessing a guru will sometimes give a disciple a small amount of the guru's urine to drink as prasad. I have since come to find out that the practice is quite common. What could this be but a remnant of the ancient Soma cult and its supercharged urine?

Consider this scenario: a guru or priest, in private, eats a large quantity of fly agarics, washing them down with water, or drinks a large amount of prepared Soma. After a period of time the guru's urine will contain the full effects of all the mushrooms or Soma previously consumed, and in a readily assimilable form that somehow bypasses the negative effects of the original forms of the substance. The guru draws off a cup of urine and gives it to a disciple, who is unaware that the guru has taken Soma, and tells the disciple to drink it. It is prasad, says the guru. A good disciple does whatever is requested by the guru even if the reasons for the request are not apparent. The disciple drinks the urine and soon discovers that the guru is indeed a holy man: even his waste products can transport one to heaven.

It is easy to see how a little deceit could go a long way in such situations. It is very important for most gurus to be regarded by their followers as having supernatural powers; the system is set up in such a way that this belief is being continually fed. The scenario presented above is not as unlikely as one might think. The following story illustrates this quite well.

Many people are familiar with Ram Dass's book *Be Here Now*. Ram Dass is the former Richard Alpert, who was fired from the Harvard faculty in the sixties ostensibly for experimenting with LSD. His cohort Timothy Leary left Harvard at the same time. Suddenly opened up to the spiritual side of life as a result of his experimentation, Alpert set off to India looking for spiritual adepts. In the book, which he wrote when he returned to the United States, we are informed that he had with him on his journey quite a few tablets of very pure LSD, which he was inviting various "holy men" and wandering ascetics to sample.

After meeting his guru, Neem Karoli Baba, in the Himalayan foothills, Alpert told him about LSD and his own spiritual experiences with it. The guru asked to see some, and was handed three tablets containing 305 micrograms each, which is about nine normal doses.

Alpert describes his horror as he watched the guru pop the tablets into his mouth and swallow; then, thinking "This should be interesting," he settled back to watch what would happen. Nothing happened. After an hour had gone by, plenty of time to be strongly feeling the effects, he asked the guru how he was feeling and he replied, "Same as always," or words to that effect. The guru's condition didn't change over the course of the day and Alpert was amazed, and convinced of his new guru's supernatural status.

The man with whom I studied yoga was there too. At the time he was running and building the guru's five ashrams and serving as his right-hand man. The guru did little else but sit with people, accept the worship (and money) of his disciples, sing, and eat. My teacher ran the details of the whole show and taught yoga. He gave me his account of what happened that day with the LSD.

Simply put, the guru palmed the LSD tablets and didn't swallow anything but air. Many Indian gurus are adept at sleight of hand and small magic tricks, and are not always above using a little subterfuge "for the good of the disciple."[23] But the story doesn't end with palming the LSD. The guru later ground the tablets into powder and mixed it with a little of the fine white ash from his sacred fire. This he then gave to two unsuspecting disciples who had been visiting from a distant place and were now departing. Ash from a guru's fire is considered prasad and yes, it is eaten. I don't know anything of the men's journey home, but it was probably quite eventful, especially considering the Himalayan roads, and filled with wondrous exclamations about the guru's tremendous powers.

Along Comes Allegro

John Allegro was an Oxford-educated philologist and Hebrew scholar, one of the original team of scholars (and the only humanist) who began working on the Dead Sea scrolls, first found at Qumran in 1947. In 1956 Allegro alienated most of the other members of the scrolls team by claiming in a BBC interview that the scrolls proved Christianity to be, at best, a derivative religion. The scrolls tell of a "Teacher of Righteousness" who was crucified for leading a failed revolt a hundred years before Jesus and who had similar teachings. Allegro claimed that this was the proto-Jesus, reinvented and restructured circa 30 C.E. to appeal to gentiles in a time of persecution by Rome and the orthodox Jewish religious establishment.

He pointed out that Jesus, who claimed to be fulfilling the Law and the prophets, was in reality challenging the Jews and their obsession with the Law by wantonly breaking the Law at every turn, while claiming all the while to be divine. These stories, Allegro said, were the work of a revisionist group that took an older story, updated and embellished it, and set about winning converts among the gentiles in order to wrest power away from the oppressive Jewish religious hierarchy and present a rabble-roused challenge to Roman authority.

Most of the scrolls team considered Allegro's claims to be unsupported by the texts. He was, his detractors said, an anti-Christian atheist who had become fixated on trying to destroy the validity of the crucifixion story and Christianity along with it. Already ostracized by his fellows, almost all of whom were believing Christians or Jews, Allegro sealed his fate in 1970 when he published *The Sacred Mushroom and the Cross,* a book that claimed on linguistic evidence, real and imagined, that Jesus was the head of a cult that took psychedelic mushrooms, namely the fly agaric or "penis mushroom," the name Allegro claims was given to the mushroom by the ancients. He went on to state that perhaps Jesus never existed at all; that the name "Jesus" was a code name for the mushroom, along with the names John, James, Peter, and others. He found what he considered evidence for a fly agaric cult in the Old Testament as well, taking the names of various biblical characters and extrapolating back into ancient Sumerian and beyond in order to speculate about what the names were secretly intended to mean.

Wasson's *Soma* was published in 1968, two years before Allegro's book. Allegro read it or heard about it and lights flashed in his head, figuratively speaking. He may have sensed that something lay hidden beneath the surface of Judaism and Christianity, but he hadn't a clue as to what it might be until Wasson identified Soma and suggested that the same mushroom was implicated in the Garden of Eden myth. Needless to say, Allegro's speculations were not well received by his peers, who in good religio-scholarly fashion proceeded to fulminate with righteous indignation and contempt-charged ridicule as they merrily set about trying to destroy his career, which effectively they did. People tend to get very sensitive in matters of their own religions and the perceived blasphemy thereof. When highly respected careers are bound up with religion things get even worse.

Allegro was attacked on every side and ridiculed mercilessly, as if his hypothesis were more ridiculous than believing, for example, that a human being created the universe, revived from a horrible death, and floated bodily up to heaven. Actually his contentions are far more reasonable than the accepted versions of Christian and Jewish mythology, but there were few who would concede even this much. The numerous mistakes he made about the mushroom itself, its life cycle and effects, didn't help matters, nor did the fact that he never even tried the mushroom.

What happened to Allegro and even, to a lesser extent, to Wasson, can be expected in today's world. There are some things concerning which people don't wish to be challenged, and religion is foremost among them. There's the irony. What good is faith that is not challenged? It is empty; its possible truth can never be known without being put to the test, yet people seem to fear the *fact* of being wrong or mistaken more than the *consequences* of being mistaken.

The present work builds on Wasson's Soma theory by presenting and interpreting stories Wasson must not have seen, but expands his scope considerably. My method is to look almost exclusively at the stories themselves, even in translation, as being the carriers of the vital cultic information. It isn't crucial to me if the name Jesus means "mushroom" in some long-lost tongue, although I will consider it to be quite significant if it happens to be true. I'm proposing that in a cult, the members of which were relatively uneducated, simpler ways of preserving vital data would have been preferred over such sophisticated means as Allegro proposes.

Wasson's work employs linguistic analysis similar to but more sound than Allegro's, as well as insightful textual interpretation and photography, to prove that Soma is the fly agaric. His work is excellent and I take little exception to it, but there is much within the Indian religious texts and myths that he missed which would have greatly strengthened his position; I present some of this material here. I also expand greatly upon his hints regarding Judaism and Christianity and their parallels to the mushroom.

The reason that Wasson's work is not as convincing, to some, as it should be may be due to the fact that he never attained the ineffable experience of light and bliss the mushroom is capable of providing, even though he tried on a number of occasions. This lack of experience in the one area that would have given him the enthusiasm only conviction can bring is, I believe, the real reason his theory has not gained even wider acceptance than it has. It is also the reason he missed some clues that were right under his nose, clues that make sense only to someone who has had the full range of experiences the mushroom offers. This also holds true for areas Wasson never dealt with in print, such as Gnosticism, the Grail myths and alchemy, all of which are treated here in later chapters. Wasson's lack of enlightening experience with the fly agaric is shared by many people in the West who have tried the mushroom, except that most of these, unlike Wasson, blame the mushroom for their failure.

Some critics grant that the fly agaric sometimes provides an elevating experience, but still discount Wasson's hypotheses on the grounds that a sacred drug this temperamental, as it were, which might make a person sick one time and unconscious the next, never could have attained the status enjoyed by Soma or imputed to the sacraments of Judaism and Christianity. To these people I say, who says it had to be easy or reliable? The Rig Veda contains a number of verses imploring Soma to have a smooth and uneventful passage through the system. The ancients knew that Soma was a capricious god, but they kept using it because sometimes it gave a reward for which it was well worth the wait or the torment. The same holds true, I believe, for the ancient Jews and Christians. In the West we want everything right now, on demand, no waiting and no effort. The fly agaric doesn't work that way; it guards its gifts. One Vedic verse succinctly sums up the problem: "Let me join with my compassionate friend [Soma] so that he will not injure me when I have drunk him."[24]

It seems unlikely that the use of Soma, whatever it was, would have ended suddenly without leaving a trace, and I don't think it did.

Where Did Soma Hide?

The Rig Veda speaks freely and often about Soma. Since there was no War on Drugs at that time, the cult functioned openly and above ground. Not only was Soma drinking condoned, it was the only way to guarantee entry into heaven. In the latter days of Soma's use patrons could pay for the staging of the elaborate and costly Soma sacrifice and thereby ensure their place in the realm of the celestials, much in the same way that Indulgences were sold by the Catholic Church. In both cases this represented a degraded stage of the religion wherein money had become a principal means of attaining "salvation."

For some unknown reason the formal, institutionalized use of the Soma drink appears to have ended about 2,500 years ago. If Soma was indeed the fly agaric then the reason for this becomes clearer or at least easier to speculate about. The fly agaric fruits only once a year and only under certain trees, as stated earlier, and only a certain amount will grow in any given season. In some years there will be an abundant harvest while in others hardly any mushrooms at all. This can be problematic for a religion that relies on the intoxication the mushroom offers. It also provides the impetus for finding ways to extend the usage of whatever amounts were available, such as using Soma only in a ritual setting, limiting its use to the priesthood, and not wasting Soma-urine.

As the invading Aryans migrated from the mountainous regions in the north of India down into the Indus valley and spread out over the vast subcontinent they moved continually farther away from the source of their cultic beverage. This greatly added to the already serious problem of supply versus demand, though for some time the cult was kept supplied by native gatherers who harvested the yearly mushroom crop and sold it to the now-distant priests; by the time the Rig Veda canon was closed the ritualized buying of dried Soma, including ritualized haggling over the price, had been written into the sacrificial procedures. Significantly, the merchant was required to display his wares on the hide of a red bull: the dried "red bull" Soma displayed upon a dried red bull's hide. Increases in population thinned the supplies, in spite of the use of harvesters, until there simply wasn't enough of the sacred substance to go around most of the time. Because the sacrifice was wrongly deemed to have supernatural importance even without Soma, it continued to be performed using various surrogates for the burning god-plant.

Once the true drink of the gods was gone the Soma sacrifice was bound to follow. After the mostly wretched surrogates had taken Soma's place, the lengthy and complex ritual lost whatever charm it may have had earlier, and it fell into disuse. Without Soma the Brahmins were forced to devise new ways to offer salvation if they wanted to keep their flocks. Brahminism was the result, a complex set of scriptural injunctions and rituals only a Brahmin priest could properly administer.

Brahminism was a direct offshoot of the Soma sacrifice and the powers it had granted to the priests. They were the ones who knew how to obtain the sacred plant and how to prepare it, but without it they might lose their credibility. So they began to write Vedic commentaries that laid new stress on their own importance in the scheme of salvation, a practice that continues to this day. With scriptural edicts such as "God is great but the Brahmin is even greater, because the Brahmin takes one to God," the Brahmins assured their place and the place of their posterity in the spiritual life of the average Indian. Other movements stressing meditation or devotion would later arise to wrest some power away from the priests and put it back in the hands of the people, but for the time being the Brahmin was king. King Soma was deposed, no longer the god-plant of immortality. "Soma" generalized into a mere concept related to the moon and to real or imagined internal "nectars." But did its use really stop?

Long ago, in prehistory, the plant called Soma (the Pressed One) became personified as a god, in the same way that fire was personified as the god Agni and the thunderstorm as Indra. The longer Soma was used, the more descriptive names he collected: Deathless, Honey, Pillar, Navel, Bull, Red Bull, and others. Wasson pointed out that a common alternative name for Soma was *Agni,* Fire, even though this was specifically the fire-god's name. The two names were often used interchangeably, as though the poet's audience would know immediately why Soma was suddenly being referred to as Agni in the same verse or poem. The fiery red of the cap is the obvious connection to fire, but there is another reason, one that Wasson missed. As I mentioned before when speaking of the fly agaric's effects, sometimes incredible perspiration is experienced after consuming the mushroom. In order to sweat like this, one must surely have swallowed Fire. More will be said about this in discussing the Shiva myths.

I took seriously this tendency to assign different names to Soma; perhaps there were still others that had been overlooked by researchers. In the next chapter we will look at the Rig Veda for clues Wasson may have missed. We will also examine a number of bizarre tales from a group of Indian scriptures called the Puranas, an apparent goldmine of hidden cultic secrets.

5

The Dwarf Sun-God

At his command the eggs that are split in half
portion out the semen of the world.

Rig Veda 1.164

The ancient god Vishnu was originally a solar god, who over time attained the status of a supreme god in the Hindu pantheon; but during the time Soma was still being used Vishnu was a sun-god. Soma, throughout the Rig Veda, is compared to or identified with the sun, and one need only look at a mature fly agaric specimen to see why: it can look like a miniature sun-disc floating above the ground. The fact that Vishnu is a sun-god should alert us to a possible connection with Soma, but that alone is not enough. There are not many stories of Vishnu in the Rig Veda; most of the time he is mentioned in the story of some other god, usually Indra, and the stories often concern Soma-drinking. But in one poem Vishnu shares so many of Soma's attributes that they could trade names; I paraphrase the poem below.[25]

The Footprints of God

> The heroic deeds of Vishnu are being sung, he who has propped up as with a pillar the upper regions and stepped forth three times.

Pillar corresponds to the stalk of the mushroom. The "three steps" can be seen as the egg, the double-sphere, and the umbrella, the three main physical changes, or steps, the mushroom undergoes (plate 3).

28

Vishnu lurks in the mountains, wandering like a ferocious beast full of semen.

In India the fly agaric is found in the mountains. It "wanders" from tree to tree, not always sprouting under the same trees every year; it can appear under the same tree in a different location from the previous year; it can also appear under a tree for the first time, having "wandered there." As explained earlier the effects of the mushroom are sometimes "ferocious." "Full of semen" refers to the young phallic stage of the mushroom. In this metaphor the white creamy veil remnants on the cap are the "semen" on the red "glans."

Vishnu lives in the mountains and takes three steps, and his footprints are inexhaustibly full of honey to make others happily intoxicated with the sacrificial drink.

The "footprints" mean the plant itself, God's little toadstool "footstools," the place where God's footprint is found. "Honey" is a commonly used "pet name" for Soma, the drink that makes people happily intoxicated.

We want to be in Vishnu's heaven, where those who love the gods are intoxicated and where one unites with the god in his highest footprint, the fountain of honey.

The "highest footprint, the fountain of honey" may be speaking of the "highest" form of Soma as the Soma-urine, the "fountain" of Soma, or may simply refer to the fact that liquid is pressed from the plant, making it a kind of fountain of its own virtues; it may refer to both. "Uniting" with the god describes mystical union.

We wish to join with the god in his heaven, where there are untiring cattle, each with many horns, and where the highest footprint of the far-stepping Bull shines down brightly.

"Untiring" is a reference to the tremendous energy one can feel under the influence of the fly agaric; "cattle with many horns" is a metaphor for the mushroom with its "horned veil" as we saw in plate 1. The Bull again is Soma. "Bright light shining down" refers to the climax of the fly agaric experience, when shafts of white light appear to stream down from above the head.

Vishnu of the Rig Veda has much in common with lightning-engendered Dionysus, the Greek god of intoxication, who was also a bull-god and dispenser of divine ecstasy. Dionysus, whose name (per Graves) means "God of the Tree," was often depicted as being surrounded by raving women called Maenads, who had among their raging appetites a maniacal craving for men. Their bodies were covered with white patches and in one story the women actually turn into cows, making them fit companions for their bull-god. It may be the white patches on the fly agaric "breast" or "udder" that are being referred to here. These women also wore the skins of fawns over their shoulders. Fawns have fur that is almost red, with bright white spots. As for being sex-crazed, compare the Maenads with the women in the story of Rudra in the Pine Forest in chapter 6.

☽

The Brahmanas are scriptures written by Brahmin priests circa 800 to 500 B.C.E., which for the most part explain the significance of the Vedas and various rituals, often using old myths to illustrate a point. In contemporary language, the priests were putting their "spin" on the data; it's the same thing I am doing here, though perhaps in the opposite direction. The Shatapatha Brahmana contains a very telling story about Vishnu and his Soma alter ego.[26]

The Contracted Dwarf

> The gods and demons, both born of the Lord of Creatures, were once again at each other's throats. The demons thought they were in control of the whole earth, and judging by how things were going, they were. They decided to divide it among themselves. The gods heard about the division of the earth and went there, with Vishnu at the head of the delegation, to claim their share. The demons were a jealous bunch but agreed to give the gods as much of the earth as Vishnu could lie upon. Even though Vishnu was a dwarf and "contracted in all his limbs," the gods agreed because the space he would occupy was big enough to make a sacrificial fire, and Vishnu himself was the sacrifice.

Vishnu is a dwarf, but one who with his "three steps" (see above) covers the whole world. In his first step, the egg, he is definitely a dwarf, but by his third step he becomes a relative giant, holding the disc of the sun above the earth. "Contracted in all his limbs" implies that this dwarf is going to expand. The fact that Vishnu is the sacrifice means that he will be killed, put in fire, and then consumed.

> The gods surrounded Vishnu on three sides with Vedic meters, and on the fourth side, the East, they placed the fire-god Agni. Then they worshipped Vishnu until they all were exhausted, and by doing so obtained the whole earth. Because the gods won the whole earth by using Vishnu they named him the Altar. The sacrificial altar was then known to be as great as the whole earth, because with it they won the whole earth.

The use of Vishnu, or Soma, gives one the strength to wrest the earth away from foes. Vishnu becomes the altar by being worshipped for some time as a contracted dwarf; in other words, with the passage of time the mushroom expands, changing from an egg to a flat-topped, fiery "altar," which in the Vedic tradition are always low to the ground and always have a fire on top (plate 4).

> Now Vishnu was exhausted, but being enclosed as he was he could not leave the place; so he went down under the earth into the roots of plants. The other gods were perplexed and wondered where the sacrificial god had gone. They reasoned among them-

selves that being enclosed as he was he couldn't have escaped. They decided to search for him right there, even though he was nowhere in sight. The only place left to look was under the ground, so they began digging. Sure enough, there he was, just three finger-widths beneath the ground.

Vishnu is "exhausted": the mushroom has released all of its spores and begins to wither and shortly after disappears altogether. "Going down into the roots of plants" appears to be a sophisticated description of the mycorrhizal relationship of the mushroom with the rootlets of its host tree. When Vishnu disappears the gods know he hasn't really left: the mushroom mycelia are always "enclosed" by the area of the tree's root system.

Even after one mushroom has reached the "altar" stage, exhausted itself of spores, and disappeared, sometimes there will be others in the immediate vicinity even if none are visible above ground. These can be located by looking for subtle bumps on the surface of the ground and digging down a little with the fingers. Here one is likely to find another little Vishnu, contracted in all his limbs, once again a dwarf. And he is seldom more than three finger-widths beneath the ground.

In a later story, retold below, Vishnu has assumed the role of the main god of the vast Hindu pantheon but there is still some Soma personification going on. The story is an interesting mix of elements from different eras, and its central theme is the obtaining of Soma.

Churning the Ocean of Milk[27]

It is difficult to be vigilant in the protection of the earth when one is a god living in the pleasures of heaven. The demons had taken control of the earth again and the gods, suffering the lingering effects of a Brahmin's curse, lacked the energy and the wherewithal to do very much about it. They went together to Mount Meru, center of the universe and abode of the great Vishnu, to ask for advice. Vishnu told them that their malaise was nothing that a little Soma couldn't cure, and he told them how to obtain it. "It's quite simple. You must churn the ocean of milk and the Soma will rise to the top. Once you drink the amrita you will have the energy to rout the demons and reclaim the earth."

Vishnu scrutinized the sorry-looking gods. He said, "I think you could use a little help in this. Go to the demons and ask them to churn the ocean with you and promise them a share of the Soma. They will greedily accept, but when the Soma has been churned up I will see to it that they don't get a drop." The gods brightened up when they heard Vishnu's suggestion, and they did what he said.

The gods and demons met on the shore of the great Milk Ocean. They used Mount Mandara for the churning-rod and the serpent Ananta for the pullcord. Stationing themselves on opposite shores, they began to churn for the ambrosia. This was very hard on the poor serpent. The gods had hold of his tail and would pull with all their might, spinning the great mountain in the ocean. Then the demons, holding his head, would pull back just as hard, spinning the mountain the other way. The snake was about to die and belched out lightning and fire in protest. This immediately weakened the demon host, but the smoke rose in the air and became clouds, which floated over the gods and rained on them, giving them renewed energy.

Finally the churning began to bear fruit, and celestial objects slowly rose to the surface. The first to appear were the moon and the sun, followed by the goddess of intoxication. Then came the white horse of the sun, and then Aira-vata, the celestial white elephant, which Indra took for his mount. A mar-velous blood-red gem born of Soma came next, which Vishnu snatched up to wear on his chest. After a time the dangerous Kalakuta poison appeared and spread over the surface of the ocean, sending the gods into a panic. They ran back to Vishnu and begged for help. Vishnu demurred, saying that the task really should fall to Shiva, the Great God. Put on the spot as he was, Shiva graciously scooped the Doomsday Poison into his hands and drank it. At first he held it in his throat and it turned his throat blue; ever since he has been known as Blue-throated. Except for this he wasn't harmed at all.

The churning continued. When the lovely goddess Shri arose, Vishnu took her as his consort. Then the Wish-granting Cow and the Magical Tree of Par-adise appeared, followed at last by the divine physician Dhanvantari, holding aloft a white pot containing the precious Soma. When the gods saw this they fell to their knees and bowed their heads to the ground.

This was all the demons needed. Swift as thought one of the brighter demons rushed forward and grabbed the pot of ambrosia, to the demented cheers of his fellows. But Vishnu was not so easily undone. He assumed the form of Mohini, an illusory woman of incredible beauty and overwhelming sex appeal. Not surprisingly, the demons were quickly overwhelmed with lust and stood there staring like dummies, at which point Mohini calmly took back the pot of nectar and gave it to the gods, who immediately began to drink it down in great gulps.

A clever demon, Rahu by name, disguised himself as a god and took a drink, but Mohini saw him. She called upon Vishnu's magic discus Sudar-shana, "Beautiful to See," and it came down from the sky and alighted on her index finger, shining like the sun, blazing like a fire. She flung it at the demon and the discus cut off his head before he had time to swallow. It was the sun and moon who had spotted him and told Mohini, and to this day his immortal head will occasionally swallow the sun or the moon in retaliation, even though they pass right out of his severed neck. We call these occurrences eclipses.

Shiva looked at the gorgeous form of Mohini and briefly lost his memory and his wits, but that's another story which we'll get to later. Vishnu resumed his male form as the demons launched a fierce attack, but his shining discus sliced and chopped the demons to pieces. Overcome, the remaining demons went into the salt ocean and the earth, while the gods rose in the sky like clouds filled with water, their shouts of victory echoing through the heavens like thunder. Indra, the Wielder of the Lightning Bolt and mighty drinker of Soma, gave the precious pot of ambrosia to Vishnu, the Diademed One, for safekeeping.

In the beginning of the story the gods are unaware of how to get the Soma. This may reflect the latter days of Soma use when it was not easy to obtain; even so, the gods know enough to seek out Vishnu, who knows the secret. One of the most common food-names for Soma, other than Honey, was Butter. The pressing-out of Soma, done with stones in a trough of water, is likened to churning butter out of milk. In both cases a new and precious substance is obtained from liquid. Using a mountain to do the churning means that the mushroom will only be "churned up" by a mountain (it will grow in India only in the mountains). The snake that spins the mountain is itself a mushroom metaphor, poking its "head" out of the ground and sloughing its "skin," the universal veil (plate 5). Other important ways in which the fly agaric can be seen as a serpent will be discussed later.

Enlisting the aid of the demons implies that this is not an automatic process; both good and bad tendencies need to be harnessed and made to work together for good in order to attain the prize, and when this is successful only the good tendencies are strengthened. This is a metaphorical way of discussing the Indian concept of *karma,* a word that means both action and the result of action; in the West it is commonly understood as meaning "fate."

When nothing had yet been churned up by the mountain, rain showers enlivened the gods and things began popping up like mushrooms. This again is showing how all things work together for good when good actions are performed; it also associates the requisite rains with the mountain and the "churning up" of Soma.

Now the fruits of the churning begin to appear, and significantly the first to appear are the moon and the sun. The "moon" is another way of describing, first, the egg form of the mushroom, white and cratered; and second, the base of the mushroom once it assumes its spherical figure eight form in conjunction with the unopened cap, showing red through the universal veil like the rising sun through the clouds. First the moon, then the sun, just as in the story. In the Mahabharata version of this tale the moon itself is called Soma, a position the god Soma was assigned in writings subsequent to the Rig Veda, when the drink wasn't being used much. Soma is identified as the moon in only one Rig Veda reference, a late addition to the canon. That the god would or could be thought of as the moon derives from the moon-like qualities of the mushroom just described, as well as from the color of the light one can sometimes see under its influence.

The appearance of the moon and sun begins an object-litany of Soma references. The goddess of intoxication is an obvious connection; the white Horse of the Sun is like saying "the moon and the sun" because the sun "rides" the horse in the way the cap (the sun) rides the base (the moon). Likewise the white elephant ridden by Indra is another Soma personification: Indra is the storm-god and has a thousand "eyes" on his body. The blood-red gem is the blood-red cap of the mushroom; Vishnu, the "Diademed One," wears it on his chest, below his crown of diamonds, the "crown" of white jewel-like flecks on the cap.

When the Kalakuta poison rises to the top it almost puts a stop to the whole operation, just as one can feel poisoned after taking the fly agaric and the "poison" rises to the top as vomit. Shiva, the god of destruction, is the natural one to swallow poison, and he knows it won't kill him.

One element of the poison-drinking episode requires a digression from the story at hand, and that is Shiva's throat turning blue. This strange occurrence may owe its inclusion in a story about reclaiming Soma to the use of Soma-surrogates. Here is another scenario to consider.

The Aryan tribes have left the Himalayan foothills where the fly agaric, their Soma, is found. It becomes more and more difficult to obtain Soma, as the current story indicates. The native Dravidian people raise cattle as the Aryans do, and also use mushrooms as they do, but the mushrooms are different. They are small, bronze-colored, and grow in the dung of cattle after rainstorms. They are species of *Psilocybe* mushrooms, possibly *Psilocybe cubensis*. The Aryans, unable to get their own mushroom, use the intoxicant of the Dravidians as a surrogate and find it to be a powerful hallucinogen. On occasion it also gives a poisonous reaction at first. Holding the mushroom by its white "neck" or "throat," (that is, the stem) causes it to stain a vivid dark blue. The always-intoxicated Shiva is white, because he rubs his body with ashes after bathing; these ashes turn white when they dry. By "holding in the throat" his white neck turns blue. An additional clue is the fact that Shiva always rides his bull Nandi, just as *Psilocybe* mushrooms "ride" the bull's dung.

Blue-staining *Psilocybe* species usually will not grow outdoors in colder northern climes such as those in which the Aryans had been living before their migrations southward, so even though they raised cattle, they may not have encountered *Psilocybe* mushrooms until they moved further south. To be able to substitute one psychedelic mushroom that was no longer easy to get, with another that grew on the dung of their highly valued cattle must have seemed providential indeed.

So that the above speculation doesn't seem too far-fetched I will include another hypothesis following the same lines. The god Krishna is one of the later incarnations of Vishnu. He lives in the plains of India. He is beautiful with delicate features. He is a cowherd. He is dark blue. When he was an infant, after sucking the life out of an ogress through her breast, he was protected by the village women who waved a cow's tail over his body, bathed him in cow urine and cow dust, and wrote the names of Vishnu on all his limbs with fresh cow dung.

In a famous story, Krishna is a young cowherd in Braj, a village near the low, golden-hued mountain named Govardhana. Krishna had been urging the townsfolk to stop worshipping Indra, Lord of Storms and Soma-drinker, telling them instead to worship the mountain whose grasses fed their cattle; he even went so far as to stand on the mountain top and shout "I am the mountain!" Indra got very angry at this slight and sent pounding rains upon the village, which threatened to wash it away. But Krishna knew what to do. He walked to the mountain and lifted it up, holding it above his head with one finger. All the villagers took refuge beneath this impromptu umbrella for seven days until the rains stopped and Indra, amazed, came to pay homage to Krishna

Krishna, the Dark One, may originally have been a Dravidian shaman or priest; we know he was extremely charismatic. The story has him trying to convince the people to give up the religion of the conquering Aryans in favor of local nature divinities. Down on the plains there was no Soma, so the Aryan religion had little to offer in terms of consciousness alteration or enhancement. But Krishna's religion of cattle worship had much to offer, especially after Indra's rainstorm. The rains, meant by the Aryan god to wash the town away, instead caused mushrooms to sprout on the cow dung. Krishna's emergency umbrella looks very much like a *Psilocybe* mushroom, even to the blue "finger" holding aloft the golden dome (fig. 1). Significantly, the "umbrella" of "cow mountain" was not created until the rains had begun in earnest.

Another famous Krishna story has similar connotations.[28] Krishna was no ascetic. He liked to eat rich food, he was a musician, and he loved women. It seems that all the women loved him back as well, a fact that was causing more than a few problems in the village, as most of the women were married. These women, cowgirls all, would drop whatever they were doing when they saw the beautiful Krishna or heard his flute on the night air. One full moon the pull was too strong and all sixteen thousand of the town's cowgirls and cow-women were lured by the Dark One to an erotic rendezvous beneath the moon. Krishna magically reproduced himself for each of the women and made love with all of them at the same time. How can one god become sixteen thousand clones of himself? He might have to be a *Psilocybe* mushroom in order to do so, able to reproduce itself under the proper conditions at an alarming rate. At least it must have been alarming to the husbands.

One more thing should be noted here before we leave the cowboy Krishna. At the time the Vedas and the Brahmanas were written, cattle, though highly valued by the Aryans, were sacrificial animals and were regularly killed and eaten. At the time when most of the stories of Krishna were written things were very different. Cattle were now protected; not only

FIGURE 1: The god Krishna as a personification
of the sacred and secret food.

protected, but slightly divine, being treated better than people in some cases. They were no longer killed and eaten. What could cause such a dramatic change in attitude and practice? Perhaps this is the reason: Soma was the Bull because it was the fly agaric, whose bullish behaviour has already been discussed. Soma and the bull were related by metaphor and homology only, but in the southern latitudes of India God and cattle were more intimately involved. Their relationship was actual. Krishna was the cow-god because the cow indirectly gave birth to Krishna, hence his "anointing" with cow dung. If even the dung of a cow or bull could cause a god to sprout, how much holier must the animal itself be?

Shiva's blue throat may well relate to the *Psilocybe* mushroom, but there is another version of the tale in the Skanda Purana that seems to throw Shiva's poison-drinking back into the fly agaric's court.[29] In this rendition the churned-up poison was flaming, but Shiva didn't drink it. Instead he carried it away and tried to pour it in the Ganga (Ganges) River, which refused to accept it for fear of being burned. Finally the flaming poison was placed upon a Shiva linga, or penis-stone, in the Great Black Forest. The stone became poisoned and killed several ascetics who happened to look at it. Shiva revived them, however, and changed the offending linga into a *health-giving* penis-stone.

The first difference we notice in this story is that the poison is flaming, and the mention of flames can be a color key for the fly agaric. Shiva doesn't drink the poison, so his neck doesn't stain blue. The flaming poison is placed atop a penis-shaped upright stone in the forest, creating the image of fire on top of a pillar, and now the fly agaric correspondence is getting stronger. Next we discover that several people "died" from gazing at it but were brought back to life by the god, who then made the flaming poison-penis beneficial. This reflects the age old taboo that whoever eats the fly agaric will die, and may in fact be a warning that special knowledge is needed before the mushroom can safely be eaten; that is, the fresh mushroom must first be dried, after which it can be beneficial and healthful, although it helps to have some initial guidance in addition to having a dried mushroom.

As the people "died" and were magically brought back from the dead, the author seems to be referring to the deathlike coma described earlier, from which everyone will "magically" revive. If this occurs it becomes prudent to find out how to avoid repeating the miserable state in the future (how to turn poison into nectar). This episode is strangely reminiscent of the story of Moses and the metallic serpent, which will be examined later. The theme of Shiva's penis will be expanded below in the Pine Forest myth and elsewhere. We now return to the shores of the Milky Sea.

After the Doomsday Poison has been dispensed with, the goddess Shri arises from the ocean. In yoga theory there are subtle energy centres called *chakras* which are said to range along the spine and through the brain to the crown of the head. The uppermost of these is named *sahasrara,* which means "thousand-petaled." Its "petals" are radiant white and point downward, like a skull cap of light. Just below this is Shri chakra. The energy that has been released by the churning up of Soma travels from the base of the spine in a subtle conduit called *sushumna nadi,* which pierces through the center of all the chakras and exits at the center of sahasrara chakra at a point called *mula,* which means "origin." Shri represents an extremely tenuous mental state just before the opening of the thousand-petaled lotus floods the body with light.

Surabhi, the Magical Cow who grants all wishes, is the next to rise from the ocean, and she just happens to give Soma from her udder. Whether or not feeding mushrooms to a cow will cause her milk to become intoxicating in the way that urine does remains untested as far as I know, but the old stories tell us that Soma flowed from Surabhi's teats. This could easily be tested by anyone with the resources. We already know that Soma was likened to an udder, so in one sense the Celestial Cow represents the hydrated mushroom. Following the Magical Cow is the likewise magical Tree of Paradise, which we may recklessly assume refers to any tree under which grows the fly agaric.

At the end of this amazing parade of mushroom correspondences comes the prepared Soma-drink itself, held in a white pot by the gods' physician. The physician represents the old tribal medicine man or shaman, indicating that Soma is more than an intoxicant: it is a panacea, a medicine for both soul and body, so powerful that it can raise the dead, as we will see below. It is kept in a white pot, just as the white potlike base of the mushroom "holds" the rest of the plant (see plate 1).

Vishnu's magic discus Beautiful to See comes down from heaven, burns like fire, is studded with gems, and rests, when not in use, on Vishnu's upraised index finger. As in the case of Krishna with the mountain, this discus-on-a-finger presents a striking mushroom image, only this time the mushroom is the fly agaric, which comes down from heaven, assumes a disc-shape, has the color of fire, and is studded with the "jewels" of the universal veil fragments. Vishnu's transsexualism will be explored below in the myths of Shiva/Rudra.

After the gods drank the Soma the weakened demons made themselves scarce. The evil tendencies are no longer in control; they have been suppressed. The gods go back to heaven thundering like clouds filled with rain, a reference to the promise of the next year's rains, which once again will churn Soma from the mountains. Indra, bringer of rains and wielder of lightning, gives the pot of Soma to Vishnu for safekeeping in heaven, until the next time the earth is in need.

6

The Red-Eyed Howler

IF THERE IS ANY GOD IN THE VEDIC PANTHEON who could take the place of Soma, and therefore of the fly agaric, it has to be Rudra, the naked ascetic wildman of the Himalayan pine forests, whose name is variously translated as Red, Ruddy, Howler, and "one who weeps or causes weeping." He is always intoxicated, so his eyes are always red; those he causes to weep also get red eyes. He has bright red hair. His body is white from being rubbed with ash. His penis is always erect. This last point is especially relevant to Rudra's iconography, as well as to my contention that Rudra gradually assumed Soma's role as the Great Intoxicator.

Only three hymns in the Rig Veda are written specifically to Rudra. He was not one of the gods to whom offerings were made in the Soma sacrifice, but he is mentioned a number of times, often with the poet trying to pacify him in some way because he was considered violent and dangerous. It was better to stay on his good side and mention him once in a while; a little praise didn't hurt either. Later mythology changes Rudra into the more benevolent Shiva, whose name means "Auspicious," though he still retains his danger and unpredictability.

In one of the hymns Rudra is called the Father of the Flashing Ones.[30] The Flashing Ones are the Maruts, storm-gods usually associated with the storm-god Indra. Identifying Rudra with thunderstorms is significant, of course, because the Soma needs rain to grow. The names of the Maruts are interesting too, and four out of seven have mushroom correspondences beyond the fact that they bring the rains: Wind-mandala (circle) can refer to the shape of the mushroom cap; Wind-flame to the flaming color; Wind-semen, like Soma's epithet "Bull bursting with semen," can refer to the white veil remnants on the red cap; Wind-chakra (disc or wheel) is the same as Vishnu's disc.

In the same hymn the poet spends a lot of time praising Rudra and trying to mollify him. After extolling the virtues of Rudra's healing medicine, the Soma, and identifying him with the storm-god Indra, the author asks to be carried across the sea of anguish to the farther shore, a plea of someone who has ridden upon a Soma-induced sea of anguish before and wishes to avoid a recurrence. He asks Rudra not to be angry, calling him "Rudra the Bull," once again using a name of Soma. Rudra has "full lips eager to drink Soma"; he is the High Bull, tawny and white, probably a reference to the color of dried mushrooms, the form with which people of the time would have been most familiar, as the dried mushroom is what was used in the sacrifice; similarly in other poems Soma is called both red and tawny (plate 6).

We are told that this fierce, tawny god wears shimmering gold on his limbs; often the mushroom dries to the same metallic color (plate 7). We are asked to praise the fierce "young god" who sits on his high seat: because mushrooms go through their fruiting cycle in a matter of days they all are quite "young"; the "high seat" is the standing mushroom cap. The poet ends with several verses of praise for the strengthening, comforting, and healing medicine and with strong pleas for mercy. He wants Rudra's "great malevolence" to pass him by (the sickness that can occur during fly agaric intoxication); he wishes to be a power-ful man speaking great words during the Soma sacrifice.

I have cited the above hymn for several reasons. The cautious and deferential way Rudra is regarded in the Rig Veda may indicate that he was a god of the indigenous people of the Himalayan foothills who was encountered when the Aryans moved through, much in the same way they encountered the god Krishna in the south. The poem appears to be an attempt to bring Rudra into the fold, so to speak. The Aryans were firm believers in a host of nature gods, and it was easier to pacify them than to take the chance of incurring their wrath. Since in the hymn all of Soma's attributes are transferred to Rudra—he is both the giver of Soma and the Soma itself—Rudra becomes a personification of Soma. Rudra may have been the original fly agaric deity of the Himalayas.

Whether or not Rudra was an indigenous deity, the poem is significant for the way in which it transfers the traditional identities of the gods. By the end of the poem Rudra is not only another Indra, once the greatest of the Vedic gods, but he is also Soma, god of divine intoxication. Even from the beginning of the Rig Veda canon Rudra was considered to have the inside track to intoxication, and it must be because he lived in the mountain forests where the intoxicant was found, as the next stories will attest.

The Penis of God

Part of Rudra's "wildman" persona is due to the fact that he is ithyphallic and runs around naked. "Ithyphallic" is a word that tries to make "ever erect penis" sound more respectable, which Rudra certainly was not. His penis plays such an outstanding role in his mythology that it came to be worshipped all over India, as it still is. The icon of his penis is called a Shiva linga, *linga* meaning penis, often depicted in sexual congress with a *yoni,* or vulva. Statues of the Shiva linga, both large and small, are found all over India, especially in shrines and temples sacred to Shiva/Rudra. While many high-sounding philosophical interpretations are given to explain what these graphic icons represent, an ancient myth retold in the Puranas claims to give the real reason for worshipping the Penis of God.

Rudra in the Pine Forest[31]

Rudra appeared in the pine forest, it is said, to show his grace to the many sages and ascetics who lived and did spiritual practices there, though his early actions seem to belie this. He wandered through the forest stark naked except for the white ashes smeared over his body. His matted hair stuck out in all directions and his teeth were pointed. He laughed and howled like a madman as he juggled burning sticks and rolled his red and tawny eyes. His erect penis was painted with red, white, and black chalk.

The wives of the Seven Sages (The Seven Sages were famous Soma priests) were bathing nearby in a stream as Rudra wandered up to the bank. The chaste women stared at the wildman as though in a trance, quickly losing all sense of decorum as Rudra did an obscene dance and waved his painted member at them. Those in the water came out in full view on the bank, while those who hadn't yet disrobed threw off their clothes, and they all begged Rudra to make love to them. This he did, being more than happy to oblige them, and then he wandered off through the forest once more, howling like a banshee.

The women looked at each other and blushed as the gravity of their offense settled upon them. They quickly decided that they should all tell exactly the same story to their husbands, saying that a terrible mendicant had surprised them at their bath and propositioned them but was driven away by their angry words. And this is just what they did.

When the illustrious Sages heard the story told by their wives they were incensed. Anger flared in their hearts as they went to look for Rudra. They didn't have to look for long, because he was still nearby; they could hear his maniacal laughter and followed the sound until they were upon him. At first the Sages were frightened when they saw Rudra, but when they thought of their wives as they stared at his gaily decorated penis their fear turned again to anger. After thoroughly excoriating him for his untoward behaviour they cursed him, and as everyone knows a Brahmin's curse cannot fail to come true. "Make your penis fall off!" they cried in their rage. Rudra looked at them and laughed. "So be it!" he said, and at that moment a bolt of lightning shot from the sky and neatly performed the surgery. Rudra's manhood fell down among the pine needles, still upright but a thing apart. Rudra just laughed as he turned and walked away. The cuckolded men stared after him until all that could be seen in the distance were his firebrands, twirling in the dark wood.

The men looked at one another as their wives had done before them, and then they looked at the proud specimen standing in the pine needles. They awoke as if from a dream and pondered the meaning of what had happened. All at once they became frightened again, because they realized who it was they had emasculated. "What has come over us? This was no ordinary naked wildman. It must have been Rudra himself, the god of these forests, and we not only have driven him off but have unmanned him!" The men took counsel and agreed to make the best of an already bad situation. They decided to make a replica of the missing linga and worship it right there in the pine forest, in the hope that Rudra would forgive them and return. And there they stayed in fearful worship until almost a full year had passed and the new grasses and flowers of springtime once again filled the forest.

Their devotion paid off. Rudra did return, in the same form, to the same forest. As a reward for their devotion Rudra taught them the supreme ritual, the Removal of the Great Darkness, which freed the minds of all the people. They all rejoiced and bathed the linga, and then they bathed the lord himself. Rudra then told them to ask for a boon. They asked him to reveal the secrets of the Left-hand Tantra and the meaning of his nakedness and bathing with ashes.

This is a strange story. Even if it were not considered scripture, which it is, it would be a strange story. It makes precious little sense either as a morality tale or as doctrine; but if we employ the simple expedient of identifying Rudra as a personification of certain salient features of the fly agaric, the story suddenly begins to take on meaning.

The pine forest gives us our first clue: pine trees are a favorite host tree for the fly agaric. Rudra has gone there to "show his grace" to the spiritual seekers who live there. The next thing brought to our attention is Rudra's appearance, which is so bizarre that it is sure to stick in our minds. His whole body except for his genitals is white, as is the whole body of the mushroom except for the top of the cap. His penis is erect and decorated with red, white, and black chalk. When the fly agaric makes its appearance under a tree, that is when it breaks through the ground and leaves or needles, it is often strikingly phallic in appearance and stands ramrod straight; the red and white of Rudra's decoration are obvious when compared to the young cap, but to account for the black it needs to be pointed out that almost always there are particles of black humus that adhere to the cap after it breaks through the ground (plate 8). More to the point, every fly agaric is stained "black" on the bottom from being in the black earth.

The author tells us that Rudra's eyes are red; not only red, but red and tawny, two key color words we encountered before in descriptions of Soma, representing the young, fresh mushroom and the weathered or dried mushroom respectively. And it should not be lost on us that red eyes accompany and sometimes indicate intoxication. Along with red eyes we are told that Rudra has large, pointed teeth. In the earlier description of the fly agaric it was mentioned that the portion of the universal veil that covers the cap is made up of pointed white cells. When viewed up close these cells can be seen as pointed teeth, especially if the red "gums" of the cap are visible (plate 9). Again, these pointed veil fragments are a distinctive identifying feature of the fly agaric.

The last items of Rudra's ensemble are his wild, matted hair and his burning sticks. If Rudra has red hair in this story (we are not told) as he sometimes has in other stories, this probably refers to the red cap on top of the "head" of the mushroom; if the hair is not red it may refer to the matted pine needles jutting in every direction that cover the cap like hair covers a head. The burning sticks have a double correspondence. The first is that the firesticks are a homologous reference to the mushroom: "fire" is the cap, on top of a "stick," the stalk. The second is that the mushroom must be dried before it is used. That Rudra always carries burning sticks implies that the mushroom needs to be placed near fire; it is an integral part of Rudra's function as a god.

By the time the author finishes describing Rudra's appearance we already have enough information to make a preliminary identification, but in order to drive home the point we are given still more. The first human/god interaction in the story is with naked women, at whom Rudra has wagged his impudent wand and with whom he has gratuitous sexual relations. This is described to impress upon the reader that Rudra's penis, already decorated and described, is going to be the star of the story, which makes real sense if the penis represents the fly agaric. With or without Rudra, his mushroom-penis is a bestower in its own right, first of "sexual" bliss and then of light; without it the whole tale deflates. The nakedness and sex also call attention to the fact that the resemblance of the mushroom to an engorged penis can be more than slight: even "virtuous" women will see it. Having sex with the women may additionally reflect a secret Tantric use of the mushroom that will be discussed later.

The episode of the angry husbands is a pretext for presenting (and thereby preserving) more vital information about the fly agaric. We now know from story clues that the red and white mushroom is to be found in the Himalayan pine forests. But when? We could scour the pine forests of India for ten months of the year or more and not find any Soma, because being in a pine forest is by itself not enough; there must also be abundant rain. The story makes this point very cleverly by having a lightning bolt perform the amputation of Rudra's penis. Lightning means thunderstorms and thunderstorms mean rain; it is only after the thunderstorms that god's brightly colored penis will fall to earth and stand among the pine needles of the forest.

The author still is not finished. Now he brings in the ancient myth of the return of the hero or the savior. The pine forest Sages didn't recognize the god for what he really was. They saw his "penis" in the forest and cut it off but didn't put it to use, a typically mycophobic reaction. There are many people the world over who have an inordinate fear of fungi and will go out of their way to kick or smash any mushroom they see. Somehow the Sages were made aware of the error of their ways (perhaps their wives tipped them off) and set about performing sympathetic magic under the very trees where the penis was last seen. And so the god returned a year later, after the rains, in exactly the same form as before, because the mushroom doesn't change from year to year except for possible variations in size.

Now that the priests were properly chastened by the penis-mushroom's yearlong absence, the great god taught them the supreme ritual that destroys the Great Darkness. This speaks of the culmination in light of the fly agaric experience as earlier described, but the darkness mentioned has two connotations: one is the darkness of ignorance, which is destroyed by the light of knowledge; the other is the comalike state of actual Great Darkness that can follow a bad experience of fly agaric consumption, when one is awash in a sea blacker than which nothing is: not the night, not the color black, nothing. It is *no thing*, a state of no reference points whatsoever. Getting out of this state and into the light is a secret worth knowing.

After the people's fears and delusions were destroyed by the new ritual they performed a significant act: they bathed the linga and Rudra. In linga worship the linga itself is often in an open, square container of some sort, either metal or stone. "Bathing" the linga today consists of pouring liquid offerings directly over it, foodstuffs such as milk, honey, and yogurt, which after the ceremony are ladled out and consumed by the worshippers as prasad. I believe the washing referred to in the story is a veiled reference to the older Soma ritual, in which the dried mushrooms were put in wooden troughs, had water poured over them, and were worked with the pressing-stones, "washed" if you will, until the liquid was sufficiently impregnated with the "semen" of the Red Bull and ready to drink.

The last part of the story has the sages asking Rudra about his strange practices: his nakedness, bathing with ashes, and "Left-handedness," a reference to secret Tantric practices involving sex and drugs. He answers them in part by declaring openly what has only been hinted at up to this point: Rudra replied, "I am Fire and I am Soma; I am Fire joined with Soma, and I am Soma mixed with Fire. The whole universe has Soma and Fire for its soul. Ashes are my semen, my seed, and I bear my seed on my body; I place my seed in ashes and sprinkle all creatures with it." Fire, Soma, Rudra, and his semen-dripping penis are all the same.

Rudra solves the mystery of his existence in a few lines, and in case we still don't get it he leaves us with one last clue: his ashes. We already know that he bears his semen on his "body" like the Red Bull bursting with semen, and that this refers to the veil remnants on the cap. But semen has the dual meaning of "seed," which Rudra now equates with his ashes, and he says that he sprinkles all creatures with it. When the cap of the fly agaric opens it begins to release its millions of white spores from the gills on the underside of the cap. Whatever is beneath the mushroom will become coated with these spores as though sprinkled with fine ash (plate 10). The rest of the spores are blown into the air, some of them eventually to sprinkle down on virtually all creatures on earth, so great is the number of spores released and so close to universal their distribution by the wind-god. And of course the "seed," in the case of the fly agaric spore, is similar to an actual seed, and infinitely more capable on its own than semen of creating another seed-bearing body.

As a result of all this ash-bearing Shiva is called "Bhasmabhuta," "Made of Ashes," and once the mushroom has disappeared, spore "ash" is all that remains. Even though Rudra makes this amazing admission of his secret identity, no one until now seems to have paid enough attention to it to realize that he was speaking literally, that he really is Soma, and the Pine Forest story is a riddle, filled with clues that reveal Soma's secret alter ego as well as Rudra's.

Eventually Rudra came to be referred to more often as Shiva, especially in later myths; it is the same god with a different name. In the Pine Forest story Rudra acts like a bachelor, even though in some versions his consort is with him; in those her presence is incidental and she is barely mentioned. In other versions of the myth he wanders the pine forest in despair after the loss of his first wife, Sati, whose death we will look at below. Most stories of Shiva, though, involve his wife/consort, Parvati, Daughter of the Mountain, also known as Uma, Girija, Gauri, Devi, and Kali. Parvati is the reincarnation of Sati and plays a significant role in many myths, with or without Shiva, and though feisty she is not quite the liberated goddess that modern times might have her be. These myths were all written by men of an extremely paternalistic society, and misogyny rears its ugly head in many of the tales, as with the fallen women in the Pine Forest myth. The following story is no exception; in it Shiva is terrified of Parvati's angry rage and women are sexually violated.[32]

Too Much of a Good Thing

The gods were in a panic, though this in itself was nothing new. It seems that Shiva and Parvati had been ensconced in their retreat on Mount Kailash for several years engaged in furious lovemaking that showed no sign of letting up. They were pursuing their own pleasure with such reckless abandon that they were unaware of its effects on the rest of the world, which is why the gods were so upset: the sheer weight of the amorous couple's activities had compressed the air of the earth to a solid and everyone was beginning to suffocate. Vishnu advised the distraught divinities to accompany him to Mount Kailash, where they might have a word with Shiva.

Brahma, the god of creation, approached Shiva's door and made a whining appeal on behalf of the other gods, falsely claiming that a terrible demon was tormenting them. All the gods began to moan and offered up lavish praise to Shiva, while Vishnu wept a flood of tears. When Shiva heard their pitiful lamentations he lost all interest in making love, though he continued because he was afraid of his wife. For their part the gods continued as well, praising and pleading until finally, in his great compassion, Shiva performed *coitus interruptus*. He assuaged the gods by telling them that past and future both are unpreventable, then quickly segued to the most important issue: "I am more concerned at the moment," the Great God said, "with the matter at hand. What will happen to my semen that is already stirred up from its place? Who will take it?" Before any of the stunned gods could think of how to answer, Shiva brought himself to orgasm and spilled his burning seed on the ground.

Once again the gods fell into a panic, each one trying to beg off before the others could. As they cried in unison that no one could possibly bear the burning seed of Shiva, all of them (except Agni) thought of Agni, the god of fire. "Great Agni, foremost among all the gods, only you are hot enough to take Shiva's seed," they shouted. Poor Agni was frightened, but seeing no way out of his predicament he became a dove and ate all the semen Shiva had so artlessly deposited.

At that moment Parvati appeared and quickly sized up the situation. She was furious at having had her pleasure not only interrupted but ended, and thus being denied a chance to have a child she roundly cursed the gods and stormed off unsatisfied to her own apartments.

Whatever is put into fire, Agni's mouth, becomes smoke and steam, which in turn becomes food for the gods. This is the way in which the gods share in the sacrificial offerings, and why they are known as "drinkers of steam." Ordinarily this process doesn't present a problem, but in this case it was semen that Agni ate, and Shiva's semen at that. All the gods suddenly found themselves pregnant from Agni's potent meal and afflicted with feverish burning. In great dismay and unbearable torment they once again repaired to Shiva's door to wail and complain. They didn't understand how this could have happened. Being pregnant was bad enough, but they also felt as though they were going to burn up from having swallowed Shiva's seed. They thought they were going to die.

Shiva listened to their toadying appeal and laughed. "All you have to do to be content is quickly vomit up the seed you have swallowed," he said. The gods took Shiva's advice. Bowing their heads they quickly vomited and experienced immediate relief. They praised Shiva for proving his affection for them in this way.

The semen that was vomited by the gods became a lake filled with golden lotuses, but Agni could not vomit and begged for help. He was told to place Shiva's semen in the bodies of certain women after they had bathed. The women happened to be the unfortunate wives of the Seven Sages, once again out bathing in the forest. After bathing, six of them warmed themselves at Agni's fire, and Shiva's semen entered their bodies through their pubic hair. They became pregnant and agonizingly hot, just as the gods had been. When they went home pregnant their husbands immediately left them, and the women, like good Brahmin wives, blamed themselves. They went into the mountains and "deposited" the seed there, where it became an embryo. The embryo was too hot for the mountain, which threw it into a river. Not surprisingly, the river found it too hot as well and threw it into a clump of white reeds, where it became the six-headed god Skanda; in this way Shiva and Parvati became parents, and milk began to flow from Parvati's breasts.

In the Pine Forest story Shiva was essentially acting on his own when he lost his penis, and the penis then became the thrust of the story; we saw that the decorated penis corresponds to the phallic stage of the fly agaric's growth cycle. Correspondences to two other stages of the mushroom's growth are depicted in the present tale. One of Shiva's forms is called *Ardhanari,* which means half-woman. It is a literal name because sometimes Shiva is considered to be a hermaphrodite. He has one female breast and, in true hermaphroditic fashion, both male and female sexual organs. Why Shiva is sometimes a hermaphrodite is never explained except by the most circuitous logic, but if Shiva represents the fly agaric a novel interpretation presents itself.

The story opens with Shiva and Parvati locked in endless sexual embrace, which can be thought of as a kind of hermaphroditism in which two people have become one through the union of their genitals. When the fly agaric grows beyond its youthful phallic appearance the outer edge of the cap begins to separate from the stalk and turn upward. As mentioned earlier, this stretches out a new veil, the annulus, which covers the gills on the underside of the cap, and it changes Shiva from an exclusively phallic god into a hermaphrodite. Here is how.

In the sexual iconography of the divine couple, Shiva's penis is called the White Vajra, vajra meaning "lightning bolt"; his is the "white lightning-bolt penis." Parvati's vulva is called the Red Lotus. If we look at the underside of a fly agaric at this stage the genital imagery just described becomes readily apparent. The red cap that had formerly been the glans of Shiva's penis has changed sex and is now the "red lotus" of Parvati's vulva. The taut annulus veil becomes her hymen, which is pierced by the stalk that now is seen as Shiva's white lightning-bolt penis (plate 11). It is the seemingly endless embrace of penis and vulva, the very act represented in the story and by millions of linga statues all over India; and it is Shiva in his form of half-man, half-woman, the ultimate hermaphrodite who not only has the organs of both sexes on one body, but has them in *coitus* with each other. The top of the cap, looking less phallic as it expands, can be seen as Shiva's one female breast, now dripping with milk instead of semen. The mushroom's round base is his single testicle.

Even though the lovemaking in the story lasts for years, it doesn't last forever, and neither does this stage of the mushroom. Once the annulus veil reaches its limit of stretchability it tears loose from the outer rim of the cap and drops down on the stalk like a skirt. Meanwhile the shape of the cap is changing radically, continuing to turn upwards until eventually it turns itself inside out, like an umbrella that has opened too far. What in the Pine Forest was likened to an engorged glans covered with drops of semen now no longer fits that description, nor is it any longer breastlike. The story addresses these changes too.

After Shiva and Parvati had their love play interrupted for the good of the world, Shiva ejaculated and Agni became a dove to eat the semen. When the mushroom cap begins to invert, the white gills take on the appearance of feathers, and when viewed from the side the cap resembles the outstretched wings of a bird; the dropped annulus takes the part of the bird's tail feathers. Because it is Agni who has undergone this transformation, he naturally becomes a firebird, just as the mushroom "bird" has the color of fire on its top. The semen that Shiva spilled can be clearly seen in the white "drops" on the firebird's wings (plate 12). Seeing this stage of the mushroom explains beautifully how and why Fire became a bird after Shiva's lovemaking was interrupted.

When Fire eats the semen of Shiva the story makes direct reference, though still veiled, to the ancient Soma sacrifice itself. In one version of the sacrifice a huge altar in the shape of a bird was constructed from a thousand large adobe bricks. The wings of the bird were outstretched, the tail was fanned and the head pointed east to the rising sun. The Soma priests would climb up onto the back of the bird-altar and kindle a fire above the spot where the bird's heart would be, creating in the process what may be history's first representation of a firebird: a homologous and metaphoric representation of the fly agaric mushroom, the "bird" with fire on the back of its wings. The relationship of this firebird to the alchemical phoenix will be discussed in chapter 12.

Once the Soma was prepared, the priests would pour some of the liquid directly into the fire, and as the steam rose into the sky they called out to the gods to come and drink. What we have then in the Soma sacrifice is a fiery bird that consumes the equally fiery liquid essense of the god, which in turn is passed on to the other gods; this is precisely what occurs in the present story.

When the gods drank Shiva's semen-steam they all became "pregnant" and feverishly hot. When one is "impregnated" from eating or drinking the mushroom the same thing happens: "feverish burning" is experienced. But the pregnancy of the gods has a dual meaning, the second being the "pregnancy" caused by having a Soma-belly, a condition analagous to what we know in the West as a beer belly. It is well known that if a person drinks any liquid immoderately the stomach distends as if one were pregnant, and it might well be assumed that at the Soma sacrifice the participants on occasion would drink to excess. So it is with the gods, who after drinking what we now know was Soma become pregnant, both metaphorically and physically, at least in appearance. This interpretation may help to clear up the ongoing argument regarding who it is that is being represented by the "swollen men" in the Rig Veda verse, why they were swollen, and just what it was they were pissing as a result.

The gods also thought they were going to die, which again refers to the "perilous crossing" stage of fly agaric intoxication. When confronted with intense sweating, nausea, and perhaps coma-like swooning, the thought of possibly dying comes to mind and the prospect can be frightening, especially for the novice user. Shiva supplies the palliative, however: just vomit, he says, and you'll be fine. If one feels like the gods did after ingesting the mushroom, vomiting usually does improve things considerably, though not necessarily, and it does nothing to ameliorate the chemicals that are already in the system.

The gods took Shiva's advice and vomited the fiery seed, which formed a lake filled with golden lotuses. Some Siberian tribes are said to roll a dampened cap into a tight sausage-shape and swallow the whole thing with water in order to bypass the digestive enzymes of the mouth. Chewing the cap releases these enzymes, which in combination with the mushroom make some people sick, and the method was devised to avoid that. Vomiting is still fairly common, however, and when one does so the analogy of a lake filled with golden lotuses is rather apt, as the mushrooms come out whole and hydrated and unfurled, like strange golden flowers in the midst of waters. The story may refer as well to the hydrated mushroom caps in the pressing trough before the actual pressing begins, when they also look like golden flowers floating on the surface.

An unusual feature of an already unusual story is the passing on of the burning liquid, which doesn't stop until it creates a new birth. This is significant, remembering that the urine of one who is intoxicated with fly agaric is suffused with the same intoxicating chemicals as the mushroom. Disregarding the gods for the moment, we see that first Agni drinks the fluid, then he passes it to the six women. There are several connotations to this particular passing, but the significant point is that the women become "pregnant" from the semen. Absorbing it through the pubic hair has its own implications, one of which is that it may have been Agni's penis that passed the liquid, which in turn leads to speculation about vaginal or rectal drug absorption, a traditional technique used in the past by witches and more recently by hippies in the 1960s. Physicians have long known the efficacy of this method of drug delivery, as any user of suppositories can attest.

But why am I discussing urine when the story is about semen? Because the authors of these stories were constantly transferring qualities from one object or person to another. When urine has become "impregnated" with Soma's seed, metaphorically it is no longer urine but seed, and this seems to be the meaning of the burning semen that passes, nearly full strength, from person to person. Considering this, and the fact that the point of origin for both semen and urine is the same, it is easy to see how the two liquids could be confused and identified with each other; both even have a role in creating "new life."

It should be mentioned that the urine of one who has ingested a large quantity of fly agaric mushrooms undergoes its own transformation, apart from its new potency. Rather than being pale yellow with the unpleasant, acrid smell that everyone is familiar with and which makes the idea of urine-drinking a repugnant proposition, the urine of a bemushroomed person has a lovely and fiery orange tint, and an odor slightly redolent of the dried mushroom, not at all unpleasant. The new color is consistent with the fiery seed of the story. This physical transformation, coupled with the intoxication it now produces, can make it seem as though one's water had been magically transformed into wine, a concept we will discuss in greater detail later.

Yet these parts of the story also contain fly agaric imagery. The women relieve themselves of their burning burdens by depositing them as an "embryo" on a Himalayan mountain, corresponding to the embryonic egg of the mushroom's early life. The mountain tosses the embryo into a river, which may refer to the need for water to produce the embryo on the mountain in the first place, or to the dry Soma being placed in water; it could also represent Soma entering the "river" of one's own circulation system.

There is yet another interpretation which accounts for all the elements of the passing-of-the-seed story. Agni is the mushroom, which when hydrated is filled with the seed of Shiva, the intoxicating liquid. He has "drunk" Shiva's seed and now is filled with it. A practicing European sorcerer or witch would have had no hesitation about inserting one or a number of these slippery sponges into the vagina or rectum "through the pubic hair," as the story says, if she knew that she might experience an ecstasy greater perhaps than any she had known with her other preparations (another version of the same story has the seed being absorbed through the pores of the women's buttocks). There, through absorption, the mushrooms (or simply the mushroom liquid or ointment) will produce the same effects as if they were eaten or drunk; the pregnancy metaphor is even more fitting in this scenario.

When finished with the mushrooms the women could easily have deposited them on the ground by squatting. Theoretically the mushrooms would still be carrying some viable spores. If they were buried beneath the proper tree it is possible that fly agaric mycelia could be established beneath the tree as a result. The notion of intentionally establishing new fly agaric mycelia, something Wasson thought was not possible, is more thoroughly explored in chapter 12.

The river tosses the embryo into a clump of white reeds, usually on a mountain. The white reeds represent the white stalk of the mushroom, upon which the six-headed god is born. Skanda's six heads, all alike, tell us that all the mushroom "heads" that appear on the mountain upon white stalks should be virtually identical; otherwise we may run into trouble by mistaking an interloper for the god we want. It is crucial to remember that the *Amanita* genus does contain a few deadly species. The six heads could also be a reference to a "heroic" dosage for experienced users, since Skanda went on to become the hero of the heavenly army.

In some versions of this myth the seed or embryo at some point in the passing is put into a pot, and it is the pot that then gets passed and finally tossed into the white reeds, there to give birth to Skanda and giving him the appellation "pot-born." We can now recognize the white reeds as mushroom stalks, as above, and the pot as the pot-shaped bottom of the mushroom, which holds the nascent Skanda in the same way the white pot held Soma in the Churning of the Ocean myth. The pot also makes reference to containers used to catch the Soma-urine.

There are echoes of the birth of Skanda in an ancient Greek myth concerning the birth of Orion. It seems that the primordial Greek gods had a habit of getting drunk on "honey," which as we have seen was a metaphor for Soma among the Vedic Aryans. One day Zeus, Poseidon, and Hermes were drinking huge amounts of this "honey" and had to urinate. They formed the hide of a sacrificed bull into a container and urinated into it. The hide was then buried, and after ten months the earth-born giant Orion arose from it.

This story contains several Soma parallels, aside from the honey correspondence. In the Soma sacrifice the gods Indra and Vayu were invoked once the Soma was prepared. Indra was the god of storms and Vayu the god of the winds. Zeus was the Greek Indra, a position probably held earlier by Poseidon, who later was associated with vegetation and all things watery. Hermes was for the Greeks the messenger between the gods and humans, the same position held in Vedic times by the prototypical angel, Angiras. The gods urinate into the hide of a sacrificed bull. Soma was the Red Bull, and the dried Soma was displayed on the hide of a red bull. Additionally, it is known that among Siberian users of the fly agaric, special containers made of reindeer hide are used to catch and store fly agaric urine. The word "Orion" is cognate with "urine" but also has the meaning "to shed seed," the identical semen/urine confusion we find in Indian writings. After ten months, about the time from the harvest of the last mushroom of one season to the first harvest of the next season, an "earth-born giant" takes birth, just as Vishnu was born from beneath the earth and became a giant. The story also implies that fly agaric urine was the cause of generating new mushroom growth. To my knowledge this has not been tested.

We are told that when Skanda was born he looked like the rising sun through the

FIGURE 2: The pregnant Agni drinks Soma from Shiva's penis (p. 50).

clouds, and Parvati's breasts flowed with milk even though she was nowhere near his birthplace. The author mentions this to make a visual connection between the newly born six-headed god, the red-orange rising sun, and full breasts covered with drops of milk, fly agaric symbols already encountered, so we don't forget that everything in this entire sequence of events, starting with Shiva and the release of his burning seed, relates to the red and white mushroom (plate 13). We should also note that even though Skanda is produced, however indirectly, from Shiva's seed, he is born alone on a mountain with no apparent father or mother. The fly agaric also is born, however indirectly, from the "seed" of a father/mother, yet to all appearances is born alone, like Skanda, without apparent parents. Having read the story, we know that his parents are a penis covered with semen and a breast covered with milk.

The story of Shiva's onanism is not the only Puranic mention of the spilling of magic semen, and some are even more graphic. In one particularly telling version of the same tale Agni says to Shiva, "Let the heavenly Soma flow, release it into my hands!"[33] Calling Shiva's "seed" the "heavenly Soma" lends a great deal of credence to the foregoing exegesis. Agni rejoiced as he took the heated issue in his cupped hands and drank it down, thinking "Elixir!" An eighth-century relief depicting this scene coincidentally shows Agni with a hugely distended stomach, as though he were nine months pregnant (fig. 2). We can see from this that pregnant gods and swollen men are not merely figures of speech; they represent having a Soma-belly.

In still another variant Shiva released his burning semen directly into Agni's mouth while thinking of Parvati, which gave Shiva supreme bliss, the author informs us.[34] I wish I'd had scriptures like these read from the pulpit when I was a boy; I might have looked forward to Sunday morning rather than dreading it. Church was never like this. Or was it? We will see.

Earlier it was mentioned that Shiva was completely taken in by Vishnu when he assumed the form of Mohini to trick the demons. After the Soma had been recovered Shiva asked Vishnu if he would show everyone that spectacular illusion one more time, and Vishnu obliged the Great God. Shiva was standing with Parvati, but as soon as he saw the beautiful Mohini he forgot everything. Tearing off his loincloth he chased after the illusory woman until he caught her, and he took her by force. So energetic was their coupling that semen flew everywhere, and the semen that fell upon the earth turned to lingas and gold, mushroom parallels we readily recognize.[35]

Shiva flew through the air making love one other time, but it was not with a temporary transsexual.[36] It was with a corpse. Shiva's first wife, Sati, killed herself because her father had slighted Shiva by not inviting him to a big sacrifice. Shiva went anyway, taking with him a small army of ghosts and demons, and ruined the sacrifice, but he was too late to save Sati. He went crazy with grief and flew into the air with the corpse, caressing it and pressing it to his body in a necrophilic ecstasy, weeping inconsolably. The gods tried to stop him but he was unstoppable. Finally Vishnu threw his discus at the corpse again and again, until there was nothing left of the body; Sati was sliced to pieces. Her various parts fell all over the Himalayas; where her vulva landed Shiva took the form of a penis to receive it.

This story is similar in content to the burning seed story. We will recall that Agni entered the women, who burned feverishly in their "pregnancy" before depositing the "embryos" on a Himalayan hillside, which after mixing with water produced the six-headed Skanda. In the present tale Sati has burned herself to death, although with typical story-line inconsistency her body has not been destroyed by the fire. Sati at first takes the part of the mushroom and Shiva "caresses and presses" her until she literally falls apart and drops to the ground. The author brings in the fly agaric symbol of Vishnu's discus to accomplish this dismemberment and to remind us of what he is really saying. Because Sati's red vulva produces Shiva's penis it seems that once again it is mushroom propagation that is being described.

The exact opposite of this story occurs in still another version of Shiva's penis amputation.[37] In this the severed organ fell flaming to the ground and kept moving throughout the entire earth, causing destruction wherever it went. Shiva told Brahma that the penis would always be moving through the earth unless it could be held in place by a vulva. The gods asked Parvati for help, so she became a vulva on the ground. The burning phallus entered the vulva and became still.

Instead of Sati's vulva causing a penis to sprout, here we have Shiva's penis causing a vulva to appear. Because the penis has already fallen to earth it continues to "move through the earth"; in other words, during the mushroom season new phallic mushrooms will continue to break ground (move through the earth) until in each instance the cap becomes the red lotus "vulva" on the underside of the cap, with its tight grip on the white stalk's "lightning-bolt penis." It represents the same stage of the mushroom's growth as the eternal lovemaking of Shiva and Parvati in the burning seed story above.

There are several different accounts of what happened when Shiva made love to Vishnu; we have already heard that phalluses and gold appeared on the ground where the semen fell. The Linga Purana, appropriately named, mixes the story with that of the primeval creation.[38] We are told that Shiva placed his golden seed in Vishnu's "womb," which we know already. After some time the seed became an egg that floated for a long time in the cosmic waters. Finally a wind arose that split the egg in two; the top became the sky, the bottom became the earth, and the yolk became the golden mountain.

When the "egg" of the fly agaric splits in two it reveals the cap clearly for the first time. Quite often the newly exposed cap is all of the mushroom that is visible above the ground. The bottom of the egg seems to have become the ground itself and is in the ground; the top of the egg, the white veil remnants, look like clouds in the sky; the yolk that becomes the golden mountain is the mushroom's cap (plate 14).

The Shiva Purana takes strangeness to new heights in its rendition of the affair.[39] After Shiva embraces Vishnu the semen falls to earth as in other stories, only this time it is gathered up and put in a pot by the Seven Sages and poured into the ear (!) of another sage's daughter. This caused her to become pregnant, of course (knowing what we do of early Indian ideas of fertilization and conception), and she gave birth to the monkey-god Hanuman.

This quirky tale makes more sense than first appears, but that's true of most of these stories. Having the fiery seed collected and put in a pot we know refers to the pot-shaped base of the mushroom, as well as to the simple fact that both Soma and Soma-urine were also kept in pots. The old semen-in-the-ear trick leaves me a little baffled, however. Knowing from other stories that pregnancy is caused in many ways, including the sniffing of semen, it may only be the author's attempt at one-upmanship. Knowing also that the burning seed is a kind of poison and that poison is sometimes administered through the ear, this may represent a typical Indian poison/nectar reversal. Then again it may just be showing us an obscure, unorthodox, and untidy way of taking drugs. Whatever the case, the most important element of the story is that Shiva's seed caused the birth of the monkey-god Hanuman.

Hanuman is a central character in Valmiki's Ramayana, a famous epic poem written much earlier than the story above, during the time when Soma use was declining. The poem tells the story of Prince Rama, whose wife Sita was kidnapped after Rama and his brother stupidly left her alone in a demon-infested forest. During their search for the princess the two met the monkey-god Hanuman, who was ultimately instrumental in bringing about Sita's rescue. A few telling episodes from Hanuman's story are enough to show us why it is that he would be born, like Skanda, from the burning seed of Shiva.

Here is the more traditional version of the monkey-god's birth. Hanuman's mother was visited by the wind-god, Vayu, who found her beauty irresistible even though she was a monkey. Hanuman was their love child. The monkey-woman gave birth in a cave at sunrise, and the baby was as red as the rising sun. Spying the bright red ball of the sun for the first time, Hanuman mistook it for a ripe fruit and leapt into the air to pluck it. In some redactions he took a bite of the sun, while in others he was just about to when one of the gods saw the fearsome monkey and went quickly to Indra, Lord of Storms. Indra didn't waste any time. Seizing a lightning bolt in his hand he hurled it at the red monkey with all his might, catching him on the jaw and sending him falling to the ground on the slope of a mountain. The gods took pity on the fallen newborn and gave him two boons: invulnerability in battle and the ability to live as long as he desired.

The next we hear of Hanuman is his meeting with Prince Rama. Hanuman has been enlisted to jump across the ocean from the tip of India to the island of Lanka (Sri Lanka) in order to find the kidnapped Sita. The fiery red monkey is now fully grown, with sharp white teeth and a scarlet rump. He is endowed with the ability to shrink his body to the size of a thumb or expand it enormously. He knows all the Vedas and is considered a great healer. Hanuman brags that he is a friend of Fire (Agni) and a shatterer of mountains, able to circulate through space in the form of the wind and leap as well as his father, Vayu. When he yawns his mouth looks like a red-hot oven set with teeth. He tells the other monkeys that when he leaps across the sea he will look like Vishnu the Dwarf with his three marks, enveloping the vault of the sky like lightning flashing from a rain cloud. Not only that, he is so strong that he could snatch Soma out of the hands of Indra. The monkeys are impressed by Hanuman's speech and vow to remain standing on one foot until his return.

They say that Hanuman ranged all over the mountain before he finally stationed himself. Finally he was ready; bracing his feet against the mountain, the red monkey jumped. It was amazing to see the way he lifted himself into the sky. He was so strong that the mountainside was torn apart by the force of his leap, and all the poisonous serpents vomited fire. He would soar high in the air and then drop down so low that he broke waves with his chest.

After some time in the air he encountered trouble when a gigantic humanoid demon with gaping jaws and huge teeth rose up before him. She was so big that she easily could have swallowed the monkey whole, and she invited him to come and rest inside her mouth. Ever polite and not wishing to offend, Hanuman flew straight down her throat and into her stomach, where he turned around and shot back out in a flash, thanking the demon for her hospitality and saying he was sorry that he couldn't stay. Even though she had tried to eat him, Hanuman didn't kill her. A short time later he found himself approaching the shores of Lanka, so he contracted himself to his smallest size and descended on a mountain peak outside the city.

The Ramayana is an extraordinarily long book, even without its tendency to repeat half of the preceding verse at the beginning of the next, so we will skip ahead to one of the most significant fly agaric correspondences. With Hanuman's help Prince Rama brought his motley army to Sri Lanka and the battle was joined. Rama's brother Lakshman was killed, and the physician was summoned. He announced that only one thing could bring the young prince back to life: a certain plant that grew on the slopes of a certain mountain back on the mainland, a proclamation that registered general dismay until they realized that Hanuman would be able to leap back across the ocean to fetch it. Hanuman was very intelligent and took pains to get the best description of the plant that he could. But what if he picked the wrong one? "It's not a problem," the doctor assured him. "These plants look like fires burning on the mountainside. You can't miss them, not even you, a monkey." Thus reassured, Hanuman again jumped over the sea.

When he got to the mountain he looked up its slopes and it wasn't long until he spotted what looked like live coals glowing on the side of the mountain. Thinking that these must be the fiery plants he was looking for, he rushed up the mountainside and was about to pick them when he noticed some other fiery-looking plants. They were definitely not the same as the others he had found but they fitted the same general description. Hanuman worried again that he might bring back the wrong plant, so to play it safe he lifted up the whole mountain, held it over his head with one hand, and jumped back to Lanka. The physician quickly chose the correct plants from among similar-looking varieties; when he went to place the plants on Lakshman's body, the prince revived before he could do so. The mere proximity of the fiery plant was enough to bring him back to life.

Fly agaric imagery is apparent from the very beginning of this myth. Hanuman was born in a cave, meaning that the mushroom's first appearance is underground. His color is red. Hanuman's father is the wind-god, the carrier of storms, and as soon as he was born he had an encounter with Indra, storm-god and wielder of the lightning bolt; the role of these two gods was of utmost importance in the production of Soma. When the Puranic story told above depicts Hanuman as being born from the union of Shiva and Vishnu it does so in order to show his identity with them, not to dispute his parentage; they all have correspondences to the mushroom.

Hanuman's run-in with Indra came as a result of the monkey-god trying to eat the sun because he thought it was a ripe fruit; this creates a triple identity of red monkey, red sun, and red fruit. The red mushroom pops into the air from below the ground looking like the rising sun, but also looking like edible red fruit of some kind. Once Hanuman had taken a bite of the sun the gods realized he was too powerful, so Indra struck him with lightning and made him fall. It was a thunderbolt that caused the red monkey to fall from the sky and appear on a mountain, just as it was a thunderbolt that made Rudra's red penis fall to the forest floor.

The list of Hanuman's qualities reads like a description of the fly agaric: he has a scarlet rump, similar to a rounded mushroom cap; he can shrink his body to thumb size (or mushroom-embryo size) like Vishnu and can also expand it to a large size, again like Vishnu; he can travel through the air on the wind, as mushroom spores travel; he is a great "leaper," springing up from out of nowhere; his yawning "mouth" looks like a red-hot oven set about with sharp teeth, as does the red cap with the white remnants of the universal veil; he says that when he jumps he will look like Vishnu the Dwarf, enveloping the sky like lightning from a rain cloud; he is strong enough to "snatch Soma out of Indra's hands," in other words to usurp Indra's place as the Soma-god. When the other monkeys stand on one foot it corresponds to Soma's ancient epithet of *Aja Ekapad,* "Not-born Single-foot."

Hanuman ranged all over the mountain, meaning that like the fly agaric he won't be found in only one spot; when he "jumped" he tore up the mountain, which we know is meant literally, and then he was "in the sky," that is, above the ground; poisonous serpents vomiting fire is a quadruple mushroom correspondence to the sometimes poisonous effects of the mushroom, the snake-like appearance of the young mushroom, the fiery color of the cap, and the nausea and intense sweating that can follow fly agaric consumption; breaking waves with his body could refer to the immersion in water of the dried mushroom.

After he jumped Hanuman encountered a giant demon who tried to eat him. The tremendous disparity of size is just what one finds between a mushroom and a human. Their meeting is presented from the clever and unusual perspective of a mushroom about to be eaten. Hanuman goes into her stomach, but once there, turns around and flies out her mouth, an apparent reference to vomiting. The author notes that the act of eating the red monkey did not result in the giant being killed; neither did the eating of Shiva's semen kill Agni or the gods. In order to return to earth, Hanuman contracts himself to his smallest size and lands on a mountainside again. This is a dual reference, first to a wind-borne spore alighting and second to the appearance of a contracted embryo beneath the ground.

The story of Hanuman's mission of mercy to the mainland is significant, because it presents us with another aspect of the plant of immortality: the power to restore life as well as grant the knowledge of unending life. As we know, this ability also plays a large part in the mythology of Jesus, and the subject will be taken up in detail in chapter 9. The theme of dying and coming back to life is inherent in the mythology of the fly agaric wherever it has been used, because of the effects it causes in the human system.

Everyone thought Lakshman was dead. The physician told Hanuman the specific mountain on which the sacred plant was known to grow. What did it look like? It glowed like fire on the mountainside. Hanuman found the mountain and spied some fiery plants but found some others that were the same color and type, throwing him into confusion. This is inserted in the story to let the reader know that just because one has found a red plant, or even a red mushroom, one may not have found the *correct* red mushroom. There are several other species of red mushroom, none of which have the properties of the fly agaric. If one is unsure, it may be

FIGURE 3: Rama (left) and Hanuman holding mushrooms.

necessary to take all the different specimens to a specialist as Hanuman did. Carrying the mountain over his head on one hand is the same mushroom analogue as Krishna holding a mountain over *his* head and Vishnu holding his discus on one finger.

Putting the plants on Lakshman's body was supposed to bring him back to life, but he revived from their mere proximity. The mushrooms are the cause of one's revival from the land of the dead just as they were the cause of entering it in the first place. One doesn't need to use them a second time to perform the "miracle" of resurrection; revival takes place automatically. If a plant has the power to "kill" people and then bring them back to life, then surely it can bring an already dead person back to life. The mushroom is the plant of immortality in more ways than one.

Since the preceding account of Hanuman and the Ramayana was written I have come into possession of a remarkable photograph (fig. 3) from a temple in South India, taken by researcher Gregory Howard. It is of a relief carving on a column in the Pattadakal temple complex (7th–8th century C.E.), a photograph of which, to our knowledge, has never before been published. The carving depicts the two aforementioned Ramayana heroes Rama and Hanuman standing beside (and touching) a strange looking Shiva-linga. This in itself is not unusual, as both were worshippers of the god Shiva. What *is* unusual, apart from the linga, is what they are holding in their other hands: mushrooms. Each is holding a large, opened mushroom with a thick stem, and each is holding it by the bottom of the stem, in such a way as to suggest that they are gripping the bulbous base of a fly agaric. Gills are clearly seen on the underside of the cap of Rama's mushroom. The odd-looking linga between them, which could be interpreted as an inept depiction of a lotus bud fused with a linga, is more accurately seen as the bud stage of a fly agaric, the unopened cap tightly gripping the thick stalk and the cap covered with pointed segments of the universal veil. The two figures touch the cap to show that the linga and the mushrooms represent the same object in different stages

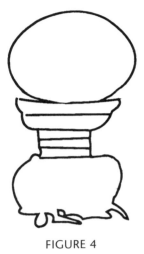

FIGURE 4

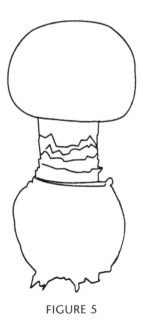

FIGURE 5

of development, and that it is to be harvested only when completely opened. Additionally, each stands with one leg raised, mimicking the one-legged stance of the mushroom.

Shiva has another name that should not surprise us. He is sometimes called *Sthanu*, which for a phallic god like Shiva is particularly apt: it means "pillar," or "post." It is reminiscent of Shiva's priapism and also of Soma's epithet, Pillar of the Sky. In a curious classical poem, Shiva and Parvati are once again having an argument.[40] Parvati has just made a pun in Sanskrit that a man of ashes such as Shiva could bear no love (oiliness) for her. Shiva says, "Your anger against me will bear no fruit, darling." Parvati replies, "How could there be fruit on a Pillar *(Sthanu)*?" At a certain stage in its development the fly agaric resembles nothing so much as fruit on a pillar (plate 15).

As we saw with the sculpture of Shiva and Agni, cultic imagery sometimes finds its way into the visual arts. An old Hindu painting seems to be a case in point (plate 16). It also may be only an extraordinary coincidence, but knowing what we do about Shiva and Soma it appears to be a case of visual encoding. The painting shows Shiva and Parvati sitting high atop a strange-looking pillar; one supposes that this must be an allusion to *"Sthanu,"* Pillar. The pillar looks as if it is rising right out of the back of Shiva's white bull, Nandi. Shiva rides Nandi whenever he goes anywhere. Shiva and Parvati are leaning against a large, red oval pillow with white accents. They are sitting on a "god stool," not unlike ancient depictions of toad-gods sitting on their toadstool thrones. Shiva the phallic pillar is white, while Parvati's body is red, the same sex and coloration references we found earlier with the lightning-bolt penis and red lotus vulva. Overhead, angels with wings that are red on top and white underneath are sprinkling white "stars" onto the couple and their red pillow. Comparing this painting to a photograph of the fly agaric reveals that the foregoing mushroom correspondences may have been intentional (plate 17). Tracing out the principal shapes makes the analogy even clearer (figs. 4 and 5). As I said, this may only be coincidence, but it could represent a secret identity of Shiva unknown in modern times.

Tantra: Sex, Drugs, and Religion

Tantra is an unusual religious form that began more or less as a reaction to the stultifying rituals of Brahminism. Its basis is a class of scriptures also called Tantra, which are said to have been authored by Shiva. Most of the Tantras take the form of Parvati asking questions to Shiva, who then expounds the Tantra philosophy in his answers. In these works Shiva says that Tantra is the religion for the new age, which in Indian terms is the opposite of what we mean in the West by "New Age." There are four ages in Hindu cosmology: *Sat Yuga,* when everything is Truth; *Treta Yuga,* when there is three-quarters Truth; *Dwapara Yuga,* with one-half Truth; and *Kali Yuga,* which starts at one-quarter Truth and finishes at zero. Each *yuga* is progressively shorter than the last and everything speeds up day by day, until by the end of Kali Yuga everything, and everyone, is in a frenzy. At this point Shiva does his *tandava* dance of universal destruction, resolving the entire universe back into atoms, after which the atoms regroup and the whole thing starts over again. The New Age for Hindus is Kali Yuga, supposed to have begun some six thousand years ago and just getting warmed up.

In Kali Yuga, says Shiva, no one has the time or temperament for the long, drawn out rituals of the Vedas and Brahmanas. People are dull and their memories are short, so easier methods are required if salvation is to be won and Dharma (righteousness) is to survive. The Tantras are said to contain these easier and shorter methods, although to the modern speeded-up brain the Tantric rites seem almost as interminable as their Vedic counterparts. They are, however, much more engaging, in part because they are performed jointly by men and women, food and wine are consumed, drugs are taken, and everyone is completely naked and has sex.

One novel aspect of Tantric practice is the idea that the body of the worshipper contains both Shiva and Shakti, the object of the practice being to bring the two together in ecstatic bliss. Shiva is said to be present in the area between the brows known as the "third eye" or *Ajna* chakra. Shakti's abode is at the base of the spinal column where she exists as the Kundalini Shakti or serpent power. This energy is said to remain coiled like a serpent until it is aroused by yogic practice, accident, dream, or drug and rises up the spine through the chakras, where, if one is successful, Shakti merges in metaphysical sexual union with Shiva and the practitioner experiences the bliss of their coupling. With practice one is said to attain the ability to merge with the Absolute at death, breaking the cycle of rebirth.

While in the coed practices all men take the role of Shiva and all women take the role of Shakti, in order to bring about their union it is necessary for each person mentally to become the goddess, the ultimate female, whose only desire is sexual union with Shiva, the ultimate male, in *Ajna* chakra.[41]

Today there exist two main branches of Tantra, Left-hand and Right-hand, although I am inclined to think that all Tantra was regarded as Left-hand when it began. This was the new religion that did the things that were not done, that broke the ancient taboos. It snatched religion out of the hands of the priests and gave it back to the people, in the same way that Prometheus stole fire, in the way the demons stole Soma from the gods, in the way Hanuman vowed that he would snatch Soma from the very hands of Indra. It was the first organized and systematic challenge within Vedism/Brahminism/Hinduism to the traditional religious hierarchy that had been created by and principally for male Brahmins. In Tantra any person of either sex, regardless of caste or status, could participate equally in the new cult. This did not, however, stop some Tantric gurus from perpetuating the abuses of the old system. Old habits die hard, and old religious habits seem to generate a life of their own. The guru system is Brahminism's legacy to the religions of India and remains to this day a dominant factor in people's lives.

It is important to understand what "Left-hand" means in the present context. In India it is the custom to perform one's most intimate personal hygiene tasks with the left hand. After defecation, for example, one pours water with the right hand and cleans the offending area with the left. Sanitary facilities and the general availability of soap being what they were in ancient India, it became the polite custom in public or private never to use the left hand in an unsanitary way, such as for eating or drinking, or touching someone. The left hand was considered unclean, and often it was. "Left-hand" became a pejorative term (cf. *sinister,* etc.) applied to anything that was unseemly or "not done." Tantric practitioners, on the other hand, went out of their way to do all the unseemly things, for they believed it was only by *experiencing* everything that one became *free* of everything, an idea that some Gnostics were busily pursuing elsewhere at the same time.

While Brahminism and later Vedanta were preaching abstinence and the control of desires, Tantra was teaching that the only way to be free from the tyranny of desire was to fulfill all desires to the point of satiety. All things were seen as being God in their essence, so whatever was done with this precept in mind was free of binding repercussions in the form of karma, which is the idea that if one does good, then one reaps good and vice versa. Tantra does not shun the world as do the more ascetic disciplines of Hinduism; it uses the world for the purpose of transcending the world.

The Tantric methodology, in general, involves use of the "Five M's"; this refers to five Sanskrit words all beginning with the letter M. Translated, these are meat, fish, grain, wine and sexual intercourse, and in Left-hand Tantra these are meant quite literally. A typical Tantric chakra, or circle, would be comprised of an equal number of males and females in couples alternately seated around and facing a central couple, the *chakreshwar* (lord of the circle) and his partner. All participants are naked and sit cross-legged on the ground. The central couple leads the proceedings and everyone else follows, doing whatever the lead couple does. The practice begins with the "placing" of God in various parts of the body by touching each part and reciting sound formulas *(mantras)*. Next the male paints a red line with a finger on the naked body of his partner, beginning at the clitoris and going straight up the front of the body, including the face, and ending at the crown of the skull at Mula, described earlier as being the center of the "thousand-petalled lotus," Sahasrara Chakra.

After these preliminaries the chakreshwar leads the group through the Five M's one at a time. These five sacraments symbolically represent the consumption of everything in creation: meat represents all creatures of the land and air; fish, all creatures of the sea;

grain, all vegetation; wine, all intoxicants; and sexual intercourse, all desires. Only token amounts of the first three items are eaten. How much wine is drunk depends on what other intoxicants are also taken at this time. If wine alone is used, each person will drink enough to get slightly, or more than slightly, drunk. One is advised in the scriptures not to drink until the speech slurs or the vision doubles. That remains good advice today.

It is also traditional to consume a drink called Five Deathless Nectars *(panchamrita)*, a throwback to earlier Soma use, which usually consists of milk, honey, curd (yogurt), butter, and *bhang*, ground marijuana. The bhang and butter both are Soma surrogates, the use of which began sometime in the distant past when Soma was no longer available. The first three ingredients were commonly mixed with fly agaric juice in the Soma sacrifice.

Once the intoxicants are taken the chakreshwar begins the first of a long series of sexual positions with his Shakti. The idea is to assume the position, with penetration, and hold still while both partners recite mantras while concentrating on their third eyes (or at least pretending to). The object, at first, is not to experience orgasm but rather to create a tremendous sexual tension, which in turn is supposed to arouse the sleeping goddess Kundalini Shakti; this happens because sexual energy, including orgasm, is thought to be a subsidiary form of Kundalini. The scriptures advise to keep the mind in the "kindling" stage of the sexual fire in order to avoid the "embers" at the end.

Many variations of the sexual portion of the practice developed over the centuries, as one might imagine. In one variant the male tries to bring his partner to orgasm without doing so himself, a practice believed to drain spiritual energy from the female and transfer it to the male, which amounts to a kind of misogynistic psycho-sexual thievery. The more clever of these selfish types will try to induce simultaneous orgasm, after which, by a yogic method, he will attempt to draw the sexual fluids (and escaped energies) of both back into his body through his penis, as though it were a vacuum cleaner. How successful this procedure is I leave to the reader's imagination.

In one of the more common variants, at the end of the series of sexual postures both partners experience orgasm, then collect and eat the spent fluid that runs out of the female. Ideally the woman is menstruating, making more fluid available to collect and share. In one text the male is instructed to release his semen into the mouth of his partner, as Shiva did to Agni. This is then passed back and forth between them by mouth until finally it is put into a dish and consumed by both.

This practice may have developed because many or most people found it impossible not to reach orgasm and didn't want to waste their precious fluids, or it may be a remnant of a much more logical practice dating from earlier times, namely the drinking of the Soma-fluids of both partners at the end of the series. If the participants had drunk the real Soma at the beginning, at the end their urine would have been infused with the divine inebriant and it would have made sense to drink it, knowing as they did its superlative virtues. This practice also would have obviated the need to get up from the circle, which no one was supposed to do for any reason until the gathering was officially dismissed by the leader. The circle once formed was believed to make a circuit of energies that would keep building until the ceremony was completed; getting up early would break and upset the energy, and everyone knew this was forbidden.

The drinking of semen and menses may again represent the confusion of semen and Soma-urine that we encountered elsewhere and may be a mere remnant of Soma-drinking. Wendy Doniger, who authored a portion of *Soma* with Wasson, points out in another book the link between swallowing semen and swallowing Soma, but not why the link exists.[42]

Since there have already been a few wild speculations up to this point, I will add another. It is regarding the use of the Shiva penis-stones, or lingas, by Tantric cults. In the story of Agni's impregnation of the women it was suggested that one way the women could have become "pregnant" from the penis-mushrooms was by using them in the manner of a penis, that is, inserting them into the vagina where the mushroom juices would be readily absorbed by the thin and capillary-rich vaginal membranes; or, as in the version in which the women absorb the seed through their buttocks, by inserting the mushrooms into their recta.

Although I already knew about similar techniques used in ancient witchcraft, the idea for this unusual use of the Soma-mushroom came from an old Tantric painting (fig. 6). It is well known that some Tantric gurus take great delight in initiating new female members into their cults, especially if a "defloration" (an unfortunate metaphor, to be sure) is performed in the process. This painting supposedly represents such an event, only using a stone penis rather than the real thing.

FIGURE 6: Tantric initiation.

Aside from the general strangeness of the painting, two things in particular stand out. The first regards the young woman, who is squatting on a stone linga over which red liquid is coursing, which we assume is the woman's blood. Granted the perspective is wrong and the representations are very stylized, but it doesn't appear that the linga is in her vagina; the labia are closed. It appears to be inserted in her rectum. The second thing we have to wonder about is what the guru is doing with *his* stone linga, which is positioned *behind* his genitals.

We are looking here at a secret cultic

practice, something that is most definitely "Left-hand." Surely no one outside the cult would have been allowed to see this painting. We should recall here the Tantric dictum that every practitioner must become female in order to have sex with Shiva, and that even Vishnu did that very thing. Could this possibly be what was meant? A hydrated mushroom cap can easily be molded onto the top of lingas such as we see in the painting, turning the device into a much more realistic representation of Shiva's penis. If one's desire is to link up with the lord by squatting on his linga during meditation, as the rolled-up eyes of the guru indicate that he is doing, one may as well equip it with the lord's "glans," a hydrated mushroom cap, and absorb his fiery seed in the process. The participants would still be able to engage in their sexual rituals as well, at least some of them, if they were so inclined. With the addition of mushrooms to the scenario in the painting we at least have a plausible explanation for the unusual behaviour exhibited by both parties.[43]

There are two secondary features in the painting worth noting: the first is that the initiation is taking place beneath a tree with all the lingas grouped beneath it, as fly agaric "lingas" are found only beneath trees; the second is that the woman's earring, the bottom of which is red, has the shape of a mushroom cap and has small white accents.

A Puranic story written during the time Tantra flourished in India may be talking about this arcane practice.[44] A male demon had assumed the form of Parvati unbeknownst to Shiva, who at the time was feeling very lustful. Shiva embraced the imposter and made love to her externally, but when he entered her he found inside her vagina a golden linga with a trident in its center. This worried the Great God, but he was so overcome with desire that he continued his lovemaking. He must have had his eyes closed, because while they were having sex the demon made a staff and a cudgel with the intention of cutting off Shiva's penis; but Shiva managed to stay one up on the demon and let flow from his mighty organ a stream of weapons. After Shiva finished making love the demon died.

In one respect this story is a multiform of the Pine Forest myth, in that the demon wishes to separate Shiva from his manhood. But the salient feature is the golden linga inside the vagina, which sounds suspiciously like a hydrated mushroom. The trident in the middle of the linga may refer to the stem of the mushroom, as sometimes the mushrooms are dried whole, with the pointed "teeth" on the mushroom cap representing the pointed tips of the trident. The trident could also be some sort of insertion device. The staff and cudgel in association with the penis make them additional mushroom metaphors; they certainly would not have been very effective in cutting off Shiva's penis.

The stream of weapons that issues from Shiva's penis corresponds to Soma-urine, which counteracts the "demonic" effects sometimes experienced from taking the mushroom initially. Another variant of the myth has Shiva putting a thunderbolt in his penis to kill the demon, who this time has pointed teeth inside his vagina.[45] The fact that Parvati is a male "demon" in both stories illustrates that such practices are not done by right-thinking folk. They are demonic. They are Left-hand.

7

The Secrets of Eden

Strange Fruit

Who would have guessed
that the fruit of Eden
that fruit forbidden
to Eve and Adam
and offered by a snake to Eve
was all along the selfsame serpent?
For the fruit was a serpent
coming out of the ground
from the roots of the tree
and shedding his skin
And the snake was a fruit
to be plucked from the ground
beneath the tree
And Eve and Adam ate him
Later Moses nailed that snake
all brazen to a cross
for everyone to gaze upon
when lost in desert sands
Sympathetic magic made
to cure the bite of serpents
Later still we find the snake
lying in a feeding trough
born again as sustenance

and saying to his followers
I must be lifted up again
just as Moses lifted up
the serpent in the wilderness
Yes he said
I am the same
The same metallic serpent
I carry my own cross and I crucify myself
And now it's time for you to eat
just as Eve and Adam ate
for I have conquered death
My death will wash your sins away
and you will know that I was born
so you may truly live
For your darkness I bring light
I am the food of my last supper
Fear me not for I have brought
the way to life
It is not I that kills
I come from deep within the earth
to remedy your ills
Upon my cross I nail myself
I give myself away
The light of God has fallen low
so you don't have to pay

Adam means Red, and Ruddy, and From the Soil. The red Adam came from the soil. Eve means Life; Eve means Perhaps; Eve means Serpent. The life of Eve is perhaps the serpent.

In the beginning, no one wrote anything down. There was no such thing as writing. But there was the Word, and the Word was the substance of God's voice. It was the same as the living God, because it was from the living God. God was the force that made things happen. Only God could give and take away. God was the One. The one responsible. God was male.

To what can we compare the Word of God? What sound did it make? It was a thundering in heaven that shook the sky, that echoed from the mountains and through the valleys. Before God spoke he would show himself in heaven as a great light, and as a fire that sometimes fell to earth. And water would fall from the sky when he spoke, but it was more than water, it was the spittle of God's mighty Word. Nay, it was more than this: it had to be the very semen of God to bring forth such abundant life. The Word of God sounded like thunder, it looked like lightning, it felt like rain; it fell like semen into the furrowed body of the Woman below, and it brought forth life.

This is one of the most ancient conceptions of God and his Word, and it is the reason that in the book of Genesis God creates light with his Word. God said, "Let there be light," and there was light, and the waters were released, and the earth brought forth.

In the Garden, Day One

No sooner had God created Adam and put him in Eden than God began to contradict himself. He told Adam that he could eat from all the trees of the garden. *All* the trees. Then God said, "Nevertheless, you can't eat from the tree of the knowledge of good and evil. If you do, you will die that very day." It appears that God was still making up his mind about things. After this, God decided that Adam needed a helpmate, so he fashioned from the soil all the wild beasts and the birds of the air and paraded them before Adam to see if he wanted one for a mate. Adam wasn't moved to take a wife from among the beasts, which is to say he wasn't attracted to them sexually; but then it was only the first day. Nevertheless God caused Adam to fall into a deep sleep and removed one of Adam's ribs, which God enclosed in flesh and made into a woman. When Adam saw her he was relieved to have someone from his own species with whom he could procreate (whatever that was).

The next thing we know, the woman is having a conversation with a serpent. The serpent asked the woman if God had really forbidden her and Adam to eat from the trees of the garden. She answered that they were allowed to eat from every tree but the one in the middle of the garden, and then she misquoted God to the snake: "You must not eat it, nor touch it, under pain of death." Of course, she wasn't there when God gave the edict to Adam, so we can't blame her; Adam must have added the bit about touching. The serpent was quick to respond, as serpents are. He told her, "You will not die. God knows that when you eat this fruit your eyes will be opened and you yourselves will become gods. Now you see everything the same. When you eat you will know the difference between good and evil." The woman saw that the tree was beautiful to look at; it pleased her. The fruit was even more beautiful, and a desire arose in her for the knowledge it would bring. She gathered some of the fruits and ate, and gave some to Adam, and he ate.

After they ate the fruits their eyes were opened, just as the serpent had said. Later that day, when the first couple heard God walking in the garden, they hid behind some bushes. If Adam and the woman hadn't yet realized that God was not all-knowing, they soon discovered this. "Where are you?" God called out.

Adam revealed himself and told God that he had hidden because he was naked, inventing prevarication as he did so, but God was not convinced. "Have you been eating from the forbidden tree?" he asked, further exhibiting his ignorance. Adam then invented the excuse: "It was that woman," he said, "the woman *you* gave me. She gave me the fruit." God still was not getting the whole picture. "What have you done?" he said to the woman. She said, "I only ate it because the serpent tempted me." She was a fast learner.

At this God became very upset. First he cursed the serpent, making him accursed beyond all beasts, which God had apparently already cursed to a lesser degree, and told the snake that he would crawl on his belly and eat dust each day of his life. All the animals were new, so perhaps God hadn't yet realized that the serpent already did this. He also told the snake that he and the man and woman and all their offspring would be enemies from that day forward. All humanity henceforth would crush the heads of serpents, and the serpents would strike their heels. Then God turned to the woman and gave her a nasty curse as well: "You will give birth in pain," he said, "and I will multiply that pain. Your only desire will be toward your husband, and he will use that against you, lording it over you."[46]

Finally it was Adam's turn. "Because of what you've done I will curse the soil. You will suffer trying to make it produce food, and it will yield brambles and thistles, forcing you to eat wild plants. When you eat your bread you will have sweat on your brow, and it will be this way until you return to the soil from which I made you." What a temper. Forget for the moment that Adam had no idea what bread was; at least God didn't kill them that very day as he had earlier said he would. God never told them they would live forever, but he did tell them they would die on the very day they ate the fruit. He either made a mistake, or he lied. Either way it's problematic.

Once God finished cursing, Adam thought it would be a good time to name his wife, who up until then was known only as "the woman." He named her Eve. After making clothes for the two chastened humans God began to talk to himself. Or perhaps he was talking to some other god; we're not told. He said, "Look. With his knowledge of good and evil the man has become like one of us." Notice that the woman is not even mentioned. "We mustn't let him pick any fruit from the tree of life, because then he would live forever." And God kicked them out of the garden, just like that. No appeal, no second chance, out they went. Then at the entrance to the garden he posted cherubs who spun swords of flashing fire. Suddenly finding themselves on the outside looking in, Adam and Eve did the only thing they could think of: they had sex.

This is a two-edged story. On the surface it is a simplistic morality tale showing us that we had better obey God or face his sure and terrible, though inconsistent, wrath. Forget that God gave an unfair test, putting the two most naive people who ever lived in front of a beautiful tree with gorgeous fruit after telling them not to eat from it. Forget that he put the subtlest of all creatures at the base of the tree to entice Eve, only a few hours old, into eating the fruit anyway. Forget that the serpent told the truth and God lied. Don't think; just obey God. And *don't* forget that it was Woman who caused it all to come tumbling down on the same day it started.

Just below the surface lie all the discrepancies I've mentioned and a bit more. The story almost invites dissection part by part, as though this were the author's intention. Aside from God's contradictions and lying, which are obvious to anyone who looks at the story critically, there are elements that are curious and suspicious. We are told that God planted *two* magical trees in the center of paradise, yet he forbade eating only from the tree of knowledge. This means that it was acceptable to eat from the tree of life even though Our Parents were kicked out just so they wouldn't.

As soon as the woman was made we find her in front of the forbidden tree, the tree of knowledge, where she encounters a serpent. It has been mentioned that Soma was likened to a serpent sloughing its skin, and we have seen that the fly agaric sometimes "sloughs" its outer skin when it pushes up out of the ground; sometimes, when the mushroom doesn't completely broach the enclosing leaves or pine needles that cover it, and opens its cap beneath them, the cap can resemble the flattened head of a pit viper (see plate 5). The stalk of the mushroom is also snakelike in its shape, and especially so when it rises out of a hole in pine needles or other leaves. If such a specimen is carefully harvested it leaves a perfectly round opening that looks like a snake hole. Snakes are said to live among the roots of trees, just as the fly agaric does. The fly agaric is the serpent at the foot of the tree of knowledge.

If the fly agaric is the serpent, then what is the fruit? Where did Eve first spy the fruit when she stood beneath the tree? Up in the branches, out of reach? Or on the ground, where one always finds the ripest fruit, down among the serpents. As much as the fly agaric might look like a serpent on occasion, it more often appears to be a ripe, round fruit that has fallen from the tree above it. It is an actual fruit, the fruiting body of the mushroom mycelium, and it resembles fruits that humans eat.[47]

When Eve approached the tree she first saw a serpent, and then the serpent started talking about the eating of fruit. In other words, the presence of the "snake," upon examination, suggests the eating of fruit. When one finds the right tree, there will be serpents that offer fruits and fruits that look like serpents, and both will be the fly agaric mushroom. The presence of the snake in the story also informs us that there is a certain danger involved if the serpent-fruit is eaten: it is possible to feel as poisoned from eating it as from being bitten by a viper, especially if it is eaten in its fresh state.

The reputation of the fruit was that it was deadly poison, but the man and woman ate it anyway, and it opened their eyes. Having one's eyes opened is positive, not negative, and in common speech implies gaining helpful and formerly hidden knowledge. In spiritual parlance it means enlightenment, passing from darkness into light. The knowledge of good and evil and the ability to discriminate between them is the gift as well as the burden of such enlightenment, signalling the end of innocence and the beginning of real maturity. It is the knowledge one needs to survive and prosper in a dangerous world. Eating the fruit of enlightenment is the act that lifted Adam and Eve above the level of the other animals. It made them godlike, as the story says. Now capable of subtle reflection, they realized their lives would one day come to an end. The idea of death had not even occurred to them before this, but now they saw things clearly. And in the clarity of this new knowledge they may have sensed that life in some form never ends.

They didn't die from eating the fruit; that had been a lie. This part of the story sounds like an echo of an ancient tribal taboo put on the mushroom by a shaman or priest. Maybe the priest wanted all the mushrooms for himself, and all the power they brought. The simplest way to prevent others from eating them would be to declare them a deadly poison. If anyone were brave enough to break the taboo and eat a mushroom, more than likely it would be eaten raw in its most visually appealing stage: young, colorful, and fruitlike. This would almost certainly cause the eater to become sick or at least nauseous. It would quickly be seen that the taboo was for a good reason and the person would feel fortunate not to have died from eating the dreadful fruit. But apparently Eve had the counsel of someone versed in the proper use of the mushroom, who assured her that she would not die; on the contrary, she and Adam would gain saving knowledge and become as gods, a fact not lost on the Head Gardener.

God's curse of the serpent is interesting; it corresponds to the "curse" placed by some societies on mushrooms in general and the fly agaric in particular. The mushroom might indeed strike someone's heel, but that same heel would crush the "head" of the mushroom. The curse illustrates the way a mycophobic society often reacts when it sees a loathsome fungus of any kind, and that is to stomp or kick it. When Eve tells the serpent what God has said about the fruit, the author has her add that even touching the fruit would cause death. Many mycophobes believe the same thing about mushrooms, especially poisonous varieties. It is, of course, not true.

The bliss of the newfound paradise did not last. Eve and Adam still had the memory of the experience and the knowledge it had awakened in them, yet afterwards they returned to mundane reality, where everything is done with effort, and pain is an inescapable part of everyday life. But they soon discovered that the state could be recaptured, albeit briefly, in the bliss of sexual union, where the true god existed in a love and joy quite apart from the stifling opprobrium of the god of the garden.

Just before giving them the boot, God realized that the two humans, with their knowledge of good and evil, had become like him. He worried that they might next eat from the tree of life and live forever, so he quickly expelled them, stationing angels with flaming swords to guard the way to the tree. We know that Soma was called the drink of immortality even though no one ever became physically immortal from drinking it, nor did anyone believe that this would happen. For untold centuries it was known that anyone who drank Soma would die like everyone else, yet the appellation was still used. The immortality spoken of refers to knowing that one's life does not end with the death of the physical body, knowledge obtainable in the fly agaric experience: this is what God was worried about. Once the humans knew this secret they would no longer remain subject to his bullying. They could tap the infinite and eternal within themselves and recognize their own inherent god-nature.

If this tale was intended to explain away persistent and nagging stories about a magical tree with even more magical fruit, it succeeds much more in piquing interest about the subject; perhaps this was the author's real intention.

The two trees are the same, unless this refers to two different species of fly agaric hosts, such as the birch and the pine. The fruits are also the same, because the mushroom grants both knowledge and "immortality." The separation could be arbitrary, made for the sake of the story, or it could be implying that although every experience with the fly agaric produces some sort of new knowledge, the knowledge of immortal life is more difficult to obtain. It may take a number of attempts before this happens, if it happens at all. Adam and Eve already knew that "God" (or a priest) had lied about the fruit killing them. What would stop them from eating it again and possibly gaining the knowledge that would put him out of a job? It was not the fruit that caused problems for Adam and Eve, it was disobeying the authorities, a problem that still exists today for those who dare to use a number of potentially beneficial and relatively harmless plant substances that happen to be arbitrarily classified as "illegal." "Original sin" is a euphemism for organized religion's condemnation of the plant-induced entheogenic experience.

How, if one wished to try this magic fruit, would one recognize the tree of life? The author supplies us with one more clue in the form of the eternally stationed cherubim or angels that guard the tree. If the right tree has been found at the right time the angels will be standing there before it dressed in white robes, fiery wings extended, spinning their flaming swords in circles of red.

8

The Prophets of Ancient Israel

Abraham and the Mountain God

The Bible is replete with characters who by today's standards would be diagnosed as suffering from paranoid schizophrenia, and Abraham is foremost among them. Newspapers today are filled with stories of people who have committed heinous crimes and blamed it on voices in their heads that told them what to do; evidently Abraham had a similar problem. From the beginning of his story in Genesis Abraham hears what he construes to be the voice of a god, usually named Yahweh, giving him all manner of commands. "Yahweh" told Abraham to leave his home and go to Canaan, so Abraham did. Later, in a vision, Yahweh promised Abraham great rewards: "You will have innumerable descendants and own all the land of Canaan." To prove this, the voice ordered Abraham to bisect a cow, a goat, and a ram, and put the halves on the ground in two rows facing each other; during the night a smoking furnace appeared, and a flaming torch passed between the halves. Then the voice assured Abraham that he would get what was promised.

Still later an apparition appeared to Abraham claiming to be El Shaddai, which means Mountain God. Mountain God told him, "You will have innumerable descendants and own all the land of Canaan. And change your name from Abram [which had been his name] to Abraham."

Now the god proclaimed an unusual condition, which, if not fulfilled, would negate the covenant they had just made. Mountain God said, "For your part of the bargain, I want you to cut off your foreskin, and the foreskin of all your descendants and anyone else who comes into your household and theirs, even if they are not related to any of you. The scars on your organs will prove to everyone forever after that we made this covenant. Any male whose foreskin is not cut off from his penis will be cut off from his people." And that very day Abraham mutilated his penis and the penis of every male member of his household, including his many slaves. The same barbaric practice continues in many places to this day, only without the promised land. And without the consent of the mutilated.

Not long after this Abraham's voices told him to send his young son Ishmael and Ishmael's mother, a servant woman, into the wilderness to fend for themselves, because Abraham's wife Sarah was jealous. So he did. It gets worse. Some years after banishing Ishmael a voice ordered Abraham to take his younger son Isaac to a mountain top, kill him, and burn him, "as an offering to me." He took the boy to the mountain (making Isaac carry the firewood) and made an altar of stones, arranging the firewood on the top. Then Abraham bound his son and laid him on the pile of wood, and took out his flint knife to kill the boy. Luckily Abraham heard the voice at this very moment.

"Just kidding!" the voice said (or words to that effect). "I only wanted to see if you would do whatever I said without questioning. You would. Because of this you will have innumerable descendants and own all the land of Canaan." This promise sounded vaguely familiar, but Abraham didn't question his good fortune. He spied a ram caught in a nearby thicket. Perhaps not wanting to waste the altar and firewood, he killed and burned the ram instead of his son. Poor Isaac. First his father cuts off part of his penis, and now this. He was scarred for life in more ways than one. We are told that Abraham named the place "Yahweh appears."

These stories are as important for their insights into the mind of a religious fanatic as they are for their mushroom correspondences. Humanity has been forever plagued by self-serving authoritarians who claim to have God's ear, or God in *their* ear, and their power can be far-reaching: I don't have a foreskin today because someone almost four thousand years ago was in the throes of a paranoid delusion and everybody went along with him. I can hear the men and boys even now: "Great idea, Abraham! Let's all mutilate our penises!"

Why would Abraham's god require him to cut off his foreskin as a sign of their special relationship? Either Abraham was truly insane, or the act represents some unusual trait of the Mountain God that Abraham was trying to emulate. Or both. We have seen that the penis fascination of the Hindus may be due in part to the resemblance between a phallus and the fly agaric mushroom. In its early stage of growth the glans-like cap is completely ensheathed by the universal veil in much the same way the foreskin sheathes the glans of the penis. The growth of the mushroom eventually causes the universal veil to separate from the mushroom's base by causing a tear along the outer circumference of the cap, a kind of self-circumcision if you will. This tearing away of the upper portion of the veil is what gives the fly agaric its distinctive pot-shaped base (see plate 1). The cap is then seen as distinct from the base, in the same way circumcision allows the glans to be seen as distinct from the penile shaft.

Certainly circumcision could also have been performed as a prophylactic measure among some desert tribes with little access to water, but the fly agaric may be the reason that circumcision became associated with the Word of God. And it is significant that it was a Mountain God who required the surgery to be performed. Soma, Vishnu, Shiva, Parvati, and Skanda were also mountain gods, and there is certainly no shortage of penis references and cutting remarks in their mythology. In the Pine Forest story the priests order God to cut his penis; in the story of Abraham God orders the priest to cut his.

Fire altars and sacrifices were an integral part of the early Jewish religion, as they were of the Soma and Haoma cults. When the voice told Abraham to sacrifice his son it told him to do it on top of a mountain, the second significant mountain reference in the story. In the Middle East as in India, *Amanita* species will be found only in the mountainous regions. Abraham built a raised altar with fire on top, on which he was going to sacrifice his circumcised child, just as the Aryans built fire altars on which to sacrifice Soma, the "circumcised" mushroom. Instead of his son a ram was sacrificed, an animal with white wool covering blood-red flesh, a fly agaric image we will meet again when discussing Christianity.

The story says the voice on the mountain was an "angel" of Yahweh, thus adding a fiery-winged messenger to the mix of symbols. The last clue comes when Abraham names the place "Yahweh appears" and the author tells us that this is the origin of the old Jewish saying, "On the mountain of Yahweh he appears." Yahweh and his Word are not different, as John informs his readers in the Christian Bible. The angel of God, God's Word in the flesh, appears at, and as, the fiery altar of sacrifice on the Mountain of God.

Moses and the Fiery God-Plant

In the colorful and often bloody history of the Jews prior to the birth of Jesus no one commands more awe and reverence than Moses does. To have frequent conversation with God and receive God's personal, finger-written correspondence are the marks of a demi-god, not a human, to those outside the faith things may look a little different. The circumstances of Moses' birth and ancestry are debated even today, but it is generally agreed that he was raised by the Egyptians and may have been groomed to become a high official, if not Pharaoh. He was steeped in the philosophy and religion of Egypt and seems to have been familiar with the solar monotheism of Akhenaton as well as the various magical practices and rites for which the Egyptians were famous. We will take up the story of Moses just after he was seen killing an Egyptian who had mistreated a Hebrew laborer.

Fleeing to an area south of the Red Sea, Moses joined a group of Midianite sheep herders. Their leader, a priest named Jethro, liked the intelligent newcomer and gave him his daughter Zipporah in marriage, and for some time Moses lived the life of a simple shepherd. One day, when pasturing Jethro's sheep on Horeb, the Mountain of God, he saw a strange sight:

a plant that glowed like fire, yet gave off no smoke and was not consumed. The story says that this plant was another angel of Yahweh. Moses moved closer so he could see why the plant was not burned. He heard a voice from the midst of the fiery plant call his name. "I am here," Moses replied. The plant said, "Stay where you are and take the shoes off your feet, for the ground upon which you stand is holy. I am the God of your fathers."

The god-plant went on to say that it had a plan: Moses was to lead the Hebrews out of Egypt and into a land overflowing with milk and honey. The land was already occupied by the Canaanites and others, of course, but that didn't matter since God had already given it to Abraham. Several times. "After you lead the people out of Egypt, come back to this mountain and offer worship to God," said the plant.

Moses was a little unsure of himself. He said, "You, a plant, want me to go to the Hebrews and tell them that I have been sent by the God of their fathers. Great. And what if they ask me what your name is?" The plant answered, "I am who I am [Yahweh]. Tell the sons of Israel, 'I Am has sent me.' Then go with the tribal elders to visit Pharaoh and tell him to let all the Hebrews go into the wilderness for three days to offer sacrifice." Moses was worried. He wondered what would happen if the Egyptians didn't believe that Yahweh had appeared to him, so the plant gave him a few tricks to convince them.

First it had Moses throw his staff on the ground, where it turned into a serpent. When he picked it up by the tail it turned back into a staff. As a result of this Moses was sometimes called "the staff of God." Then Moses was told to put his hand into his bosom and draw it back out. When he did so the hand was covered with white leprous patches. When he put it back into his bosom and drew it out again the hand was free of the white patches. Next the plant instructed Moses in the subtle art of equivocation: "If the first trick doesn't convince them, the second surely will. But if neither one works, take some water from the river and pour it on the ground in front of them, and the water will have turned bloody. Now go."

Moses was still worried. He said, "I have uncircumcised lips. Why should Pharaoh listen to me?" The plant said, "Look, I am making you into a god before Pharaoh. Your brother Aaron can speak for you as your prophet. Besides, it really doesn't matter, because I will make Pharaoh say 'no' every time you ask him to release the Hebrews, regardless of what sorts of magic you show him. I do this so that I can visit many plagues upon Egypt to prove to them that I am God. I will allow Pharaoh to say 'yes' after I have killed his first born child, his son, and the first born of every creature in Egypt, including the cattle."

After saying goodbye to Jethro Moses took his wife and son and began his journey, but then the strangest thing happened: when they stopped for the night Yahweh came to meet Moses and tried to kill him. The same Yahweh who had just finished telling Moses to go on this journey was now killing him on the first night of the trip! This is one of those incidents that theologians tend to skirt, and for good reason. How the almighty God could have failed in the attempt to kill Moses is not told, but in a fit of inspiration Zipporah grabbed a flint and cut off the foreskin of their son; she then touched the bloody prepuce to Moses' penis, saying, "Truly you are a bloody husband to me!" Because of Zipporah's bizarre actions Yahweh spared Moses.

When they arrived in Egypt it was as the god-plant had said. Moses and Aaron showed all the tricks of their god but the court magicians duplicated most of them, even, stupidly, the plagues on their own people. It didn't matter, of course, because Pharaoh found himself unable to say anything but "no" to Moses' request. After a series of terrible plagues Moses finally got to play his trump card. He warned Pharaoh that Pharaoh's son and all the first born of Egypt would be dead in the morning unless Pharaoh let the Israelites go. Pharaoh couldn't help himself: "No," he said.

Some days earlier Yahweh had said to Moses, "Tell all the Israelites that they should paint the lintels and posts of their doorways with blood on the night before I kill the first-born of Egypt, so that I will know to pass over their houses," and this is what the Israelites did. Also, on that day they were to eat only unleavened bread; no leaven should even be in their houses. Later, after the killing was accomplished, Pharaoh summoned Moses and told him to leave, and take all the Israelites with him. That very day Moses and over 600,000 Hebrews left Egypt, loaded down with jewelery, gold, and vast herds of animals, amazing booty for slaves to come away with.

Moses hadn't told anyone exactly where it was they were going, but he knew their first destination was Horeb, the Mountain of God. After wandering for some time with little food the people began to complain. Yahweh assured Moses that he would supply the people with food. At night Yahweh sent flocks of quails flying into the camp, and the people ate them. It must have been a vast covey to feed so many people. In the morning there were little white balls the size of coriander seeds covering the ground, but it was not from the birds. When the people saw it they said, "Manna?" which means "What is it?" For some reason manna became the name of the substance. The people were instructed to gather what they needed for the day and eat it, but not to save any for the next day. Those who disobeyed found that in the morning the saved manna had bred maggots and smelled foul.

When the horde was nearing the Mountain of God they camped at a place that had no water, and the people complained to Moses. Yahweh instructed Moses to take his staff, gather the elders of Israel, and go to a certain rock at Horeb; once there he should strike the rock with his staff and water would flow out. This is what he did, and the water flowed.

Finally the sojourners reached the Mountain of God. Now Moses was a clever man, and the first thing he did was mark out boundaries around the base of the mountain. He told the people that Yahweh had told him no one was to cross the boundary and go up the mountain, or even touch the foot of the mountain, or that person would be put to death. No one would even be allowed to touch the condemned person: the execution had to be by arrows or stones. Even animals that touched the mountain would be killed. Then

Moses told the people that he would be speaking directly with Yahweh, who would appear in the form of a dense cloud. "What sounds like thunder is actually God's voice," Moses said, "but only I will be able to understand what is being spoken. I will tell all of you what it is that Yahweh has said." With this Moses led the people to the foot of the mountain. Clouds covered the mountain top and violent thunderstorms rent the air. Fires and smoke could be seen on the mountain's summit.

Moses' first translation of the thunder took the form of what has come to be called the Ten Commandments. The people said, "Fine, whatever God says, just don't make us talk with him." The people kept their distance as Moses approached the mountain and faced the raging storm. Yahweh took this opportunity to present, through the mouth of Moses, a long and specific list of laws, ending with the admonition not to boil a young goat in its mother's milk, a despicable Canaanite practice of which God didn't want any part. Then he promised that if the people kept all the laws he gave them he would send his angel before them to destroy utterly the multitudes living on the lands the Israelites were about to ransack. "Exterminate" is the word he used, and although he didn't do what he promised, this is exactly what the Israelites themselves did when they met in battle the Canaanites, the Amorites, the Hittites, the Perizzites, and all the other peoples they ruthlessly slaughtered on their way to establishing Yahweh's righteous kingdom on earth; in many instances they killed every man, woman, child, and animal.[48]

Moses built a stone altar at the foot of the mountain and instructed some young men to begin slaughtering bulls to burn on the altar; half the blood Moses put in basins and half he threw on the altar. Then Moses turned around and threw blood on the people, telling them that it was the blood of the covenant that God had made with them. Thick clouds covered the mountain for six days, and on the seventh day Moses went up into the cloud. He stayed on the mountain for forty days, during which he must have been taking dictation much of the time, so long was the list of God's orders Moses carried with him when he finally returned to camp.

The first thing Yahweh told Moses on the mountain was that he, Yaweh, was now accepting costly donations from the people, which Moses should collect and use to build a sanctuary in which Yahweh could "dwell with the people." The second command was to construct a wooden box, an ark, plated with pure gold inside and out, and with moldings of pure gold. Four rings of cast gold would be mounted (two to a side), through which two gold-plated poles would be inserted for transporting the ark. A seat of gold would then be made for the top, a "seat of mercy," with two cherubim of gold mounted at either end, their golden wings forming an arch over the seat. Inside this ornate box would be kept the tablets of the Testimony. Henceforth it would be here, on the mercy seat, that God would appear to give his many commands to the children of Israel.

The third item of note that came out of these discussions was God's directive to construct a large tent called a tabernacle. The walls of the tabernacle were to be made of red, crimson, and violet linen embroidered with golden cherubim. Covering the tabernacle would be large sheets of wool sewn together. Over this would be placed a covering made of ram skins dyed red and over this a covering of fine leather. The framework of the tent was to be made of acacia wood plated with gold, and all the clasps and fittings would also be gold. Within the tent would be a square partition made again of hanging fabric of red, crimson, and violet wherein the ark and mercy seat would rest. Only the high priest could enter this Holy of Holies. The rest of the list contained the many minute details regarding the accoutrements of the tabernacle, the clothing and investiture of the priests, and other details. When God had finished telling Moses what to do he gave Moses two tablets of stone on which were written the Ten Words of the Testimony.

Moses didn't return for a long time. The people began to fear that he wasn't coming back, so they went to Aaron and asked him to supply a god to go before them as Moses had done. Aaron didn't hesitate. He had the men collect all the gold earrings in the camp and bring them to him. These Aaron melted down and cast into the likeness of a bull. The men cried out, "Israel! Here is the god who led you out of Egypt!" The next day a sacrifice was offered.

About this time Moses was making his way down the mountain, and he heard the sounds of music and chanting. When he saw the golden bull and the people dancing and fornicating before it he broke the tablets on the ground and went berserk. Running up to the altar in a rage he grabbed the bull by the horns; first he burned it, then he ground it into powder, mixed it with water, and made all the people drink it. Calling out to the crowd he said, "Whoever is for Yahweh, come and stand with me!" All the Levites rallied around him, and he ordered them to draw their swords and slay every man, woman, and child who had not come to his side. The number of people said to have been murdered that day ranges from 3,000 to 23,000.

After the butchery Moses praised the men who had so mercilessly slain their kinsmen, and in some cases their parents, brothers, sisters, wives, sons, and daughters: "Today you have won investiture as priests of Yahweh, and today he grants you a blessing." Maybe there is good reason to demand that freedom of religion become part of the constitution of every nation.

After his little fit of pique Moses returned to the mountain, wrote the ten words once again on two tablets of stone and, after forty days, returned to camp. He was troubled when Aaron and the others backed away from him, until they told him that his face was so radiant it frightened them. Moses called them to him and told them what Yahweh had said; then Moses put a veil over his face so he wouldn't continue to scare them. After this he always kept the veil over his face, except when he spoke with God in the tabernacle tent. Once inside the tent Moses would remove his veil and leave his face uncovered until he came out to tell the people what Yahweh had said; then he would put it back on until the next time. Each time Moses returned from talking with God his face was radiant.

Moses spent the rest of his life writing laws and the punishments for violating those laws, many of which were draconian. Any men or women who are magicians? Stone them to death. The daughter of a priest who prostitutes herself? Burn her to death. A man who wants to marry? Only a virgin from his own family. Curse Yahweh (a fickle and arbitrary god if there ever was one) and what happens? Death by stoning, of course.

Shortly before the Israelites finally attacked the land of Canaan, after they had left Mount Hor and were near Edom, they ran short of food, and the people again complained that Moses had brought them out of Egypt only to die in the wilderness. God heard their complaint, the story says, and as an answer sent fiery, winged serpents to attack them. Many people died from the poison of the serpents and in their fear the survivors repented and apologized to Moses for all their complaining. They asked him to fix things with Yahweh and protect them from the serpents. Yahweh told Moses to make a fiery serpent out of metal and put it on top of a pole, which he did, probably using copper and perhaps some gold to get the fiery effect he wanted. After this, those who had been bitten by the fiery serpents had only to look upon the metallic serpent and they would not die.[49]

The Hidden Symbols

Moses may or may not have been a religious man before he went into hiding, but he certainly was after his first encounter with Yahweh on the Mountain of God. A burning plant, indeed. After all the stories of Agni and Shiva that have been presented it is difficult not to think of the fly agaric once again, and the setting is perfect. It is in the high mountain conifer forests of the Middle East that the *Amanita* genus is found, and if there were any segment of the desert population with a knowledge of mountain mushrooms it would have been shepherds. Few people had reason to climb to the high mountain meadows, but shepherds routinely did so. During and after the rainy season the mountain forests fill with grasses and flowers, so during these times desert shepherds drive their sheep to the mountains to feed. The rain also brings many species of mushrooms to these same meadows. The only "burning" plant that enables one to speak with God, at least the only one I have found, is the fiery fly agaric (plate 18).

It is possible that the burning bush story represents Moses' finding the fly agaric on his own accidently, but it is more likely that he was initiated into a shepherdic mushroom cult by Jethro, the Midianite priest whose flocks Moses was pasturing. This part of the tale hides several other mushroom analogies, in addition to the "flaming plant" correspondence these other parallels seem to be cultic details intentionally inserted into the story. For example, after getting Moses' attention the first thing the god-plant says is, "Take off your shoes! The ground on which you are so carelessly stamping is holy!" This is vital information, not a pious religious observance, if the plant doing the talking is a mushroom. A cult would want its novice foragers to know that when hunting for the fiery prey, as soon as the first mushroom is sighted it is a good practice to stand still and look around carefully, especially in the immediate vicinity of one's feet, because if a person can see one mushroom there are probably others nearby, possibly underfoot and unbeknownst to the hunter. Walking through a fruiting grove barefoot is not only more respectful of the god, but it is also more prudent. There is less likelihood of damaging the harvest.

Moses was made aware that he was in the presence of a god; one can sometimes feel the same way during fly agaric intoxication. One can also feel extremely energetic and strong, and this strength is not an illusion. It is well known among Siberian users of the fly agaric that feats of tremendous physical endurance are possible under its influence. After "meeting" the god-plant, Moses felt strong enough to come out of hiding and try to right the wrongs being done to his people. He could now speak forcefully enough to argue with the Pharaoh, and well enough to convince the Israelites to follow him. This from a man with formerly "uncircumcised lips," which implies a speech impediment of some kind. We are reminded by this phrase of Abraham's similar conversation with God on a mountain top and must wonder about the inordinate interest these men had in circumcision.

Moses protested that he wouldn't know how to name the god when people asked him on whose authority he spoke, and the god said his name was, "I am," and "I am who I am." On one level this can be viewed as sophisticated philosophy, a way of forcing people to accept that the god exists within them by making the god's name an act of identification with the person. "Who is God?" "I am." Moses realized that "I am" is the nature of God because when Moses ate the mushroom he felt the god within himself as himself. And because this is a difficult concept to grasp without personal experience, Moses kept it to himself once he arrived in Egypt to round up the Israelites, since there wouldn't be enough mushrooms for everyone anyway.

The two "signs" Moses received from Yahweh may be signs of the mushroom and not tricks to show Pharaoh. The first sign, his staff turning into a serpent and back again, is reminiscent of the serpent and the tree in the Garden of Eden story as well as the "Pillar" appellation of Soma and Shiva. The "stiff staff" that changes into a "wriggling snake" and back again is undeniably phallic as well as being another mushroom parallel.

The second sign occurred when Moses put his hand "into his breast" and it came out covered with scaly white patches. These patches correspond to the white veil fragments covering the "breast" of the fly agaric. The somewhat sticky pieces sometimes adhere to the skin when handling the fresh mushroom but are easily wiped off, just as they can be wiped off the cap.

If the serpent-staff and the white patches failed to convince, Moses was told to pour water that would "turn bloody." Dried fly agarics immersed in water turn the water a dilute red as though a quantity of blood had been mixed with it. The same thing happens to urine, as noted earlier.

These were the signs given to Moses to convince others that he had found the correct god-plant: the plant grows in the mountains, low to the ground; it contains the power of a god; it resembles a serpent in several ways; it stands on one "staff" and is phallic in appearance; it has white patches covering its "breast"; and it glows red like a live coal.

Scholars are at a loss to explain why Yahweh tried to kill Moses just as Moses was leaving to perform the task Yahweh himself had assigned. Anyone wishing to demonstrate the perfidy of the ancient God would have to go no further than this verse, so its inclusion here is curious. Since no one has been able to come up with even a remotely plausible explanation of the episode, I will offer one.

We know that sex magic was used extensively by the Tantrics and others in India who also used the fly agaric, and I have conjectured that the fly agaric was used in the sexual practices. The foreskin of the penis is related to the cap of the fly agaric. It could easily be construed to refer to the whole cap and not just the universal veil, and since the entire cap separates from the base at "circumcision," cutting off the cap still leaves the phallic stalk intact. Moses' wife touches her son's "foreskin" to the penis of her husband and says, "Surely you are a bloody husband to me." What could this possibly mean? We know that Shiva found a golden "linga" that had been placed in a vagina, perhaps with a penis-stone. There is no reason an actual penis couldn't be used for the same purpose, which would certainly have made Moses a "bloody husband" to his wife, given the way "bloody" juice flows from the moistened cap. A woman using the fly agaric in similar fashion by herself could also address the mushroom directly with the same statement, "Surely you are a bloody husband to me." For that matter, so could a man.

The story also appears to record a near death experience that Moses suffered, because "Yahweh tried to kill him"; a fly agaric consumer sometimes unexpectedly experiences the same thing. The same god-plant that had revealed mysteries and given Moses new-found strength now appeared to be taking his life; his wife may actually have made a desperate offering of her son's foreskin to placate the penis-mushroom that was raging inside Moses, touching it to his penis in an act of sympathetic magic. Or perhaps the near death experience prompted Moses to experiment with ways of bypassing the digestive system in order to avoid getting sick, as explained in chapter 5.

Moses recovered, of course, and made his way to Egypt. He and Aaron met with Pharaoh and showed him their magic, but Pharaoh was not impressed by it. What he was impressed by was the series of natural disasters the area was going through at the time, which probably included earthquakes and climate-altering volcanic activity. With crops failing, livestock dying, and food stocks running low, the thought of suddenly having 600,000 (or whatever the real number) fewer mouths to feed every day must indeed have seemed providential to Pharaoh, and he let the Israelites leave. Yet it appears Moses played one last trick on Pharaoh.

The angel of death passed over the houses of people who had painted blood on their doorposts and lintels, an act that is curiously and specifically linked with unleavened bread.

The people had to leave so quickly, the story says, that they had no time to leaven their bread dough, and this odd fact is mentioned a number of times; it was considered so important that unleavened bread became incorporated into the Passover ritual. Yet it wasn't because they had to leave quickly that the Israelites ate unleavened bread; Moses had already told them not to eat leavened bread on that day. What is the reason for this pretext?

A dried fly agaric cap bears a resemblance to a small loaf of unleavened bread and has a similar consistency. Perhaps this is a reminder to eat the mushroom only in its "unleavened" or dried state, not its expanded blood-red state, so that the angel of death will pass by.

There may be more, however, to this story of a petty god who mercilessly slew innocent people to prove a point. There are documented reports even in modern times of the poisoning of whole villages due to the consumption of contaminated grain, usually in the form of bread. The last large-scale outbreaks occurred in France in 1816. The poisoning agent was a fungus, *Claviceps purpurea,* a sac fungus that attacks the ripening heads of grains; it is a powerful hallucinogen that is effective in minuscule dosages. Commonly called ergot, the plant has long been used in obstetrics and is the source of the extremely potent drug LSD.

Ergotamine poisoning is of two types: gangrenous and spasmodic. The gangrenous type is characterized by the cessation of circulation in various parts of the body, resulting in gangrene of the limbs. If the respiratory muscles are affected death quickly follows. The symptoms of the spasmodic type are more LSD-like in nature and include itching and tingling of the skin, visual distortion, twitching and spasms, deafness, hallucinations, and psychotic episodes. The different reactions are caused by two or more different species of *Claviceps,* one of which, *Claviceps paspilli,* is significantly more benign in its effects.

Ergot poisoning can occur wherever grain is grown and consumed; a trained eye can easily pick out infected heads of grain. Moses had been trained in the wisdom of both the Semitic tribes and the Egyptians. He was familiar with their magic and their pharmacopoeia; it is entirely feasible that the knowledge of the various ergot species was part of his education from either or both sources. The growing of grain, after all, is thought to have come to Egypt by way of Palestine.

Although there are no Egyptian records of the Israelite "sojourn" in Egypt, it appears from Hebrew writings that by the time of the Exodus a large part of the working class was comprised of Hebrews. There is no reason to assume that they were only brickmakers, the only Jewish trade mentioned in the story. If the circumstances required it, foreigners were employed at virtually every type of work that needed to be done, including farming, milling, and baking; cooks and housekeepers were especially prized among the upper classes. If Moses had really wanted to impress Pharaoh with the power of an angry Yahweh, he could have made a great show of threatening Pharaoh in front of witnesses, as he did prior to the killing of the firstborn; if Yahweh had done nothing by the next day Moses would lose face and leave defeated, but if Yahweh performed according to Moses' threat,

Pharaoh would be forced to recognize Yahweh's power and capitulate. The story tells us that Moses won: there were dead people throughout the city, yet the Israelites were all healthy and unharmed.

Barring as unreasonable partisan complicity on God's part, what should we assume happened here? Could Moses have poisoned the Egyptians' bread supply with ergot? Logic dictates that if the story has any validity at all the people were poisoned. Moses could have delivered poison to virtually every Egyptian in the city and many of their animals if he had somehow been able to get it into the daily bread, which was the staple food of the whole country; large bakeries were common in the cities. The only poison possibly available to Moses, which could have caused such widespread sickness and death overnight, seemingly selective in its bizarre symptoms and with low, effective dosages was ergot. But how would this have been accomplished?

Consider this: Moses has word sent secretly to Jewish domestics and bakers throughout the city, especially those in the Pharaoh's palace and the homes of influential citizens, that the bread of the Egyptians is to be leavened on a certain day with leavening "from Yahweh," which will help the Israelites win their freedom. They are supplied with a lump of leavening that is infected with species of *Claviceps* fungus, dried and ground into fine powder. In those days all leavening was done in the "sour dough" method; that is, for each day's baking a small amount of fermented dough kept over from the previous day was kneaded into larger amounts of fresh dough, leavening the whole amount. On the given day the Israelites are to use only this "special" leavening when they make bread and must eat none of the bread themselves. Only the Egyptians are to eat it. To be sure of their own safety the bakers must eat bread with no leavening whatsoever.

The same prohibition is given to all other Israelites as well: on that day eat only unleavened bread and do not even have leavening in the house. When the fateful day arrives everyone does as instructed, and soon most of the Egyptian population is in the throes of a very bad LSD-type experience (or worse). There is wailing in the streets; there is bedlam everywhere. Many are extremely sick or dying; many are completely out of their minds. Pharaoh, whose own firstborn son was among the dead, summons Moses and orders him and the Israelites to leave Egypt immediately. Pharaoh realized then that Moses was not the smalltime magician he had appeared to be; he had the ear of a powerful and cruel god. Pharaoh's whole city was sick or dying, yet the Israelites were all fit and healthy. Pharaoh had no choice; he let them leave.

Yahweh, through Moses, told the Israelites to "ask" the Egyptians for silver and gold to take with them, each one asking his or her neighbor. The author says the Egyptians complied because "Yahweh gave the people great prestige in the eyes of the Egyptians, and they gave what was asked of them." Sure. In the midst of unparalleled misery and death the whole city revives just long enough to cheerfully give all their gold and valuables to the Israelites, the same Israelites, who were despised slaves.

Now imagine a city filled with sick, hallucinating, and dying people who *don't* quickly revive when the Israelites walk into their homes, and the inappropriate generosity of the Egyptians suddenly makes sense. They were too sick or out of their minds to put up any resistance whatsoever; the Israelites, as the story so indelicately phrases it, "plundered" the Egyptians; they robbed them blind. Leaving with vast herds of animals and all the gold, silver, jewelery, fabric, and clothing their animals could carry, the only thing the Israelites seem to have neglected in their looting was a raid on the granaries; as a consequence they ran out of staple foodstuffs quickly on their journey.

Before reaching the Mountain of God the wanderers experienced the miracle of the manna. What this was is anybody's guess, but it does have certain mushroom parallels that, while probably not relating directly to the fly agaric in this instance, may be a remnant of a story that does. The manna made its appearance overnight, just as mushrooms seem to. They were round and white, as some mushrooms are, notably puffballs and embryonic fly agarics. If the manna-balls were kept overnight they bred maggots; mushrooms are vulnerable to maggot infestation, and this is a real problem with the fly agaric. Many is the time I brought home what seemed to be an uninfected specimen only to find it teeming with maggots in the morning. The manna kept overnight also stank: rotting fly agaric flesh smells like carrion, truly horrid. Fly agaric also has an anorexic effect when eaten which lasts for many hours. The mushroom correspondences indicate that the story is a conflation of cultic lore and an early survival tale.

The next miracle we encounter is the striking of a rock to obtain water. As well as looking like an egg in its early life, the young fly agaric also resembles a rough white stone, an image later encountered in Christianity and alchemy. This means that an unusual reference to a magic stone could possibly be a reference to the fly agaric.

We've seen that the pillar gods of India correspond to the fly agaric, as does Moses' "Staff of God." Not only does he *carry* the serpent-staff of God, he becomes *known* as the Staff of God; Moses becomes a personification of the god-plant as well as a user of it, the same thing that happened to Soma, Vishnu, Agni, Shiva and Hanuman. "Staff," like "pillar" and "serpent," also has the alternative reading of "penis," as we saw with Shiva. Moses had a staff that sometimes was like a serpent and sometimes like an erect penis, which suggests that perhaps the staff Moses used to strike the mushroom-stone to release the pent-up waters was his penis, which is not a satisfying image. But the same elements can be stated in a different way: Moses "makes water" from the mushroom-stone; it manifests magically through the agency of his "staff." A gloss puts the location of the miracle at Horeb, home of the fiery god-plant known for its ability to produce two types of magic water.

It is interesting to note in this regard that Perseus, beheader of the snake-festooned Medusa and recent convert to the worship of snake-festooned Dionysus, named the city of Mycenae after a toadstool he found growing on the site. A stream of water poured forth from the toadstool. Later, as we will see, the European alchemists likewise extracted divine water from a stone.

When the vast caravan finally reached the Mountain of God it was the rainy season and thunderstorms were raging on the mountain's slopes. Moses' timing was perfect: the rainy season meant it was also mushroom season. The first thing he did on arrival was to issue a spurious decree from Yahweh: "Anyone who so much as touches even the foot of the mountain will immediately be put to death." Then he put up boundary markers along the base of the mountain so there would be no question about the point past which it would be deadly to tread.

Let us assume that Moses came back here primarily (or wholly) to harvest mushrooms during the rainy season. These mushrooms could serve him well in his new role as leader and priest of a small nation in terms of the spiritual counsel and sheer physical energy they would provide. But if the people found out, two things could happen. They might want mushrooms for themselves, which due to the limited supply would mean he wouldn't end up with any; or they might brand him as a magician or necromancer and kill him (which wasn't as likely since the people seemed to *like* magicians and necromancers at the time). It was the Moses the magician's—I mean God's—own laws that made these practices a capital offense.

So it was probably for reasons of supply that Moses kept the real purpose of his expedition secret as well as the unavoidable fact that the mushrooms gave him an immense advantage in his dealings with the people. It allowed him to operate at another level of consciousness entirely; the Israelites believed anything he told them because when he was under the influence of the fly agaric, which appears to have been often, he spoke with the power and authority of a god. These people were not twentieth-century sophisticates; they were conditioned to superstition and magical thinking, a trait that Moses exploited to the maximum degree.

Moses didn't want anyone even to *see* a fly agaric, because they are so striking that they elicit immediate interest. They do not go unnoticed. If secrecy is the intent it becomes imperative to keep people away from the whole area in which the mushrooms are found, in this case an entire mountain or range. And this was not a half-measure; the death penalty assured that the prohibition would be taken seriously. Once the taboo was established (the second taboo of the Hebrew Bible; the first was the fruit of Eden) Moses had free run of the mountain and its forests. He knew exactly where he was and where he was going, and he also knew that he would not soon pass that way again, if ever. As a priest of the fiery god-plant Yahweh he was duty-bound to harvest every fly agaric he could get his hands on. The story tells us that Moses spent a total of at least eighty days alone on the mountain, which in a bumper year could have resulted in numerous specimens. A harvest can easily extend to that length if the rains are propitious and evenly spaced.

A bumper crop would have presented problems to someone who wanted to keep his harvest a secret. It would have been difficult keeping *anything* secret among the thousands of people living together in the most intimate conditions imaginable; trying to hide several large bags of dried mushrooms would have been nearly impossible, especially for Moses, whose every move was scrutinized. His solution was ingenious: he told the ever-gullible throng that Yahweh had ordered them to construct a box of certain dimensions and out of certain materials, and that the box was to be used exclusively for storing the tablets of the Word of God; Moses even showed the people the two small tablets that would go inside. No one seems to have noticed that the ark itself was vastly overbuilt: measuring 52 inches x 31 inches x 31 inches, it could have held dozens or even hundreds of such tablets. Or thousands of dried mushroom caps.

No sooner had Moses issued the decree to build the ark than he pronounced still another taboo: once construction was complete, anyone who so much as *touched* the ark would be put to death immediately. It was carried by rings and poles so that even the bearers would not be in danger of touching it. There were no exceptions. Years later when a faithful steward reached out and righted the ark when it was about to tumble to the ground, the man was executed on the spot, even though he had saved the ark from desecration.

There had to have been as great a secret attached to the ark as there was to the Mountain of God for the same excessive taboo to be applied to both. There was, and it was the same secret: the fiery god-plant, grown on the Mountain of God and carried away in the Ark of God. And for those who inadvertently discovered the secret, or simply got too close to it, the penalty was the same: instant execution.

After his first forty days on the mountain Moses returned with the Tablets of the Pretext and was shocked to see the people dancing and fornicating in front of a gold bull. The worship of God as a bull was happening at the time in several places, including Canaan, Syria, and of course India, where the "bull" was the red mushroom that turns to gold when it dries. Which form of bull worship the Israelites were performing is not known, but once again there are curious similarities to the ritual use of fly agaric in other areas.

We are told that Moses "burned" the bull and ground it to powder, which, unless the bull had been made of wood and merely coated with gold, would not have been possible. He then put the powder in water and made all the participants drink. This sounds more like a ritual than a form of punishment, but punishment comes swift and sure after the drinking episode. "Put the bull-plant next to fire until it becomes golden and so dry that it is easily powdered. Mix the powder with water and drink." These imagined instructions give a sophisticated recipe not only for bringing about the vital chemical changes that drying produces, but also for getting the mushroom into the stomach without chewing it. Whatever the Israelites were really doing in Moses' absence is unknown, but the inclusion of the bull-burning episode in the story seems to be another misplaced remnant of cultic mushroom practice.

After ordering the slaughter of thousands of innocent people Moses issued instructions for constructing the ark and the tabernacle and then went back to the mountain for forty more days. When he returned his face was glowing so much that people thought something was wrong with him. When a user consumes a large quantity of fly agaric mushrooms this is what happens: the face glows like a red lantern. Capillaries in the skin dilate and the face can become engorged with blood to the extent that others become concerned for the person's well-being. It is not a subtle blush; it is extremely noticeable. Adding to the overall effect is the fact that portions of the face can drain of blood while the rest of the face remains engorged, creating an even stranger sight: a bright red face with white spots. This is what happened to Moses every time he "talked" with God in private, and it was so unusual and noteworthy that it has a prominent place in the story.

The veil Moses wore to cover his brightness can be seen as symbolic of the veil that covers the face of Yahweh's angel, the cap of the mushroom, and therefore can be seen as an act of sympathetic magic on Moses' part. It appears though that Moses used the veil as another ruse. The story says he wore the veil at all times except when he came out of the tabernacle tent with face aglow to reveal Yahweh's latest messages to the people; then he would again put on the veil and wear it until the next time talked to Yahweh. I propose that far from being worn to hide his illuminated countenance, the veil was instead worn to hide his ordinary, non-illuminated face during the times he was not intoxicated. It would have been more advantageous for Moses to have the people think that he was always in such an exalted condition.

Toward the end of their wanderings the Israelites passed through a mountainous region near Mount Hor and the people were attacked by "fiery winged serpents," whose poison evidently killed some of them. Moses was asked to intervene with Yahweh on their behalf and was told by Yahweh to make a fiery serpent of metal and put it on a pole: this would stop the poisoning. Once again we seem to have cultic information masquerading as a historical event, although it is entirely possible that an actual event forms the basis of the story.

We are told that the people had no food, then that they were poisoned by fiery winged serpents, which we immediately recognize as a metaphor for the fly agaric. Hungry people forage for food; if fly agarics were found it is likely they would have been eaten, which would have resulted in numerous poisonings, some of them fatal if the hungry person in question could have wolfed down enough of them. In order to stop the poisonings the simple expedient would be to turn those fiery serpents into fiery *metallic* serpents; that is, dry the fresh mushrooms to make them safer and more tolerable.

It has been pointed out that when a mature fly agaric specimen is viewed in profile it resembles a bird. If that same mushroom is allowed to dry intact the bird disappears and is replaced by a "fiery serpent," due to the changing shape of the cap and its new metallic color. It is the fiery winged serpent on a pole that eliminates poisoning (plate 19).

PLATE 1 *above left:* A young fly agaric with the "horns" of the universal veil covering the unexpanded cap (p. 20). Other references: Pot-like base (p. 37). Thorns of the mystic flower (p. 93). Crown of thorns (p. 123).

PLATE 2 *above right:* A fly agaric digging up the ground with its horns like Soma the bull (p. 20). Other references: The pointed buckler (shield) protecting the cap from harm (p. 96). Adam, "the luminous man of blood," with earth spread over him (p. 147).

PLATE 3 *below:* The three main stages in the fly agaric growth cycle: the egg, double-sphere, and umbrella shapes. Also shows the difference in color between the rounded cap and expanded (flat) cap (p. 28).

PLATE 4 *facing page:* Altars of sacrificial fire (p. 30). Other references: Straight-legged hoofed angels (p. 102). Base and stem resemble bones (p. 163).

PLATE 5 *above:* The poisonous serpent coming out of the ground (p. 33).

PLATE 6 *right:* Dried skins of the red and tawny bull (p. 39).

PLATE 7 *above:* Shimmering gold worn on the limbs of the fierce god Rudra (p. 39).

PLATE 8 *right:* The decorated penis of Rudra, the god of the pine forest (p. 41).

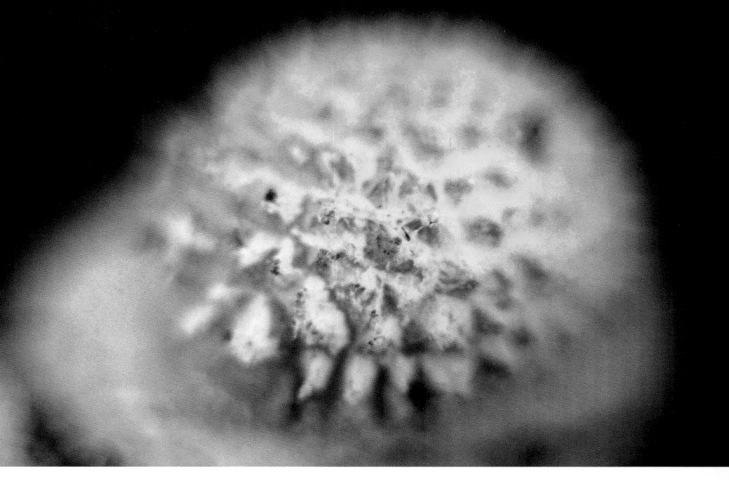

PLATE 9 *above:* Rudra showing his pointed white teeth (p. 42). Other references: The crowned head of the alchemical dragon (p. 179).

PLATE 10 *left:* Rudra's ashes, his seed, with which he sprinkles all creatures (p. 43). Other references: Ashes left in the nest by the burning phoenix (pp. 148, 175).

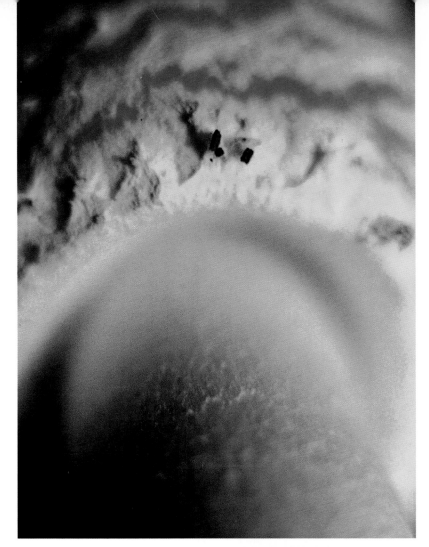

PLATE 11 *above:* Shiva's white lightning bolt penis and Parvati's red lotus vulva in coitus (p. 46). Other references: Intercourse of the sun-moon hermaphrodite (p. 173). Hermes' birds in the closest bonds of wedlock (p. 183).

PLATE 12 *below:* Agni as the firebird, with drops of Shiva's semen on his wings (p. 47). Other references: The white dove over Jesus' head (p. 117). The cup of Jesus' blood (p. 124). The phoenix in its nest (p. 148). The Holy Grail filled with blood (p. 157). One of Hermes' birds tries to fly away but can't escape (p. 183).

PLATE 13 *facing page:* The six-headed god, the red-orange rising sun and full breasts dripping milk (p. 50).

PLATE 14: The golden egg of
creation, born of the union of
Vishnu and Shiva
(p. 53).

An Italian artist of the late fifteenth century seems to have been aware of the secret meaning of the fiery winged serpent in his depiction of the same event (plate 20). The painting shows a fiery serpent attacking the Israelites. The serpent is directly under a tree, where one finds the fly agaric. Its back, or top, is red with white spots and a convex curve in the manner of a mushroom; his underside is not only white like the mushroom's underside is but also has thin, protruding scales that resemble mushroom gills. The beast looks directly at the viewer with a conspiratorial smile on his face. The two lower victims, already dealt with by the monster, have the look of wishing they were dead; the one with his fingers on his chest looks as though he is about to vomit. More examples of suspicious medieval and Renaissance artworks will be explored later.

Elijah and Elisha, the First Messiahs

The stories of the wildman prophet Elijah and his successor Elisha are notable for their many similarities to the myth of Jesus. Although some of the "bigger" miracles are cited as proof that Jesus is God, Elijah and Elisha did most of the same miracles first, and more besides. Not only that, but Elijah beat the system: he was carried up to heaven without having to die first. He was such a rich character that his story, though brief, could later be played by two people: John the Baptizer and Jesus the Nazarene.

Elijah was a wild prophet who wore a leather loincloth and a hair cape and lived in caves; he was the last of the "priests of Yahweh," the others having been put to the sword by Baal-worshipping Queen Jezebel, wife of King Ahab. This happened during a severe and prolonged drought. Three years into the drought Elijah was on Mount Carmel when he saw signs of an impending storm on the horizon. He decided immediately to set out for Mount Horeb, his pace quickened by the knowledge that Jezebel was now seeking his life. Once in the wilderness he fell asleep under a small tree only to be awakened by an angel, who told him to get up and eat.

When Elijah looked around he saw a round cake that had been baked over hot coals, and a jar of water to drink. He ate and drank and then lay back down, but the angel urged him to eat and drink a second time. On the strength of this "angel" food Elijah was able to walk for forty days and nights until he reached Mount Horeb, the same "Mountain of God" upon which Moses had his conversations with the burning god-plant. When Elijah arrived he spent the night in the same cave where Moses long ago hid when Moses viewed Yahweh's hinder parts. The word of Yahweh told Elijah to stand outside, and when he did Yahweh himself passed by. This was followed by violent storms and fire; finally Yahweh reappeared as the sound of a gentle breeze. A voice told Elijah to go and anoint three men, two of whom were to become kings; the third, Elisha, would become Elijah's successor.

After anointing the two future kings Elijah met Elisha and the two traveled together on a long journey that brought them to the banks of the Jordan. Elijah asked Elisha, "What can I give you before I am taken away?" Elisha asked for a double portion of Elijah's spirit. Elijah replied, "If you see me during the time I am being taken away you will get what you want; if you don't see me, you won't get it." A chariot of fire and flaming horses appeared between them and Elijah was carried up to heaven in a whirlwind. The brotherhood of prophets saw that Elijah's spirit now possessed Elisha, and they bowed before him. They asked Elisha if they could go out and search for Elijah, for perhaps he had been taken up in the air by Yahweh only to be dropped on some mountainside or valley. Elisha told them it was too late but they went anyway. After three days of searching they came back empty-handed. "I told you," Elisha said.

Elijah first appears in the text during a severe drought, which to a mushroom user means no mushrooms; this coincided with the introduction of Baal worship in Israel, possibly because the Yahweh priests weren't as convincing without their yearly supply of "Yahweh," the fly agaric. Once in power the Baal priests killed all of the Yahweh priests with the exception of Elijah, whose habit was to live in the wilderness.

From Mount Carmel Elijah could see rain clouds on the horizon, and coincidentally decided to go to Mount Horeb, home of the fiery plant of God. He wasn't going to miss the first opportunity in over three years to harvest mushrooms. On the way he met an "angel" who gave him coal-baked cakes to eat and water to drink. This angel represents either the mushroom itself or someone Elijah met who had some mushrooms; alternately, Elijah himself may have cached some for just such an emergency.

The dome-shaped cakes are similar to mushroom caps; the "fiery coals" reference alludes to their color and to their having been dried. The water could have been just that, or it could have been either of the two liquid forms of the mushroom already discussed. To make sure the initiated reader knew that the fly agaric was the real topic, the author says that Elijah ate twice his normal amount; this gave him supernormal strength, enabling him to walk the rest of the way to the Mountain of God on the strength of that food alone, the sort of prodigious feat of stamina for which the fly agaric is justly famous.

Dierick Bouts, a Flemish painter of the fifteenth century, may have come to the same conclusions regarding Elijah's cake-eating. His painting *Elijah in the Desert* depicts the angel waking Elijah from sleep (plate 21). The cake has been placed by the angel on top of the water cup, an unusual arrangement, creating a homologue of a round-bottomed fly agaric. The colors of the "mushroom" are not quite right, but Elijah's red cap and cloak compensate for this. The cake and the red cap are both positioned directly beneath a tree, and in both depictions of Elijah only one foot is showing, corresponding to the one-footed mushroom. Literal sleep and figurative waking from sleep have always been associated with the fly agaric, and it is an "angel," the mushroom itself, that provides the food, the drink, and the awakening.

It should also be noted that the painting is part of a triptych containing five separate paintings, all of which involve the eating of sacred food: the central panel depicts the Last Supper of Jesus; another shows the high priest Melchizedek offering sacred bread and water to Abraham prior to the circumcision episode; two others depict the feast of the Passover and the gathering of the manna; the fifth is the painting of Elijah. Was Dierick Bouts trying to tell us something?

When Elijah reached the mountain he went directly to Moses' cave (which certainly indicates Elijah had been there before), and the word of Yahweh came to him that night. It would have been well into the mushroom season by the time Elijah arrived. Once the mushrooms have been growing for a few weeks it is not difficult to find specimens that have dried standing, if weather conditions have been propitious. Assuming that Elijah was collecting mushrooms as he made his way through the mountain forests, it is not surprising that the "word" of Yahweh came to him on his first night in the cave. If the fasting man consumed fly agaric mushrooms he would have ascended very quickly to the realm of the speaking god.

No sooner did Yahweh appear to Elijah than a violent storm broke upon the mountain, probably as much within Elijah's own mind as outside the cave, and there was a "fire," but at last the turbulence subsided and nothing stirred but the gentlest of breezes. It was then Elijah knew that God was there with him.

The rainstorm meant that there would soon be even more god-plants to harvest. Elijah faced a difficult task and needed the help of the fly agaric to carry it through to completion. The other "inspired" priests of the secret cult had been killed, no one had been initiated during the three-year drought, and he was under a death sentence for murdering the priests of Baal. He decided that the best course was direct action: he would initiate three very powerful and capable people into the cult of Yahweh so that the religion would not die out; two became kings who reestablished Yahweh-worship and the third became their spiritual adviser. Words alone were not sufficient at this juncture, and these were men who needed to feel the strength of God's word within themselves if the plan was to succeed. So when the rains finally arrived Elijah had made straight for the mountain on which he knew the Word of God could be found down among the pine needles, glowing like fire.

The purpose of anointing has been variously explained over the centuries, and none of the explanations of this rather strange practice is especially satisfying, given the great prominence the rite enjoys in the literature. It could have begun merely as an extension of cosmetic hair-oiling, but it is probably more significant than this. Investiture to a position of secular or spiritual authority often included anointing the person with a mixture of costly oils and fragrant balsam, which was poured ceremonially over the head. Because of its inclusion in the sacred ointment, balsam has come to symbolize anything that heals, soothes, mitigates suffering, or ministers to the mind. The last quality is particularly telling and implies the practice once had more than ceremonial meaning.

Since the great majority of those so oiled were men, some have suggested that the anointing represented semen flowing over the head of the penis, a way of identifying the person with the superpotent male deity; this may have been true in some cases. In the ancient Indian medical system known as Ayurveda oil is poured on the head in a constant stream for long periods of time as a mental health practice. The ancient Jewish kings and priests were always anointed ceremonially, and among the early Christians anointing with the chrism or sacred ointment was performed on all new initiates, hence the name "Christian": those who have been chrismed, or christened. Jesus was said to have received the chrism from God.

Whatever the original reasons for anointing or chrisming, one thing is sure: some of the oil used in the rite is absorbed through the skin. A very powerful concentrate can be made by thoroughly soaking dried fly agaric caps in warm oil for a long time and then carefully and completely pressing out all the absorbed oil. The process can be repeated over and over again, each time using new specimens but the same oil. The more this is done the stronger the concentration of the mushroom's virtues in the oil. If the impregnated oil is then massaged into the head or body the oil carries the chemicals into the skin, where they enter the bloodstream. It is the same type of drug-delivery system sometimes employed by sorcerers and witches; the latter were known for rubbing psychedelic ointments into their armpits, vulvas, or any other site that afforded easy absorption. A similar method could have been employed by Elijah when he anointed the three men.

I wouldn't be surprised if the recipients were uninformed beforehand of the unique nature of the anointing they were to receive, in keeping with the secrecy and deception employed by Moses. What better way to convince two prospective kings of the power of Yahweh and his priest than by giving the unsuspecting men drugs unawares in the name of God, as the gurus of India and Persia seem to have done. Elisha, though, would have needed to know the secret in order to carry on the cult.

A few of the reported miracles of Elijah and Elisha seem designed solely to put them on an equal footing with Moses, such as when both men struck a river with Elijah's rolled-up cloak and the waters parted like a miniature Red Sea. If they were mushroom magicians the identification would be appropriate, since they would have had access to the same "powers" that Moses used. The same technique of identification with former prophets, notably Moses and Elijah, was often used in the mythology of Jesus.

In Siberia, mushroom users report that there are mushroom "spirits" with whom they communicate when they are bemushroomed, and among the ancients of the Middle East and elsewhere it was well known that a good magician had the help of one or more spirits who would do his or her bidding. When Elisha asked Elijah for a double portion of his "spirit" he was not asking for a portion of his soul or vigor; he was asking for the supernatural spirit who served Elijah to become his own servant after Elijah died. Elijah answered that Elisha would get the spirit only if he saw Elijah while he was being taken away; if not, he would not get it. If this story reflects Elisha's initiation into the mushroom cult it may refer to the necessity of being shown the sacred mushroom grounds before the season ended and before Elijah left for good; otherwise Elisha wouldn't be able to repeat the experience or initiate anyone else into Yahweh's inner circle. Elijah's spirit was the spirit of the mushroom, and Elisha needed to know where and when it grew.

It was at this point that Elijah was "carried up to heaven" in a whirlwind by a fiery chariot. Now it is possible that Elijah was picked up by an actual whirlwind or tornado, but it seems more likely that once again the fly agaric is being symbolized, especially when the chariot is considered. A fiery chariot has fiery wheels; the fly agaric is the wheel of fire that descends from the heavens to the depths of the earth and then ascends back to the heavens, sometimes "carrying" a human passenger on the journey. More will be said later about chariot wheels and ascensions.

The story, however, has Elisha's companions taking the whirlwind tale at face value: fifty of them went out searching for Elijah in case the Yahweh-whirlwind had dropped him somewhere on the way to heaven. People have been picked up by whirlwinds, after all, and they always land somewhere. Either that or the men were trying to find more specimens of fly agaric on the mountainsides, perhaps after a late rainstorm, even though Elisha had told them the harvest was over for the year. Hope may well eternally, but once the mushroom season is over no amount of searching will produce a "body."

The Song of Songs

The Song of Songs is the most passionate piece of writing in the entire Judeo-Christian canon and also one that nearly neglects to mention God, doing so only once in the last verse. It was important enough to the ancient Jews to make it the first of the five rolls that were recited at special feasts; the Song was recited at Passover. Some insist that the Song is to be taken literally; that its sexy verse represents and celebrates pure physical love between two people as sanctioned by God. Others, due to the Song's enigmatic imagery and repeated phrases, are convinced it is allegorical, referring to the love between God and the individual soul. Still others think it refers to the love between God and Israel or between Jesus and the Church. Certainly it can be read in all these ways.

This is the same work referred to centuries later by a critic of alchemy when he complained that the alchemists were treating the whole Bible, especially the Song of Songs, as though it had been written expressly in honor of their Art.[50] If the assertion is true, why would the alchemists treat the Bible in this way? Perhaps because they share the same secret.

My suggestion that the Song is written in praise of the divine mushroom should come as no surprise. What may be surprising are the number and density of the fly agaric correspondences in so brief a work. It is debated whether the Song is actually one distinct composition or a collection of songs, but this really does not matter for our purposes. The personified mushroom's point of view switches back and forth in the verses, regardless of which character is speaking.

The author doesn't waste time or mince words; from the very first verse onwards the Song is replete with fly agaric correspondences.

> Let him kiss me with the kisses of his mouth. Your love is more delightful than wine; delicate is the fragrance of your perfume, your name is an oil poured out, and that is why the maidens love you. Draw me in your footsteps, let us run. The King has brought me into his rooms; you will be our joy and gladness. We shall praise your love above wine; how right it is to love you.

In this most intimate of relationships, the love that can be experienced far surpasses alcoholic intoxication. The dried mushroom, especially so if it is aged, has a delicate, honey-like fragrance. The name "like an oil" corresponds to the method of infusing oil with the mushroom as described above; ". . . that is why the maidens love you" may refer to vulval or vaginal absorption of the infused oil. The "footsteps" are the mushrooms themselves ranging like fiery footprints in the forest, as we saw in the footsteps of Vishnu. Running indicates the elation and physical energy the mushroom imparts. The "King" is both the mushroom and God, and his rooms are the realms of light. He does indeed produce joy and gladness. The love experienced is much better than wine. It is right to love something or someone so obviously good.

> I am black but lovely . . . like the tents of Kedar, like the pavilions of Solomon. Take no notice of my swarthiness, it is the sun that has burnt me.

What woman, to better describe her loveliness, would compare herself to a couple of tents? A mushroom is a kind of tent. The blackness "burnt by the sun" may refer to a mushroom that has dried to a very dark color, which sometimes happens depending on the circumstances of drying. This swarthiness does not affect the mushroom's real "beauty."

> Tell me then, you whom my heart loves: where will you lead your flock to graze . . . that I may no longer wander like a woman veiled.

The chorus tells the woman to

> follow the tracks of the flock . . . close by the shepherds' tents.

Following the tracks of the flocks driven to the mountain meadows is one way to find the fly agaric. The "veiled woman" is the mushroom with its veils. Remember that Moses also was veiled.

> Your cheeks show fair between their pendants and your neck within its necklaces. We shall make you golden earrings and beads of silver.

The "fair" cheeks are not "pale" but beautiful; later he says they are red. They correspond to the cap of the mushroom. The pendants are the veil remnants. "Golden earrings" probably refers to the golden mature or dried cap, while "beads of silver" again means the "beads" of the veil fragments (see plate 7).

> How beautiful you are, my beloved, and how delightful! All green is our bed. The beams of our house are cedar, the panelling of cypress.

This is a very clever metaphor. The "green bed" is the green earth out of which the mushroom grows, specifically the new grasses that blanket the hillsides when the mushroom sprouts. The references to cedar and cypress denote the kinds of trees under which the mushroom grows; the beams and panelling are the branches and trunks of the trees.

> I am the rose of Sharon, the lily of the valleys. As a lily among the thistles, so is my love.

I used to think this verse referred to lily-white and rose-red, which would make this a color key for the fly agaric. But I have since discovered that there is much debate surrounding which actual plants were being referenced. One opinion is that the rose of Sharon was a narcissus or crocus, both of which have white varieties, and the lily of the valleys was the red Palestine lily. This reverses the colors but they remain the same: white and red. The "lily among thistles" comparison may refer only to the fly agaric's beauty as compared with other mushrooms or plants, but if a red lily is meant, then it is analagous to the red cap among the "thorns" of the veil (see plate 1).

> As an apple among the trees of the orchard, so is my beloved . . . In his longed-for shade I am seated and his fruit is sweet to my taste. He has taken me to his house of wine, and the banner he raises over me is love. Feed me with raisin cakes, restore me with apples, for I am sick with love.

In this, the Song's second tree reference, is the additional mention of fruit; not only fruit but reddish fruit. Even if the apple in question originally meant "apricot" in the Middle East, as some scholars believe, the beautiful red-orange of a ripe apricot still fits the fly agaric. All of the fly agaric's host trees become the "apple" tree in this metaphor. The "longed-for shade" is a multiple allusion. These were primarily desert people, to whom the word "shade" has special meaning. There is the physical shade of the trees under which the mushrooms grow; there is the shade created by the open mushroom, which is itself a shade or umbrella; and shade has for desert dwellers the additional meaning of salvation and rest. "Fruit sweet to my taste" is the dried mushroom, which has a slightly sweet taste, as opposed to the fresh, which is almost bitter. The lover has been taken to the house of wine (or intoxication) where there is much drinking. The "raised banner" over the lover is both the "raised" mushroom itself and the overspreading light and bliss that are the true fruit of this union. "Cakes" and "apples" again correspond to the mushroom at different stages. The phrase "I am sick with love" expresses, like the two horns of a bull, the eternal dilemma of fly agaric intoxication: sickness and bliss.

> I charge you, daughters of Jerusalem, by the gazelles, by the hinds of the field, not to stir my love, nor rouse it, until it please to awake.

This is another key admonition for the initiate. Its main message is, "Do not pick the mushroom until it is mature and don't disturb it either." It is couched in odd animal references because both animals relate to the fly agaric. A hind is a female red deer. Deer have a special fondness for the mushroom, as reported by Wasson and others. My own experience proves this as well: I have often seen deer bites on fly agaric. The gazelle referred to was probably *Gazelle dorcas*, a small, horned, fawn-colored animal. The fly agaric is also fawn-colored, that is, reddish with white spots, and has "horns." If the mushroom is disturbed or picked in its early stages its growth will be severely stunted. It is best to let them reach their full upturned maturity before harvesting, both in terms of the mushroom's effects and to allow maximum spore dispersal.

> See how he comes leaping on the mountains, bounding over the hills. My beloved is like a gazelle, like a young stag.

Again we have the gazelle and deer metaphors, this time coupled with the mushrooms' "leaping" and "bounding" into existence on the mountains.

> See where he stands . . . he peers through the lattice.

As the mushroom's veil separates, the cap beneath can take on the appearance of eyes behind the lattice-work of the veil. More generally, just as we can look through the "lattice" and see the cap, the personified cap can look out and see us. The other "lattice" that can be looked through is that formed by pine needles covering the mushroom (plate 22).

> For see, winter is past, the rains are over and gone. The flowers appear on the earth.

The winter rains make the mushroom "flowers" appear.

> My dove, hiding in the clefts of the rock, in the coverts of the cliff, show me your face, let me hear your voice; for your voice is sweet and your face is beautiful.

The birdlike mushroom is often well-concealed; it is very beautiful; it is the word of God manifest on earth. Sometimes the word is audible to the inner ear.

> Catch the little foxes for us, the little foxes that make havoc of our vineyards, for our vineyards are in flower.

Animals can ruin the mushroom crop. The admonition is similar to God's telling Moses to take off his shoes. "Vineyards" alludes to the hydrated mushrooms being pressed for their juice like grapes, which also yield an intoxicating liquid when fermented with yeast, a type of fungus.

> He pastures his flock among the lilies.

If the red Palestine lily is being referred to, the image is of white wool next to shiny red flowers.

> . . . return! Be, my beloved, like a gazelle, a young stag on the mountains of the victims cut in half.

"Return" is the eternal plea of the user to the mushroom. "The victims cut in half" is the literal rendering of what is usually translated as "the covenant," recalling Abraham's bloody offering on the mountain. The harvested mushroom is indeed a victim, and it "cuts" itself in half when the cap tears away from the base. Also, if the cap is separated from the stalk for ease of harvesting and drying, it is literally cut in two.

> On my bed, at night, I sought him whom my heart loves . . . but did not find him.

The supply of dried mushrooms has run out and the new season has not started. Later she finds "him" and there is a repetition of the verse about not stirring or arousing "until it please to awake."

> King Solomon has made himself a throne of wood from Lebanon. The posts he has made of silver, the canopy of gold, the seat of purple; the back is inlaid with love.

Again the reference is to the mushroom-trees of the mountains of Lebanon. The throne is where the king, the mushroom, sits. "Posts of silver" are the white stalks of the mushroom, while the "canopy of gold" is the expanded cap, usually red-orange or gold, with the red concentrated at the center, the "seat." When this was written, "purple" usually referred to any of several shades of red ending with crimson, although dried specimens sometimes end up with the cap in shades of modern purple, especially in the center. The throne is "inlaid with love" just as the banner was love; "inlaid" may also refer to the veil fragments.

> How beautiful you are, my love . . . Your eyes, behind your veil, are doves . . . Your teeth are like a flock of shorn ewes as they come up from the washing. Each one has its twin . . . Your lips are a scarlet thread . . . Your cheeks, behind your veil, are halves of pomegranate. Your neck is the tower of David built as a fortress, hung round with a thousand bucklers, and each the shield of a hero. Your breasts are two fawns, twins of a gazelle, that feed among the lilies.

First we had the beloved looking through the lattice, and now the lover looks out through her veil with "dove eyes." Many varieties of doves and pigeons have red eyes. The teeth are the same teeth we encountered in Rudra's mythology, white and very much alike. "Lips like a scarlet thread" is another way of describing the scarlet cap beneath the veil (plate 23). The cheeks earlier described as "fair" are now seen to be pomegranate red. The "neck like a tower" is the beautiful white stalk. The "thousand bucklers" (shields) are the same as the thousand eyes of Indra: the white veil fragments that have actually shielded the cap, each pointed "buckler" breaking up and turning aside the soil and leaves that first covered it (see plate 2). "Shield of a hero" has the additional meaning of the individual shieldlike cap, the hero being the brave soul who consumes the mushroom (we will see such a shield in action, wielded by an angel, in chapter 12). The last image, when the man compares his lover's breasts to two feeding fawns, is neither very romantic nor even a good metaphor; that is, unless it is a metaphor for the fly agaric, in which case the comparison is as precise as it is obscure (plate 24).

> You are wholly beautiful, my love, and without a blemish.

The unexpected beauty and symmetry of the fly agaric is matched only by the perfection of form and delicacy it exhibits. Beneath its veil the young mushroom reveals a round, perfect, shining face, a face without a blemish.

> Come from Lebanon, my promised bride, come from Lebanon, come on your way. Lower your gaze from the heights of Amana, from the crests of Senir and Hermon, the haunts of lions, the mountains of leopards.

Again the author mentions Lebanon and its mountains as the place from which the "beloved" comes. Additionally, the mushroom is spotted, like a leopard.

> You ravish my heart . . . you ravish my heart with a single one of your glances, with a single pearl of your necklace. What spells lie in your love . . . How delicious is your love, more delicious than wine . . . Your lips, my promised one, distill wild honey. Honey and milk are under your tongue: and the scent of your garments is like the scent of Lebanon.

The "ravished heart" is reminiscent of Rig Veda poems to Soma: it corresponds to being overwhelmed with ecstasy from the mushroom; even the mushroom's appearance is ravishing. "Spells" corresponds to the trance states that one can experience, as well as to possible magical uses. It appears that the author was familiar with mixing the mushroom juice with milk and honey as the Aryans did. The result is both delicious and intoxicating, like wine but much better. "Lips" and "tongue" probably refer to the dried mushroom itself; the curled edges of dry specimens can be seen as "lips" or "tongues." Additionally, the color of the dried gills (which are "under the tongue") is the color of milk mixed with honey.

> She is a garden enclosed, my sister, my promised bride; a garden enclosed, a sealed fountain. Your shoots form an orchard of pomegranate trees, the rarest essences are

yours . . . Fountain that makes the gardens fertile, well of living water, streams flowing
down from Lebanon.

This is a very apt metaphor. The young fly agaric is indeed sealed. Not only is the entire
mushroom enclosed by the universal veil, but the gills have their own seal as well, the
annulus.

Using a fountain as a metaphor colorfully describes the way the mushroom springs up
into existence as a result of water, occasionally even resembling a fountain (plate 25). It also
alludes to the pressing of juice from the hydrated cap and to the fountain the individual user
becomes after drinking. The author goes on to describe the fruits of this garden as "shoots,"
once again a very fitting metaphor for a mushroom. What do these shoots produce but
pomegranates; round, red pomegranates, like Shiva's "fruit on a post." Fruit on a shoot. This
"fountain that makes the gardens fertile" does so because it is also the penis-mushroom covered with semen, in coitus with the very earth. It creates living water out of ordinary water,
a concept later embraced by Jesus. These streams flow ultimately from the regions in which
the fly agaric is found.

> I come into my garden, my sister, my promised bride, I gather my myrrh and balsam, I
> eat my honey and my honeycomb, I drink my wine and my milk. Eat, friends, and
> drink, drink deep, my dearest friends.

This verse appears to be a list of the vital ingredients of the sacred meal, although the
foods and drinks listed are euphemisms for the real items. It is possible that literal myrrh
and balsam were used, but "honey" and "honeycomb" correspond to the dried mushroom, just as Soma was called Honey in the Rig Veda. "Honey" is the mushroom's juice,
probably mixed with honey, while "honeycomb" is the dried cap with its comblike gills.
"Wine" in this context is either the mushroom's expressed juice or the user's. The "milk"
could be for drinking with the honeyed mushroom-water as the Aryans did, or it could
refer to the drinking of semen, a practice of some Tantric and Gnostic sects. The poet's
dearest friends are invited to share in this ritual love feast, to eat and drink deeply.

> I sleep but my heart is awake. I hear my beloved knocking. "Open to me, my sister, my
> love, my dove, my perfect one, for my head is covered with dew, my locks with the
> drops of the night. I have taken off my tunic, am I to put it on again? I have washed my
> feet, am I to dirty them again?"

Deep, sleeplike trance states of various kinds are sometimes experienced in fly agaric
intoxication. "Sleeping with the heart awake" is a good description of the state. "Opening" to the beloved might refer to some of the more unusual uses of the mushroom
described earlier because it is certainly a sexual reference. It is directly followed by a
description of the beloved's "head" covered with "dew," Rudra-fashion, and pubic locks
covered with drops of nocturnal emission. The mushroom "takes off its tunic," the

universal veil, in the same way Soma sloughed his white vestments. Every fly agaric has a very distinct base or foot, unlike many mushrooms, and every foot is planted in the soil. When the mushroom is picked the foot is always dirty, and often removed for this reason.

There are still more fly agaric correspondences, as well as significant repeated phrases, in the remainder of the Song. Once again "sick with love" is mentioned; the beloved is fresh and ruddy; his head is purest gold; his legs are alabaster columns set in sockets of pure gold; the flock is among the lilies; the teeth are like sheep; the cheeks are like pomegranates; the lover is like a dove, "who arises like the dawn, fair as the moon, resplendent as the sun." Her navel is described as a well-rounded bowl with no lack of wine, and we know that the fly agaric also becomes a well-rounded bowl of intoxication.

After one final admonition not to stir or rouse the beloved "until it please to awake," comes the concluding verse:

> I awakened you under the apple tree, there where your mother conceived you, there where she who gave birth to you conceived you. Set me like a seal on your heart, like a seal on your arm. For love is strong as death . . . The flash of it is a flash of fire, a flame of Yahweh himself. Love no flood can quench, no torrents drown.

Significantly, the Song ends beneath the "apple" tree where the mushroom was conceived by Mother Earth; no mention is made of a father. Seals are mentioned again, one on the blood-filled "heart" and one on the "arm," or stalk. "Love is strong as death" is a last reminder for the initiates that they will not die from the mushroom even though they may feel that way. The promised love is real; it is simply not as available on demand as one might wish. This fungal love is a true "flash of fire" in more ways than one, and is Yahweh's own flame, just as Moses described it, though Moses seemed a little deficient in the love department. Yet even though this love is aflame, torrents of water cannot drown it, because it is torrents of water that cause it to shoot into existence beneath the trees, and it is water that releases its virtues. And the love it is capable of producing is a power unto itself; it is the unquenchable flame of the divine, light irresistible and blissful.

Isaiah

Halfway into the first chapter of Isaiah, after Yahweh has told the people of Judah that he is sick and tired of them and their endless sacrifices to him, we are struck by an unusual verse: "Come now, let us talk this over," says Yahweh, who is not usually one to do that. "Though your sins are like scarlet, they shall be as white as snow; though they are red like crimson, they shall be like [white] wool."[51]

What is the purpose of this repetition? One example would have sufficed, unless it is not sins that are being spoken of but colors and form. The universal veil of a young fly agaric is white and fluffy; both "snow" and "wool" are good descriptions of what it looks like. "Scarlet" and "crimson" both are associated with the color of blood, the same color as the cap of a young fly agaric. One look at such a specimen and the metaphors become descriptions (see plate 24). These two vivid color keys are followed directly by talk of eating: "If you are willing to obey, you shall eat the good things of the earth."

The career of the prophet really took off after his first big vision, and what a vision it was. He saw Yahweh seated on a high throne with two seraphs, "burning ones," standing above, each with three sets of wings: one set to cover their faces, one set to cover their genitals, and one set for flying. The fiery ones cried out to each other, "Holy, holy, holy is Yahweh Sabaoth. His glory fills the whole earth."

Isaiah was terribly humbled by his vision; he felt unworthy to behold the glory he was witnessing and was loudly bewailing his wretchedness and unclean lips when one of the seraphs flew up to him and touched his lips with a burning coal from Yahweh's altar. The angel said, "See now, this has touched your lips, your sin is taken away, your iniquity is purged." And Isaiah heard a voice that said, "Whom shall I send? Who will be our messenger?" Isaiah answered and said that he would do it. "Send me," he told Yahweh. Yahweh told him, "Go then, and say this to the people: "Hear and hear again, but do not understand; see and see again, but do not perceive." Make the heart of the people gross, its ears dull; shut its eyes, so that it will not see with its eyes, hear with its ears, understand with its heart, and be converted and healed."

This is very odd. First Yahweh asks for a messenger, and as soon as one is found he is told to make sure no one sees, hears, or understands the word of God so that no one will be converted and healed. What is going on here? Let us first look at the vision itself and the clues it offers.

Once again Yahweh is seated on a high throne like Shiva atop his pillar. He is flanked by two angelic beings called "burning ones," with wings for covering and wings for flying. The covered "face" of the burning ones is the veil-covered cap of the fly agaric. "Covered genitals" corresponds to the phalluslike young mushroom "covered" with the same veil. "Wings for flying" parallels the mature mushroom with its cap expanded and outstretched like the wings of a bird in flight. These flaming angels do nothing but speak the holiness of Yahweh. One of the burning ones puts a blazing coal to Isaiah's lips, which launches his prophetic career in earnest. Suddenly he is not bound up with self-pity and weakness; now he is strong and filled with God's word. The blazing coal has touched his lips: Isaiah has eaten the sacred mushroom.

But now Yahweh makes strange demands of Isaiah. Either God is terribly petty and this represents a temper tantrum, or we are witnessing another call to secrecy for the cult. "Hear . . . but do not understand; see . . . but do not perceive" is a way of saying that the cultic secrets, as before, will be kept hidden in such a way that even though they are told openly they will not be understood by anyone but initiates, due to the use of metaphorical language; in this way the power and primacy of the priesthood will remain inviolate.

Because if the people, on their own, can understand with their hearts and be converted and healed, of what use is the priesthood? After Isaiah's pledge of secrecy he begins prophesying in the usual fashion until chapter eleven, when he says,

> A shoot springs from the stock of Jesse, a shoot thrusts from his roots: on him the spirit of Yahweh rests, a spirit of wisdom and insight, a spirit of counsel and power, a spirit of knowledge and the fear of Yahweh.

This and the following verses were later appropriated and cited by Paul and the Christians as proof that Jesus was the Messiah. Leaving that aside for now, what is the verse saying? Is it using shoots and trees and roots as metaphors to describe some wished-for person of the future or is it using those words to describe actual shoots and trees and roots? "A shoot springs" and "a shoot thrusts" are words one would use to describe the growth of a mushroom, not the birth of a child. If the shoot is a mushroom then "the stock of Jesse" refers to a certain kind of tree. A "shoot thrusting from the roots" of the tree is an accurate description of the fly agaric's mycelium home among the roots of trees, from which it sends forth its thrusting shoots. What do the shoots contain? They contain the spirits of wisdom, insight, counsel, power, knowledge, and the fear of God.

> The wolf lives with the lamb, the panther lies down with the kid . . . They do no hurt, no harm, on all my holy mountain, for the country is filled with the knowledge of Yahweh as the waters fill the sea. That day, the root of Jesse shall stand as a signal to the peoples. It will be sought out by the nations and its home will be glorious.

The first line refers again to the dual nature of the fly agaric experience, and also to the generally passive and peaceful state it produces. When one is sufficiently bemushroomed the thought of doing anyone harm is far from the mind, although if the situation arose in which one had to make a defense, the strength to do so could be marshalled easily (in most cases). The last two lines are significant in that they refer to the root of Jesse as "it" rather than "he," forcing us to think of literal roots and trees rather than someone's ancestor. We already know that the root of Jesse produces thrusting shoots; on God's mountain a root with shoots stands as a beacon, sought by the nations for the salvation it offers. Its home, in the realms of light, is glorious to behold.

> I give thanks to you, Yahweh, you were angry with me but your anger is appeased and you have given me consolation. See now, he is the God of my salvation. I have trust now and no fear, for Yahweh is my strength, my song, he is my salvation. And you will draw water joyfully from the springs of salvation.

The anguish of an unpleasant mushroom experience has passed; the fear of death is gone, replaced by the conviction that one has been saved and made whole. "Springs of salvation" refers to the liquid forms of the saving, healing fly agaric.

Later on Isaiah says,

> When the Lord has given you the bread of suffering and the water of distress, he who is
> your teacher will hide no longer, and you will see your teacher with your own eyes.
> Whether you turn left or right, your ears will hear these words behind you, "This is the
> way, follow it."

"Bread of suffering" and "waters of distress" are picturesque metaphors for trials and
tribulations, but they also are metaphors for the dried fly agaric and its liquid products.
Speaking of them in this way stresses the volatile and uncertain nature of the substances;
this is not a meal that should be eaten lightly. But once they are consumed the inner
teacher is revealed in light that can be heard as well as seen, and the way becomes clear.

Ezekiel and the Wheels of Fire

The book of Ezekiel begins conveniently with a huge thunderstorm, and we know one
thing that signifies: mushrooms. In the heart of the "fire" of the storm Ezekiel saw what
appeared to be four animals with vaguely human features. Each creature had four faces,
four wings, straight legs and hoofed feet. Each one had the faces of a man, a lion, a bull,
and an eagle. Each had wings that turned upwards and wings that covered its body. Firebrands and flaming torches seemed to pass between the animals. On the ground beside
each animal was a glittering wheel, each one looking like the other, and each one seeming
to have another wheel within it. When Ezekiel looked at them they seemed enormous,
and their rims had eyes all the way around. The moving wheels made a noise. Over the
head of each animal was what looked like an arched vault. Above the vaults was a throne
on which was seated a being apparently made of fire.

A voice came from the midst of the fire and spoke to Ezekiel. It said, "Open your
mouth and eat what I am about to give you." With these words a hand appeared and
unrolled a scroll on which was written, "lamentations, wailings, moanings." The voice
continued: "Son of man, eat what is given to you; eat this scroll, then go and speak to the
house of Israel." Ezekiel opened his mouth and was handed the scroll to eat. The voice
said, "Son of man, feed and be satisfied by the scroll I am giving you." Ezekiel ate the
scroll, and it tasted as sweet as honey. Soon he felt himself lifted up by the spirit. Behind
him he heard the boisterous shouting of heavenly throngs, "Blessed be the glory of Yahweh in his dwelling place." The spirit took him, and his heart overflowed with bitterness
and anger, and the hand of Yahweh lay heavy on him. Finally he came to Tel Abib, where
he stayed for seven days "like a man stunned." Another thunderstorm, another prophet.
There seems to be a pattern developing.

As a result of the storm Ezekiel saw some strange creatures. What could they have
been? They reminded him of various animals, they looked a little human, but most of all

they looked like angels, like the "burning ones" of Isaiah's vision. They even had the same sort of "wings," some covering their bodies and some extended as in flight, and the same fly agaric correspondences apply. Additionally, these burning ones had straight legs, an odd thing to mention unless it is meant to imply that the legs are *only* straight; that is, they don't bend at all. Straight as the stalk of a fly agaric. The angels also had hoofed feet, which is one way to describe the club "foot" of the fly agaric, more like a hoof than a foot (see plate 4).

Between the creatures were burning torches and firebrands, more distinct fly agaric imagery: fire on top of a stick or pole. On the ground were glittering wheels with "eyes all around the rims." A fly agaric is certainly a wheel; the "eyes" all around the rim are the veil remnants (plate 26). These wheels also had wheels within them. Seen from the top, the cap of the mushroom is a solid wheel. Seen from beneath, another wheel, within the first and with "spokes," reveals itself. There is even an "axle" at the hub (plate 27). Another significant point mentioned by Ezekiel is that the rims "seemed enormous" when he looked at them, which indicates he may have been experiencing the macrovision described earlier. In that condition a mushroom user is able to see things in extreme close-up, as though the objects themselves had grown to huge proportions. It is a known side effect of fly agaric intoxication.

To Ezekiel, the wheels were moving and making a noise, and there was also the noise of storms and the sound of wings in the fiery air. A fly agaric legend of the Anishinaubeg, the native people of the Great Lakes region in North America, describes the characters' first sight of the mushroom: "They saw a beautiful meadow in which grew many tall red and white mushrooms—handsome *wajashkwedeg* they were—turning and revolving, buzzing and murmuring, singing a strange song of happiness under a brilliant sunny sky."[52] To stop the mushrooms from turning, the feather of a "thunderbird" was stuck into the stalk below the cap, indicating that the author was aware of the correspondence of feathers to gills; the mushroom *is* the thunderbird. Ezekiel's angels also had feathered wings, and in both stories the feathers are associated with thunder.

A voice emerged out of the sounds Ezekiel was hearing and told him he must go and preach to the Israelites, a scenario nearly identical to the experiences of Moses and Elijah. The voice then told him not once but *four* times to eat the proffered scroll, and the author mentions the eating of the scroll two additional times. Perhaps we are supposed to come away with the impression that something is actually being eaten here. When the scroll was unrolled three words could be seen ("lamentations, wailings, moanings"), all of which can apply to fly agaric sickness; this is how Ezekiel felt after he ate the scroll. Dried caps can be rolled and unrolled like a scroll, and sometimes appear to have writing on them.

Ezekiel felt as if he was rising bodily in the air after he ate the scroll. In profound fly agaric intoxication the same sensation is experienced. The body feels amazingly light, as though one had been inflated with helium. There is a definite perception of waves of energy rising through the body unobstructed, moving from bottom to top in a continuous flow. It is the same blissful feeling that can be experienced in dream-flying. It appears that Ezekiel's "flight" wasn't quite as blissful, though; he experienced some of the physical discomfort for which the fly agaric is infamous. His description makes it sound like motion sickness. Yahweh's hand lay heavy on Ezekiel during his trip, and though unpleasant it was nonetheless profound.

Jonah the Dove

The book of Jonah is one of the shortest and strangest of the Hebrew canon. To this day no one can agree on what it means, though nearly everyone is certain it means something beyond its surface story, which in itself is patently unbelievable. Briefly stated, the story goes like this:

Yahweh ordered Jonah to go and tell the people of Nineveh that their wickedness was known. Jonah responded by booking passage on a boat bound for the ends of the earth. He wanted no part of playing the prophet. A terrible storm arose at sea and lots were cast to determine who was responsible for bringing the catastrophe; the lot fell to Jonah, and he was sacrificed to the sea in the hope that this would appease the gods' wrath and spare the ship. As soon as Jonah hit the water the seas calmed. Yahweh had arranged for a great fish to be there at precisely that moment, and Jonah was swallowed whole by the beast.

For three days and three nights Jonah languished in the fish's belly. Finally he prayed a desperate prayer that lamented his utter misery and called out to Yahweh from "the depths of Sheol" where he lay tossing and drowning in the terrible billowing waves of the abyss. Yahweh told the fish to vomit Jonah onto the shore, and it did. Yahweh again told Jonah to go and warn the people of Nineveh, and this time he went. We're told he went there and said, "Nineveh is going to be destroyed in only forty days." Remarkably, the people believed him. They all put on sackcloth, even the animals, and everyone fasted and renounced their evil ways. God was impressed by their efforts and decided not to destroy them.

Jonah got very angry when Yahweh didn't destroy Nineveh on the fortieth day or any day thereafter. He was humiliated. If the city had been destroyed the people at least would know that Jonah was a real prophet; but when it didn't happen, how could he prove that it would have if not for God's mercy? He went and sat down in the city to see if anything might still happen to it. Yahweh caused a "castor bean" plant to spring up overnight and make shade for Jonah, but at dawn the next day he sent a worm to attack the plant and make it wither. Jonah got very angry again. Yahweh asked Jonah if Jonah was right to be upset about the plant and Jonah replied that he was, and he was angry to the point of death. Yahweh said, "You're only angry about a plant that you did nothing to create and which sprouted in a night and perished in a night." Yahweh then asked if Yahweh shouldn't feel

sorry for the people of Nineveh, who can't even tell their right hand from their left, and so
ends the book.

The name "Jonah" means "dove" in Hebrew. The Vedic fire-god Agni also became a dove,
and the lovers in the Song of Songs were "doves." "Dove" is a metaphor for the fly agaric,
which begins life as an egg and ends as a "bird" with wings extended. The dove of this
story became a sacrificial victim just as Soma, Agni, and Vishnu were the sacrifice. Jonah
was sacrificed to the ocean where he was "swallowed up" by a great beast. If Jonah is a personification of the fly agaric then this part of the tale literally represents, from the mushroom's point of view, being eaten and regurgitated, the exact thing that happened to the
red monkey-god Hanuman. But as happens in so many myths, sometimes Jonah seems to
be the mushroom and sometimes the one who has consumed the mushroom. His prayer
from the belly of the beast, the "belly of Sheol," is the plea of one caught in a seemingly
endless and unbearable fly agaric agony. This agony is sometimes relieved by vomiting,
which is what the fish did to relieve Jonah's agony.

When Jonah sits in the city God causes a plant to spring up "overnight" to provide him
with shade. The identity of the plant in question is uncertain; it is generally regarded as
being either a gourd plant or a castor bean plant. One scholar says the Semitic name for
the plant means "pod-plant," which could apply to a mushroom, its cap being the "pod"
that opens up. Everyone knows that mushrooms look like little umbrellas or parasols,
which makes them literal shades; Jonah's plant became a shade. They are also the only
"plant" of their size that can spring up virtually overnight.

After one day Yahweh sends a worm to attack the plant and make it wither, which
sounds like the maggot attacks to which the fly agaric is so vulnerable. Worms also
attacked the manna of the Israelites overnight. Jonah was upset that his prized shade-plant
withered, and God offered consolation in one last fly agaric metaphor, asking Jonah how
he could be upset over a plant that "sprouted in a night and has perished in a night"; in
other words, a mushroom.

9

Living Water and the Bread of Life:
The Story of Jesus

THE STORY OF JESUS IS ONE OF THE MOST mysterious in all of religious history. The mystery is not that Jesus was considered to be God by his followers; there are many such "gods" in history and even a number of claimants in the present day. It is not that he is supposed to have died and come back to life, because he is not alone in that claim either. The mystery of Jesus is that there is no longer a Mystery in Christianity; everything has been explained. The official position of all the differing branches and sects is the same, one of the few things they agree on: Christianity today has no secret rites. Yet Jesus himself was the head of a heretical mystery cult, the initiates of which met secretly to share sacred food and drink while their master explained to them the hidden meanings of his teachings. We know of this from the Christian Bible.

The Christianity of today is a far cry from the cult of Jesus. Many of today's Christians have taken it upon themselves as their primary task in life to make Christians out of us all, as though this were possible and desirable. But Jesus himself used parables in his public teaching expressly so he *wouldn't* be understood by the masses, as he told his disciples: "The mysteries of the kingdom of heaven are revealed to you, but they are not revealed to them [the crowds]. For anyone who has will be given more than enough; but from anyone who has not, even what he has will be taken away." This from the man who supposedly sent his disciples to the ends of the earth to spread the word and make converts.

The writer continues later saying, "In all this Jesus spoke to the crowds in parables; indeed, *he would never speak to them except in parables.* This was to fulfil the prophecy: I will

speak to you in parables and expound things hidden from the foundation of the world."
[Italics mine.] Now if Jesus is the savior of the world, why is he acting with such duplicity?
And where is the promised expounding of the ancient hidden teachings? Even the ostensible exposition in private to the disciples is nothing short of pedestrian and certainly reveals
no secrets except that most people are destined never to join his élite inner circle.

But if we accept that Jesus was a man of secrets, as he is quoted as being, then we should
realize that the most important secrets of his cult never made it to the page. As Clement
of Alexandria wrote to a questioner who had heard of a secret gospel containing sexual references, it was known among the more privy followers of Jesus that his teachings were of
three kinds: the first consisted of the homely parables, admonitions, and warnings we are
so used to hearing and seeing in print; these became what we know as the New Testament.
Second, there was a secret written gospel that was passed hand to hand among the initiates and which contained secret teachings meant to steer disciples to the third level of
teaching, which was never written down.

Clement says, referring to Mark,

[Thus] he composed a more spiritual gospel for the use of those who were being perfected. Nevertheless, he did not divulge the things not to be uttered, nor did he write
down the hierophantic teaching of the Lord, but to the stories already written he added
others and, moreover, brought in certain sayings of which he knew the interpretation
would, as a mystagogue, lead the hearers into the innermost sanctuary of that truth
hidden by seven [veils] . . . [Mark] left his composition to the church in Alexandria,
where it even yet is most carefully guarded, being read only to those who are being initiated into the great mysteries.

Clement advised the writer to keep all of this a secret and even to lie about it if that were
necessary. The reason for this he explains later in the same letter:

the Wisdom of God, through Solomon, advises, "Answer the fool from his folly," teaching that the light of truth shall be hidden from those who are mentally blind. Again it
says, "From him who has not shall be taken away," and, "Let the fool walk in darkness." But we are "children of light."[53]

Clement goes on to explain that yes, the secret gospel does say that a youth "whom Jesus
loved" wished to be initiated into Jesus' mystery. He was told by Jesus what to do in order
to become one of the elect, and the youth came to Jesus that evening with only a linen
cloth covering his naked body. The boy spent the night with Jesus and was taught the mystery of the Kingdom of God. Clement's letter breaks off just after telling his questioner
that "naked man with naked man" and the other things he had written about "are not
found" in the secret gospel.[54]

All of this flies in the face of traditional Christianity. What is the meaning of the secrecy, and what is the real secret? Perhaps the answer lies in what was eaten and drunk at these secret nocturnal meetings. What were the great mysteries to which Jesus purportedly had access, and how did he initiate people into his cult? I think that these are reasonable questions to ask. Have we been missing out on the true Christianity?

That Jesus even existed is a matter of some debate, but whether or not he ever lived is unimportant for the purpose of our hypothesis, because even if he did, many events of his life could have been invented and ordered in such a way that the unwritten secrets of his cult were hidden within the story, much as we have seen in the stories of Rudra and others. One such purposeful ordering of events is already evident in the way the New Testament writers shamelessly invented sayings and stories designed to make Jesus appear to be the coming Anointed One mentioned in the Hebrew Bible; yet there may also have been secret reasons for doing so.

There may well have been a real Jesus, or Yeshua, who performed the duties of hierophant, "the one who shows the sacred." It is also possible that Jesus/Yeshua was a cultic title designating the position of Initiator within the cult, as in the Soma sacrifice. We also know that the name "Jesus," the Greek version of Yeshua, was considered to have magical properties of its own. It was even used by some non-Christians of the time in exorcisms and other forms of magic. This is similar to some beliefs held by the Hindus, who elaborated on the idea of magical sounds and words to create the philosophy of mantra yoga. But again, this is incidental. My intention was not to prove whether or not Jesus existed but rather to look for correspondences between the Jesus *story* and the life cycle of the fly agaric mushroom. I found many obvious parallels, as well as a number that are more hidden. We are, after all, dealing with a man of secrets.

Even though among non-Christian authors of the time Jesus was known to be a *mamzer*, a bastard, the gospels present us with a somewhat less likely scenario. We are told that the spirit of the Most High came upon Mary, a virgin, and that the power of the Most High covered her with his shadow, impregnating her. This is more than a little reminiscent of the spirit of Zeus covering Danae and Io and impregnating them, as well as the Ramayana story of the conception of Hanuman. That all these stories have parallels to the fly agaric should not surprise us.

The Birth of Jesus

When Mary was about to give birth she and Joseph were travelling and had to be put up in a stable for the night. Tradition holds that the stable was in a cave. Mary gave birth that same night to a boy. She wrapped the baby in white swaddling cloth and placed it upon straw in the animals' manger. After a time three men arrived. They were obviously foreigners, for their elegant and mysterious dress betrayed them. They were magicians from

Persia, they told the new parents, and had journeyed a great distance to find the newborn child. Their names were Gaspar, "White," Melchior, "Light," and Balthasar, "the Lord of the Treasury." When asked how they knew where and when to find the infant, a feat that seemed most unlikely, they answered that the rising of a certain star in the night sky gave both the general time of the birth and the direction in which to travel. Approaching the manger where the child lay, they fell to their knees and praised God for their good fortune. It is ironic that these professed magicians, members of a profession elsewhere in the Bible condemned as satanic, are given an honored place at the beginning of the story of Jesus.

At about the same time an angel appeared to a group of shepherds who were tending their sheep in the nearby hills. They were surrounded by heavenly light as the angel spoke to them. He told the shepherds that their savior had been born, the Anointed Lord, and told them this would be the sign of the divine child: he would be found wrapped in swaddling cloth and lying in a manger. The shepherds hurried to find the child, and when they found him they told everyone there the astonishing things said by the angel.

Circumcision

When the child was eight days old he was circumcised according to the covenant of Abraham and was given the name Jesus (actually he was named Yeshua, "Yahweh is Salvation," but for the sake of convention he will be referred to as Jesus).

When Jesus was twelve years old his parents took him to the Passover feast, but after a time he abandoned them. After much searching they found him in the temple with the elders, both asking and answering questions, even though he was still in puberty. His full power was not yet manifest.

Nothing of the next eighteen years of Jesus' life is known with any certainty. Most assume that he worked as a carpenter during this time. Some stories have him visiting Egypt and India.

Initiation

At the age of thirty Jesus heard about a wild man named John the Baptizer, who was preaching in the Jordan district along the banks of the river. He gave the people salutary and practical advice, and taught them the virtue and symbolism of simple bathing. Jesus went to John and submitted to his initiation. At the end of the rite, after being dipped in the water, it seemed to Jesus as though the very heavens had opened above his head, and he was flooded with light as white as a dove. A voice from above told Jesus that he was the son of the heavenly father.

This experience was very powerful. Jesus went into the wilderness to ponder the meaning of what had happened at John's initiation, and there he fasted for many days. After some time he began to imagine that he could work miracles, such as producing bread from a stone or throwing himself off a cliff and surviving, but he realized these were only hallucinations. He also experienced delusions of grandeur, imagining himself to be the ruler of the entire world and all of its wealth. But again he came to his senses. "Angels" appeared to look after him in his delicate state of mind. After this he returned to Galilee, advising people to turn from their bad behavior because heaven, as he himself had so recently discovered, was very close at hand.

Ministry

Jesus wandered all over Galilee preaching his new revelation. He was a changed man. He carried with him a jar of ointment and a pouch of herbs, and with these he healed many. His fame as a healer began to grow. Being rejected himself because of his illegitimate birth, he did much of his preaching among the poor and outcast, promising them unlikely rewards if they followed his teachings. The authorities began to think of him as a rabble-rouser and feared that he might be trying to foment a revolution by claiming to be the long-awaited Jewish messiah. He was openly critical of the Jewish priests and scribes, and enjoyed humiliating them in debate in front of others.

Even though he claimed not to be trying to abolish the Jewish law and the teachings of the prophets, he kept reinterpreting them in the light of his own experience. His central themes were love for one another, generosity, and forgiveness, qualities that the Jewish and pagan religions of the time were not practicing to his satisfaction. His public teaching can be summed up by what has become known as the golden rule: "So always treat others as you would like them to treat you; that is the meaning of the Law and the Prophets." He himself did not always follow it, but it was good advice.

Jesus preached love but at the same time railed against "false" prophets, telling people that his magic was the only magic that came from God. He promised terrible tortures throughout eternity for those who chose not to believe the doctrine of love he was preaching. Stories began spreading of his magical powers and many people were afraid of him. Sometimes he was chased out of town, and other times narrowly missed being stoned to death. The delusions of grandeur he had experienced after his initiation seem to have returned, and Jesus began to claim that he was God in the flesh. "If you have seen me, you have seen the Father," he said. This did not go over well with devout Jews; it was blasphemy. He told people that if they fed and cared for him and his disciples they would go to heaven for doing so. The Brahmins in India, the priest caste, were saying exactly the same thing about themselves to the people there.

Secret Teaching

It soon became apparent that Jesus had a secret teaching or ritual. He said,

> Everything has been entrusted to me by my father; and no one knows the son except
> the Father, just as no one knows the Father except the son [Jesus] and those to whom
> the son chooses to reveal him. Come to me . . . and I will give you rest . . . and you will
> find rest for your souls.

More and more people accused him of being an evil magician, of which there was no
shortage in those days. He began to speak publicly only in parables, which not even his
disciples could understand. He told them that only they were privileged to get the true
teaching. The outsiders were out of luck, regardless of what he may have told them to the
contrary. One day someone in a group asked him for a sign to prove the claims he was
making, for by then his reputation had outstripped his ability. He became very angry, calling his audience an evil and wicked generation for daring to ask for proof. The only sign
he would give them, he said, was the sign of the prophet Jonah, who spent three days in
the belly of the beast. He got very testy when challenged.

Miracles

While much of the healing attributed to Jesus can be thought of as a combination of hyper-
bole and the temporary curing of hysterics such as one finds with faith healers today, he
apparently was able to cure some people with a combination of herbs and unguents and
the teaching of better hygiene, the outward farm of the "baptism" for which he and his
disciples were becoming well known.

Several of the so-called miracles with which Jesus is credited are worth noting. His first
major miracle was at a wedding he was attending in Cana. After some time the host ran
out of wine, and Mary told Jesus. He answered her saying his time had not yet come, but
he quickly changed his mind or was mistaken, because he immediately told the servants
to fill six stone jars with water. What happened next we are not told, but afterwards the
jars were found to be filled with a wine so superior to the wine that had run out that even
the drunken guests noticed the difference.

Another story says that Jesus fed a multitude of people with only a small amount of
bread and fish; this is said to have happened on two occasions. Sometime between these
two public events his disciples saw him walk on water.

Jesus' powers of telepathy are shown in two different stories. In one he tells Nathanael
that he knew his name though they had never met, and that he saw him beneath a fig tree
even though the tree was not visible from where Jesus was standing. The other story finds
Jesus at Jacob's well in Samaria. Resting there, he asked for a drink from a woman who
had come to the well to draw water. Because Jews notoriously despised Samaritans, the

woman was surprised that Jesus had asked her for a drink. Jesus told her that if she had asked *him* for water he would have given her living water. When she then asked him for some he told her first to go and bring her husband to the well. She answered that she had no husband and Jesus said, yes, the man you are living with now is not your husband, though you had five husbands before him. She was impressed that he could have known this.

Just then his disciples returned from begging for food and tried to get Jesus to eat some. He answered, "I have food to eat that you do not know about." They were perplexed and asked, "Has someone been bringing him food?"

One day Jesus and his disciples were in a boat on Lake Tiberias when a violent storm arose. Jesus was asleep, but they woke him because they thought they were going down. Jesus stood up and rebuked the wind and the water and all was calm again. He told all aboard the boat that they had no faith.

Jesus had been staying away from Judea, because the last time he had been there the Jews had wanted to stone him. He received a message from Mary and Martha that their brother Lazarus, "the man Jesus loved," was very ill. Jesus announced to his disciples that the sickness would not end in death but in God's glory, and that he, Jesus, would be glorified as a result. He waited two days before he left for Judea (which by Jewish time-reckoning could have been far less than forty-eight hours), telling his disciples that Lazarus was only resting and that he was going to wake him. By the time they arrived Lazarus had been dead "two days" and was entombed. Jesus rolled away the stone door and called out Lazarus' name, and the man came out of the tomb alive.

The Last Supper

At the end of his ministry Jesus was having Passover supper with the disciples in a secret upper room. He took some bread and told them to eat it. "This is my body," he said. He took a cup of wine and told them all to drink from it. "This is my blood," he said. Then he told Judas Iscariot to go and do quickly what he must do.

In the Garden

After the supper Jesus went to Gethsemene with Peter, John, James, and an unidentified young man. He posted John, James, and Peter as guards, that he and the young man might not be disturbed. He asked God, we are told, "for this cup to pass me by." But he drank it anyway. He had to go and awaken his three guards two different times during the night. When he found them asleep a third time he told them rhetorically to go on sleeping, because his capture was at hand and it was too late. Then quickly changing his mind he told them to get up, they all had to get out of there. Just at that moment Judas arrived with a mob of armed men sent by the priests, scribes, and elders. When Judas kissed Jesus they knew they had their man.

The disciples of the prince of peace were armed with swords, and Peter cut off the ear of one of the men. Although Jesus said at the time that he could, if he wanted, summon twelve legions of angels to protect himself, for some reason he chose not to do this and was arrested. The young man with whom he had spent the night ran away when the mob arrived. They tried to hold him but he slipped out of the cloth that was covering him and ran away naked, an occurrence mentioned only in Mark's gospel. The three disciples ran away as well.

The Death of Jesus

Jesus was condemned to death. There are two differing accounts of how his execution came about. In the traditional story, of course, Jesus was crucified on Golgotha, "the Place of the Skull." They forced him to wear a scarlet cloak over his naked body and a crown of thorns was put on his head. The thorns drew blood. He was forced to carry his own cross uphill to his crucifixion. The cross was a simple post and beam, a tau cross, easy to make and very strong. His cross was flanked by the crosses of two other condemned criminals, both of them thieves. Mary, his mother, was at the foot of the cross during the whole ordeal.

One of the criminals mocked Jesus, saying, "If you are the anointed one why don't you save yourself and us too?" The other thief told the former to be silent. "We deserve what we are getting," he said, "but this man was innocent." Jesus promised the good thief that on that very day they would be together in paradise.

The afternoon sun was hot and Jesus lost water rapidly. "I'm thirsty," he said, and a sponge soaked with vinegar was put on the end of a reed and held up to his lips. When Jesus was near death he cried out the first line of the twenty-second Psalm, "My God, my God, why have you deserted me?" And finally, saying, "It is accomplished," Jesus died. After he had hung for some time unmoving, a Roman guard pierced Jesus' side to see if he was dead.

Some say that Joseph of Arimathea also stood beneath the cross that day. He was holding the chalice from which Jesus had ritually shared his blood with his disciples the night before, and when the guard stabbed Jesus with his lance, Joseph held up the cup and caught the blood and fluid that flowed from the wound. He was the same man who arranged to take Jesus' body for burial. Jesus was buried in the new tomb Joseph had just finished for himself. It was Friday evening.

This has been the traditional account of Jesus' crucifixion; the other version states that Jesus was never crucified at all. Crucifixion was a Roman punishment. Jesus was convicted of blasphemy by the Jews for declaring that he was God in human form. To the Jews this was the worst form of blasphemy, punishable only by stoning, and the punishment could only be carried out by Jews. There were scriptural methods of execution prescribed according to the severity of the crime, and crucifixion was not among them. The Jews had full authority to punish their own criminals, those who had broken the Jewish laws, especially those who had committed this gravest of all offences.

Jesus had been very careful not to offend the Romans, as when he instructed his disciples to pay the Roman tax, but he attacked the Jewish religious establishment relentlessly while claiming to be God. As a result he suffered the ritual insult of being stoned to death by his own people. After the stoning he was hung by his hands from a tree, the ultimate indignity, so that all could see what happened to a Jew who blasphemed. There are five references in the New Testament to Jesus being hung on a tree.

One reason the new Christian cult would have changed the story of Jewish stoning and hanging into Roman crucifixion was to win over the gentile proletariat and turn them away from the religion of Rome. These people were already far too familiar with Roman crucifixion and were its usual victims. The Jews, for their part, wanted nothing to do with either the gentiles or Jesus and his blasphemous cult. Therefore, the cult concentrated on recruiting gentiles rather than Jews, even though Jesus and all the apostles were themselves Jews. The story of the crucifixion of the Jewish God-man who loved the poor gave the gentile lower classes even more reason to hate the Romans. They began flocking to this new religion that boasted a powerful magician, now "risen from the dead," as its leader and god, and a doctrine of salvation that promised everything to the lowly and despised, regardless of how unlikely this was ever to materialize.

If the new converts didn't receive their just desserts in this lifetime, and the vast majority did not, they were assured of getting them in Jesus' exclusive heaven, where they (and Jesus, one assumes) would enjoy the added bonus of being able to watch their former social superiors writhe in hellfire for all eternity.

Whatever way Jesus actually died, the subsequent events of the tale remain essentially the same among Christian believers. It should be mentioned that some researchers believe Jesus didn't die on the cross *or* by stoning but rather that his death and resurrection were faked by him and his disciples in order to give the cult supernatural status. Cult competition was fierce in those days, as it is today. The incredible zeal they employed in forcing the "good news" on everyone after the supposed death, especially the resurrection aspect, lends some credence to this theory. Apparently it was easy to convince people that Jesus had been sucked up to heaven just because his body was missing. A variation has Jesus dying and the disciples stealing the quite dead body and disposing of it for the same reasons. Probably the only thing we will ever know for certain is that no one rose from the dead that day and floated bodily up into the sky, carried by the clouds to a heaven somewhere in space.

The Resurrection

On Sunday morning Mary Magdalene went to the tomb and found it empty. Nothing remained but the cloths that had wrapped the body. An angel told her that Jesus had risen from the dead, but when Jesus appeared before her she thought he was the gardener. The man she had loved and seen so often she now could not recognize. He claimed to be Jesus, though, and at last Mary was convinced. He told her not to cling to his body as he had not yet ascended to the Father (which at that point should have been obvious). Apparently not yet fully omniscient, Jesus instructed her to find the brothers and tell them that he was ascending.

Later Jesus appeared to two disciples on the road to Emmaus, but strangely they could not recognize him either. Jesus spent the rest of the walk to the village trying to convince them who he was, apparently to no avail. In the village they went into a house to eat. Jesus took some bread and gave it to them, and after they had eaten it they finally recognized him. "Their eyes were opened," the text says, but he had disappeared. A little while later he appeared to the eleven main disciples and the two with whom he had just broken bread, and still no one recognized him, not even the two men. Only after showing them his wounds did they believe him.

Later still, we are told, Jesus appeared on the shore of Lake Tiberias while the disciples were out fishing. For the fourth time in as many appearances Jesus was unrecognizable at first, although after a time the disciples were pretty sure it was him. Yet, even though the text says "they knew quite well it was the Lord," immediately after this it also says, "None of the disciples was bold enough to ask, 'Who are you?'" If they knew, then why frame the question at all?

During the last earthly appearance of Jesus to the disciples, recorded in Acts, Jesus told them that soon the power of the holy spirit would come upon them. After saying this, as they watched, he rose up into the air and a cloud carried him away. As they stood staring, two men dressed in white asked them why they were looking at the sky and told them that the same Jesus who had just departed would come back to them in the same way he was taken; that is in the clouds.

As mentioned earlier, Jesus may have been the actual leader of a messianic cult or he may have "existed" as a cultic office, a hierophantic role that any qualified person could take on during the secret ritual, as today the Pope is said to be Jesus' special representative on earth, even to the point of being considered infallible (though a glance at the history of the papacy quickly reveals the absurdity of the assertion). A third possibility is that Jesus, like Soma, was a personification of the sacred food and drink of the Eucharist and not vice versa, and the elements of his life story had been shaped to correspond to qualities of the sacred foods. I believe the truth may be some combination of the three, but I leave that for the reader to determine after seeing the evidence.

Assuming for the present that Jesus existed, it now should be apparent that he was a shamanic figure with secret teachings and initiations. If I am correct in my earlier speculations concerning a Jewish mushroom cult then it seems likely that Jesus was taking upon himself the ancient prophetic mantle, the "veil" if you will, of his ancestors. Even if he didn't learn about the fly agaric from John the Baptizer or some other Jewish initiator, as I believe he did, he could have learned of it through the trade routes to India, or perhaps more likely, Greece, which has a probable history of ancient use and where the fly agaric is found in abundance. The appearance of the Magi at his birth also suggests a Persian connection. It is also quite possible that Jesus was familiar with the ergot fungus used by the Greeks at Eleusis in the Greater Mysteries. Though I believe that most of his myth reflects the use of *Amanita muscaria,* I will also point out the places where ergot is a possible candidate.

The Parallels

The Birth of Jesus

Like Jesus, the fly agaric is born of a virgin, that is, the unplowed earth, and has no apparent father, other than the heavenly father who comes in the clouds and with his fertilizing rain causes the mushroom to break out of the bowels of the virgin earth. In its infancy the mushroom is within the earth as in a cave, wrapped completely in the white universal veil as though in swaddling clothes (plate 28). When it appears above the ground it is down among the leaves and grasses that are the common food of animals. The mushroom itself is often eaten by animals. Lying in a manger also foreshadows the last supper of Jesus, during which he became the food and drink of his followers, as it implies that he was born to be eaten.

Three magicians arrived at the birth, signifying that the newborn had magical value. Their names are White, Light, and Lord of the Treasury. White light is the gift that the fly agaric gives to the one who finds it and knows the "magic" involved in its use, and it is a treasure indeed. "Treasury" also refers to the golden color the mushroom gains when it is properly dried, a part of the magical art. The three men were able to find the divine child by noting the rising of a certain star or constellation. This corresponds to the yearly fruiting season of the mushroom, which, depending on location, will be accompanied by the appearance of stars that are visible or in a certain position only during the time of the mushroom's fruiting. This is similar to the Vedic reference to Rohini (red deer or red cow) or Alpha in Taurus, a constellation that appeared in conjunction with certain others during the Soma season in India.

The fact that the three men are Persian magicians is very significant. Even though the

Hebrews used all kinds of magic throughout their history, other magicians were held in contempt and considered to be evil. It would not have been considered a good omen for them to arrive at the birth. Strangely, and unlike everyone else who paid homage to Jesus during his lifetime, the men do not become worshippers of the new god. These magicians of Persia were probably Haoma priests, and Haoma, at least originally, was the same as Soma: a sacred drink made from the fly agaric mushroom. Their presence at the birth of Jesus makes a direct connection with the ancient Aryan religion of the sacrificed and eaten god.

That the divine birth was announced to shepherds is also noteworthy in the light of the other shepherdic connections already discussed. We will recall that among a desert people shepherds were among the few who ever ventured up into the mountain forests of pine, fir, and cedar, driving their flocks there to feed on vegetation unavailable in the lowlands. Also important is the fact that the message was brought by an angel, which as we have seen is itself analogous to the fly agaric. The angel calls the newborn the Anointed Lord (see plate 28), a reference to the "head" of the young mushroom being completely coated with an "anointing" of the damp, soft material that comprises the universal veil. At this early stage the veil can be smeared or wiped off easily, as could an ointment. Lastly, the angel gives the shepherds the signs by which they will know the child: he will be wrapped in swaddling clothes and lying in a manger, a repetition of two clues already mentioned in the story.

Circumcision

After eight days Jesus was circumcised. The time between the first budding of the fly agaric under the ground to the separation of the cap from the base of the mushroom is roughly seven or eight days, depending on the conditions under which it is growing; this is the "circumcision" of the mushroom as previously described.

At puberty Jesus was able to ask and even answer a few spiritual questions, but he wasn't up to full power yet. Eating the mushroom at its correspondingly early stages causes certain symptoms of intoxication, but only a mature mushroom will yield its full potential.

The fly agaric moves quickly from its phallic stage to maturity; the story of Jesus from puberty to maturity also moves quickly, as there is no record of what he did between the ages of twelve and thirty. He is said to have been a carpenter, the only other occupation besides sheepherding that required an occasional visit to the mountain forests. Apocryphal stories also place him in India and Egypt during this period, where he could have picked up magical practices, but no one knows where he was or what he did during this time.

Initiation

The next recorded event in the life of Jesus is his appearance at the Jordan river, asking to be baptized by John the Baptizer. John, like Elijah before him, may represent the last of his line. Jesus was an exceptional person but still he lacked the knowledge that only John could impart: initiation into the ancient Jewish fly agaric cult. Elaborate interpretations have been put forth over the centuries to explain away what has always stuck in the craw of Christian apologists everywhere: the fact that God himself (by their reckoning) submitted to the discipline of a mere human. Stripping Jesus of his godhood, however, reveals the episode for what it is: an initiation into the mysteries of God, the same initiation Jesus later imparted to his inner circle.

In part of the story Jesus personifies the mushroom, but in the main it tells of his remarkable experience of light and the fatherhood of God. A mature and dried mushroom is ready to be put into water to extract its essence; a mature Jesus went under the influence of the water and revealed his essence and his "mission." The zenith of the fly agaric experience is an outpouring of white light streaming down from above the user's head; a heavenly voice proclaiming godhood and kinship might be heard. The absolute profundity of the experience cannot be denied, neither can it be adequately expressed, though one is moved to try.

This is what happened to Jesus. He already had a natural talent for the job but his initiation into the mysteries focused his life and created a mission. He saw the big picture in a flash and the world was forever changed, for better or worse. Jesus' experience of light is symbolized as a white dove coming down from heaven over his head. Additionally, when the cap of the mushroom inverts and reveals its white "feathers," a "white dove" sits where the "head" of the mushroom used to be (see plate 12).

The story says that when Jesus first appeared at the place where John was baptizing, John said, "Look, here comes the Lamb of God that takes away the sin of the world." This is Jesus' second connection with sheep and his first identification as one. For shepherds the terms "lamb" and "blood of the lamb" were not metaphors; they represented the daily reality of a shepherd. The terms became metaphors the first time a shepherd found a fly agaric mushroom with its fluffy white "wool" covering its blood-red skin (plate 29). The birth of the mushroom, "announced" to shepherds, gave birth to a metaphor clothed in the terminology of shepherds: the Bloody Lamb of God.

After his initiation Jesus went off alone into the wilderness. He is said to have fasted, which may have produced his hallucinations of grandeur. Given the nature of what he had just been through a little hubris is understandable, but again I think the story is hiding something else. "Turning stones into bread" is shorthand for the fly agaric lifecycle. A white, rough "stone" grows and expands as though it were full of yeast and produces a round, dome-shaped "loaf," which when "cooked" (that is, dried) becomes fit to eat: a metaphorical Bread of Life that even resembles a round of pita bread.

In fly agaric intoxication a person commonly feels immense physical strength and vigor. One feels invincible, the way Jesus felt when he looked over the cliff's edge and imagined he could survive the fall. One also clearly sees how easy it is to gain the wealth of the whole world but lose one's soul in the process. Jesus was integrating his experience at the river with the new directions his life was suddenly taking. When "angels" appear to look after him, as they did to other Jewish prophets, we must suspect that the fly agaric, the fiery-winged angel of God, is intimately involved.

Ministry

Jesus now had tremendous dispassion, if not active aversion, toward the world. This is characteristic of the state of mind the user enters when the mushroom is taken over a period of time. A person can feel as if the universe is taking care of everything. Why worry about what to eat or what to wear when God is providing everything for the entire world? The main thing is to make sure that God is known before death. This world is not our home, so we shouldn't try to hold on to it. Our true home is on the other side. Sell what you own and give the money to the poor. Lay up your treasure in heaven. Love one another. Turn the other cheek. Help others. Treat others the way you want to be treated. All of this is perfectly consistent with fly agaric use.

Jesus also exhibited a dark side. His story indicates that he had schizophrenic tendencies leaning towards paranoia, which may have been fostered by the abuse he surely suffered all his life as a Jewish bastard. Bastards were regarded with undisguised contempt in Jewish society. For example, he was called the "son of Mary"; in Jewish society a male would have been called the son of his father, not his mother, unless he was illegitimate. "Son of Mary" was a term of derision. This made Jesus somewhat defensive; he could curse as well as bless, and this, combined with his reputation as a magician, made him feared by many.

Secret Teaching

When asked for a sign that he was the messiah Jesus got angry and said the only sign he would give was that of Jonah, who lay in the belly of the beast for three days. The story of Jonah, as we saw, is rich in mushroom imagery: being swallowed by the fish/beast is a metaphor for the deathlike coma that can be induced by fly agaric consumption. Jonah's description of sinking under incredible weight to the depths of the sea is very apt imagery, as is the image of the fish vomiting. How odd that the only sign Jesus would give to his questioners was the sign of Jonah, unless it was meant to identify him further with the ancient and secret mushroom cult. (I am fully aware of the Christian contention that Jesus was foreshadowing his three days of death prior to his revival; the two interpretations are not mutually exclusive.)

PLATE 15: "How could there be fruit on a pillar?" (p. 57).

PLATE 16 *above:* Shiva, god of the pillar,
on his high throne with Parvati (p. 57).

PLATE 17 *right:* A young fly agaric corresponding
in shape and color to the painting of Shiva's throne
(p. 58). Other references: The same mushroom as
shown in plate 30, before drying (p. 125).

PLATE 18 *facing page:* Moses saw a plant that glowed
like fire yet was not consumed (p. 78).

PLATE 19 *above:* Moses made a metallic serpent arid put it on a pole (p. 87).

PLATE 20 *right:* God sends fiery winged serpents to attack the Israelites (p. 87).

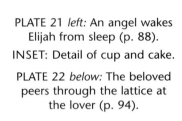

PLATE 21 *left:* An angel wakes Elijah from sleep (p. 88).

INSET: Detail of cup and cake.

PLATE 22 *below:* The beloved peers through the lattice at the lover (p. 94).

PLATE 23 *right:* Teeth like shorn sheep, eyes like a dove, and lips like a scarlet thread (p. 96).

PLATE 24 *below:* "Your breasts are two fawns . . . that feed among the lilies." (p. 96). Other references: "Though your sins are scarlet, they shall be as white as snow . . ." (p. 99). Milking the full breasts of the Father (p. 152). The goddess of alchemy gives milk and blood from her breasts (p. 188).

PLATE 25 *facing page:* The sealed fountain gushes forth (p. 97).

PLATE 26 *above:* Ezekiel saw a glittering wheel with eyes all around the rim (p. 102).
Other references: The many horns and eyes of the lamb (p. 132).

PLATE 27 *below:* Each wheel Ezekiel saw had another wheel within it (p. 102).

Miracles

At Cana Jesus turned water into wine. This is one of the miracles that could reflect the use of ergot fungus, although the story also works for the fly agaric. At Eleusis, in ancient Greece, grain contaminated with a species of the rust fungus *Claviceps* was stirred into a large bowl containing mostly liquids. The LSD-like state that followed the drinking of the potion was an intense and visionary experience, but in greater dilution (which may be the reason for mentioning *six* large water jugs in the story) the effect is much diminished and an anti-depressant euphoria is experienced.

Albert Hofmann, the discoverer of LSD, has said privately that he considers a dose of ten micrograms, which is only one-tenth of a normal dose, to be the world's best antidepressant, one with no toxic sideeffects. (He also complained that no one in the medical or pharmaceutical establishment would even consider this idea.) This type of low-dosage euphoria seems to be what the drunken guests at the party experienced, rather than the vivid hallucinations and disorientation common with larger doses.

Fly agaric also releases its active ingredients in water, as we know. It doesn't go well with food, though, and sometimes causes nausea even on its own; so in the context of the wedding feast fly agaric doesn't appear to fit, although if the story is taken to another level it does. A wedding is a symbol of the *hieros gamos,* the union of opposites. To celebrate this union properly sometimes a little "magic" is needed. After taking fly agaric a person can be close to the celebration of a perfect union between the soul and God but not quite there. If a sufficient amount of the mushroom has been eaten, and enough water drunk in the process, then when nature calls a user finds that "making water" has taken on a different cast, and literally so: the urine turns a fiery light orange hue. It loses its ordinary acrid and repugnant smell and takes on a neutral fragrance. If one were to taste it at this point (not that one would), the flavor could truthfully be described as not unpleasant. And if someone were to collect all the burning issue in a vessel and drink it (not that one would), one might suddenly arrive at the full celebration of the divine wedding.

The other New Testament stories that appear to involve ergot are the two mass feedings Jesus performs with very little food. Loaves of bread figure prominently in both stories, and bread can readily be made from infected grain or by adding a water extract of the same; the right strain can cause the type of euphoria described earlier. LSD, and by extension ergot, is a powerful anorexic as well as hallucinogen. The merest nibble from an ergot-infused loaf would completely take away one's appetite for the whole day and make one spiritually energized enough to sit happily through hours of exhortations by long-winded preachers. This appears to be the scenario at the two mass feedings, and it makes perfect sense. We needn't look for supernatural explanations for events when there are reasonable natural explanations available. Such natural explanations are not always apparent or desirable, however, so usually we either accept that an event is a "miracle" or reject it as being impossible. Psychoactive plants provide a third alternative, a bridge between the natural and supernatural worlds.

Like ergot, *Amanita muscaria* is also an anorexic but not effective in extremely small amounts in the way ergot is. LSD, for example, is measured in the millionths of a gram (micrograms). As little as ten micrograms of LSD can keep a user happy and active all day. Approximately a million times as much dried fly agaric would be needed to feel similar effects.

Jesus was said to have walked on water. In mushroom-language this says that an "immortal" dried fly agaric cap will float in water. Mortals will sink.

Jesus offered the Samaritan woman "living water" at Jacob's well. We have seen that living water is produced in two ways: when the mushroom is put in water and "vivifies" it, and when someone eats or drinks the mushroom and urinates streams of "living water." A person who drinks such water never again "thirsts after righteousness," because, as he told the woman, ". . . the water that I shall give will turn into a spring inside him, welling up to eternal life." A person who drinks from this secret spring is also capable of occasional feats of telepathy such as Jesus displayed with the woman. Even though Jesus and the disciples hadn't eaten, when the men returned with food for Jesus he refused it, saying he had food to eat that they didn't know about, a statement always given metaphysical interpretation; perhaps he really wasn't hungry. Perhaps he simply *had* eaten something they didn't know about and was temporarily anorexic.

Jesus' calming the storm on Lake Tiberias is similar to the events of the Jonah story. Jesus was sleeping while everyone else was seasick and sure they were going to die, all of which—sleep, nausea, and fear of death—are common fly agaric reactions. They woke Jesus, who through the power of his "word" was able to calm the storm. Then he criticized the other "passengers" for having no faith; in other words, for thinking they were going to die from eating the mushroom when he had already told them they wouldn't.

Sleep again plays a role in the story of raising Lazarus. The first thing we notice is how nonchalantly Jesus took the news of his good friend's impending death. He waited two days before leaving, telling his disciples that it wasn't a sickness unto death; Lazarus was "sleeping" and Jesus was going to wake him. When Jesus finally arrived everyone thought Lazarus was dead, and Lazarus was already in the tomb. Jesus awakened him by calling his name, a revival that once again recalls the fly agaric near death state. A body in this state can appear dead to the casual observer: cold, clammy, with a barely discernible pulse and heartbeat, and dead to the world, yet the simple passive act of hearing one's name called can be enough to bring one back from the brink of the void. I will say more about this later.

Toward the end of his life Jesus made another strange comparison. He identified himself with the fiery metallic serpent lifted up by Moses, saying that he must likewise be lifted up, and that whoever believes in Jesus will not die. As in the story of Moses, this can be read as a reference to the harsh qualities of the fresh mushroom and the way to avoid these effects by drying, at which time the cap takes on a metallic sheen. "But even if you still get a bad reaction," Jesus seems to be saying, "keep remembering what I told you: you will not die."

The Last Supper

By now it should be evident that the Last Supper has a one-to-one correspondence to the ritual consumption of the dry and liquid forms of the mushroom in a feast of thanksgiving. Here is the way Jesus explained himself to his disciples:

> I am the living bread that has come down from heaven. Anyone who eats this bread will live forever; and the bread that I shall give is my flesh . . . if you do not eat [my] flesh and drink [my] blood, you will not have life in you. Anyone who does eat my flesh and drink my blood has eternal life . . . for my flesh is real food and my blood is real drink . . . As I, who am sent by the living Father, myself draw life from the Father, so whoever eats me will draw life from me. This is the bread come down from heaven . . . anyone who eats this bread will live forever.

If this quite specific and literal-sounding exhortation is not about the fly agaric mushroom then it is one of the most bizarre passages in the history of religion. Christian apologists argue that Jesus is speaking symbolically, but even symbolic cannibalism is an extremely strange practice, to say nothing of literal cannibalism; yet this and similar passages are routinely danced around as though they don't sound like something out of a black magic ritual. I agree that symbolic language is being used, but not when Jesus implores us repeatedly to eat and drink. He is speaking of real eating and drinking. The only symbols in the passage are Jesus himself and the "bread come down from heaven," which he informs us are one and the same; we are to eat the "flesh" of this "bread" and drink its "blood."

Humans and their flesh are not like bread, nor does bread have blood, and the images of eating human flesh and drinking blood are perverse regardless of the context; but the dried fly agaric mushroom is analogous to bread, and it bears its red "blood" on its body. When placed in water the cap releases its "blood," and after it is thoroughly saturated it feels like human flesh. Both the flesh and the "blood" of the mushroom are edible and contain the stuff of heaven, which is more than can be said for the literal body and blood of Yeshua ben Miriam: Jesus, the son of Mary.

At the end of the ritual dinner Jesus informed the disciples that after a short time they would not see him, but later still they would. This corresponds to the end of the mushroom season and its promised return the next year; it also makes a secret secondary reference to the mushroom's second liquid form. When they eat the mushroom it will disappear, but a short time later it will reappear as "living water."

The influence of the mushroom may have emboldened Jesus to the point of revealing the secret focus of his cult. This may be what the story of Judas represents, since Jesus is portrayed as knowingly sending him on his way. More likely, however, is the idea that this is the fate—a horrible death—that awaits such a cult and such a leader should their secrets be exposed to a hostile and uncomprehending world. What was it Jesus said about casting pearls before swine?

In the Garden

The Garden of Gethsemene story is a mix of several elements. We know from the canonical Book of Mark that a fifth person was with Jesus, Peter, James, and John at Gethsemene after the sacred meal, though this mysterious man is conveniently ignored by apologists. Here is one possible scenario. Everyone at the supper took the two forms of the mushroom, the "bread" and the "wine." Jesus had arranged to initiate a young man afterwards at Gethsemene. Meeting the youth at the garden, Jesus posted his three most trusted disciples as guards so the secret rite wouldn't be disturbed. Jesus then went off with the young man, who was naked except for a linen cloth around his body, to initiate him into the mysteries of the Kingdom of God. He may have given the man mushrooms to eat, the liquid from soaked mushrooms to drink, or both.

It is also possible that, in order more easily to impress his divinity on the young man, Jesus, having already eaten and drunk ample quantities of the mushroom beforehand, simply produced on the spot the living waters that the Bible tells us will flow from the inward parts of a man. If such a drink was offered to the young man he surely would have asked, or at least wished, that the cup would pass from his lips; nevertheless, the young man knew that he must obey the hierophant in order to ascend to heaven. The words "may this cup pass from me" may have been part of the liturgy of the cult, expressing in ritualized form the aversion an initiate would naturally feel toward the indelicate act of drinking urine, especially if it is someone else's. Drinking the dreadful cup would surely have convinced the man that he was in the presence of a god, namely Jesus. More evidence for this interpretation will be brought to bear in the Gnosticism chapter.

The three guards could not stay awake. Again, deep sleep is a common reaction to fly agaric consumption. Sometimes sleep will come with a vengeance no matter what a user does to remain awake.

I have speculated that the ancient Jewish mushroom cult was a secret of the priests (and maybe a king or two), a number of whom were former shepherds. Initiation was probably an individual affair, with vows never to divulge the secret except to a successor. We saw this with Jethro and Moses, Moses and Aaron, Elijah and Elisha, and several initiating "angels." In the case of Jesus it appears that he broke the tradition of initiating only one person into the secret priesthood. Slowly the circle of initiates under Jesus grew until its activities could no longer be kept secret. The initiates were led into the kingdom of heaven and could not contain their enthusiasm for what their teacher had "given" them.

Word of the miracle-working teacher who claimed to be God spread like wildfire; it wasn't long until the authorities found out that secret initiations were being conducted overnight and caught the blasphemous participants red-handed, so to speak. The raid on the Garden of Gethsemene may represent, at least indirectly, history's first drug bust.

Whether the disciples were made aware that some of Jesus' power came from a mushroom is unclear. The stories can be read either way, though it seems likely that at first he may have initiated people unawares, the better to impress them with his divinity. If this is so then the last supper may represent the first time he revealed that a magic plant was behind the whole thing. He knew that the Jewish authorities were after him for being a blasphemer, and that the penalty for this crime was death. Even though he broke other traditions, he couldn't die without revealing the truth. Jesus may have been the only one, since the death of the baptizer, who knew the real secret; Jesus found himself in the same predicament as Elijah.

Though Jesus enjoyed being thought of as God, he may have felt guilty about not perpetuating the cult. If Jesus did reveal his use of drugs, it didn't seem to diminish his disciples' regard of him, at least not publicly. They couldn't reveal the secret on a large scale either, due to supply problems and the overzealous authorities; neither would they have wanted prospective converts to find out. Later it perfectly suited their proselytizing purposes to have a "resurrected" and absent leader who was thought of as God; this explained away all the strange stories circulating about the cult that might otherwise have caused suspicion.

The Death of Jesus

There are two accounts of the way Jesus was killed. I believe the conflicting stories, of death on both a tree and a cross, were intentionally included in the texts to identify the fly agaric more completely. Every fly agaric specimen experiences symbolic death on a tree. It must go through its whole life cycle in conjunction with its host tree and always ends up by meeting its "death" in some form at the same tree. There must be a tree involved if it is a fly agaric. The reason for the cross has been explained: the mushroom becomes cruciform at the end of its life. And the crossbeam, that is, the lifted-up mushroom cap, turns into a metallic serpent on top of the upright, as Jesus implied would also happen to him.

Jesus was given a scarlet cloak to wear over his naked body, just like the red "cloak" of the mushroom. A "crown of thorns" was placed on his head, which caused his head to become bloody. A look at a young fly agaric with its veil "thorns" intact will reveal the intended meaning here (see plate 1).

Jesus was forced to carry his own cross. The mushroom also "carries its own cross" in potential and design until the time when, at maturity, it is "lifted up and crucified." Being nailed to the cross corresponds to the points of the veil fragments on the cap and also calls attention to the need for nailing both feet together on the upright, effectively giving Jesus only one leg: the stipe of the mushroom.

The bad thief taunts Jesus, telling him to save himself as well as the two thieves. He doesn't understand that Jesus must be sacrificed so he can be eaten by his followers. The good thief recognizes the need for Jesus to die and merely prays that the thief might go with him to paradise. There are "thieves" who pick any mushrooms they see in order to destroy them, and there are those who pick only mushrooms they can put to good use.

Jesus makes two significant mushroom utterances while on the cross. In the first, Jesus asks God why he has been deserted, another correspondence to postingestion agony and the feeling that God must certainly be trying to destroy the consumer, as we saw with Moses. Resignation follows the cry for help. The second pronouncement comes at the end, when, arms outstretched, he announces, "It is accomplished." In the life of the fly agaric "it is accomplished" similarly when, in full extension, the crowned and bloody cap has released its millions of spores into the world.

Mary, the virgin mother earth, is always found at the foot of the cross.

When Joseph of Arimathea catches in the chalice of the Last Supper the blood and water flowing from the side of Jesus it signifies the final cup-of-blood configuration of the mushroom at the end of its life (see plate 12); it also suggests that the "body," having been hung out in the sun for a sufficient time, should be put into water, and the mix of water and "blood" from the mushroom should be drunk. When this happens, after all the vital juices have been pressed out of the mushroom, its body can be left behind, of no more significance than Jesus' burial cloths after the "real" Jesus left them.

The Resurrection

In every fly agaric cult that has ever existed, one feature is central and overriding in importance: the mushroom is regarded by cult members as a living, divine creature, an angel or a god, who must die and be eaten by its own devotees. We have seen how the fly agaric dies on the cross; how it is itself both cross and savior. Once the mushroom is "dead," that is, thoroughly dry, it can be brought back to life by immersing it in water, by "baptizing" it. It then resurrects before our eyes. Feel the flesh; it feels like human skin. Press the revived body and watch its blood flow out, the holy blood of the savior, the saving blood of the resurrected lamb. As Jesus says in the Book of John, speaking of Jesus' upcoming resurrection,

> I will come back to you. In a short time the world will no longer see me; because I live and you will live. On that day you will understand that I am in my Father and you in me and I in you . . . *I call you friends, because I have made known to you everything I have learnt from my Father* . . . The Father himself loves you for loving me and believing that I came from God. I came from the Father and came into the world and now I leave the

world and go to the Father . . . Father, may they be one in us, as you are in me and I am in you . . . *I have given them the glory you gave to me, that they may be one as we are one. With me in them and you in me* . . . [Italics mine]

Once when some people were challenging him Jesus said, "Do you know why you cannot take in what I say? It is because you are unable to understand my language." On top of this no one close to Jesus could even *recognize* him after he resurrected. What can this mean? It is very strange, and it is stranger still to include this fact in the story. Why couldn't the closest disciples to Jesus recognize the one with whom they had spent countless hours in the most intimate proximity? He must have looked very different after the crucifixion for this to have happened. While just hours before he was firm and ruddy-cheeked, now he was soft and pale. Perhaps his shape had changed as well; his body, drained of fluids on the cross, had become much smaller and was now limp. Upon closer examination it could be seen that it was indeed the same body as before, but it didn't look at all the same.

The unrecognizable resurrected body of Jesus corresponds to a dried fly agaric that has been placed in water. Jesus' close disciples couldn't recognize him after he resurrected because the three types of mushroom bodies, fresh, dried, and rehydrated, look so different from one another. Someone who had seen and handled a fresh fly agaric specimen might not recognize the same mushroom either dried or rehydrated, but careful examination would soon show that it is in fact the same mushroom. Look, here are the "thorns" on the crown; here are the "nails"; here is the "blood"; here is the wound where the stem was cut. It is the same flesh and blood, the same body, but nearly unrecognizable (plate 30, the same mushroom, dried, as shown in plate 17). The two disciples at Emmaus couldn't recognize Jesus until he gave them "bread" to eat, after which "their eyes were opened."

Resurrection has a triple meaning in the story. The first meaning is the resurrection of the "dead" mushroom by rehydration; the second is the resurrection within the user, when after it is consumed the mushroom "comes to life" in both the body and the "wine"; the third resurrection occurs when the mushroom reappears the following year in the same form at the same location, as Rudra did in the Pine Forest story.

After the disciples talked to the resurrected Jesus for the last time he was taken up to heaven in a cloud. Two white-robed "angels" assured them that Jesus would come back to them in exactly the same way: in the clouds, a most fitting reminder for those who had perhaps eaten their last sacred supper and were lamenting that the holy food was now gone. He was here for only a time and a season. He told them there would come a time when they would seek him and not find him, but still they should have faith, for before long they would again see the Holy One riding on the clouds of heaven, descending to earth once more in majesty, wearing his red cloak and crown of thorns. As always, since before even Abraham was, Jesus' reward is with him when he comes.

Pentecost

Pentecost was an ancient Jewish harvest festival, probably appropriated from an even older Canaanite fertility festival. It was a common practice in the ancient world for a conquering religion to usurp the old religion's sacred holidays and make them over in the new religion's image. Christmas and Easter, for instance, were pagan celebrations of the changing seasons before Christianity reinvented them. The Christians even usurped the birth date of rival god Mithra, December twenty-fifth.

So it was also that the Christians created their own version of the Jewish Pentecost festival, as the Jews had recreated the earlier Canaanite festival. It was at the Pentecost festival in Jerusalem, after Jesus' death, that the apostles chose to exhibit publicly their ability to become God-intoxicated. This was their way of "Christianizing" the holiday. What happened that day is a matter of some controversy. Of course we have only the Christian account, but the elements sound familiar.

The apostles had met privately in a room. Like Elijah and Ezekiel before them, they heard what was described as a mighty wind from heaven; then something that looked to them like tongues of fire appeared and came to rest on their heads. At this they became filled with the Holy Spirit and began to speak in other tongues. We are told that a number of non-Galileans heard the commotion coming from the room, and when they approached they all understood what was being said, as if their own languages were being spoken. Most of those present were amazed, but some, strange to say, laughed at them, saying the apostles must have been drinking too much new wine.

Peter was aware that they were being mocked, so he stood up and loudly proclaimed that they were not drunk. He exhorted the mockers with specious arguments about the divinity of Jesus and his supernatural bestowal upon the disciples of their "drunken" state. After hearing Peter's defensive tirade everyone immediately saw the error of their ways and converted on the spot to the new religion of the dead savior, or so we are told. The text says three thousand people were baptized that day.

This passage begins with an unexplained sound of heavenly wind. The sound of rushing wind is familiar to some who have had experience with psychedelic drugs or certain yoga practices; this sound can be especially noticeable as a person passes out of normal consciousness of the physical world and enters a different, more subtle world. The appearance of "tongues of fire" sounds suspiciously like the fly agaric once again, called "tongue of the way" and "fire" by the Vedic Aryans, among others; we have already seen the numerous fire references in the utterances of the earlier Hebrew prophets.

The text says the fires separated and came to rest on the men's heads. This probably refers to the way energy seems to move upward through the body during fly agaric intoxication and internally lights up the head area. It also corresponds to the red flushing of the face and to the "fire" that sits on top of the mushroom, yet it could represent something even more obscure.

Tonsuring, the shaving of the head for religious reasons, is an ancient practice that predates Christianity but was adopted by Christians. In the Eastern Church the entire head was shaved, while in the Roman Church a circle was shaved out at the crown of the head. As described earlier, a powerful ointment can be made using dried fly agaric mushrooms and oil. Rubbing this reddish, fiery oil into the scalp can be an effective way to take the mushroom, bypassing the digestive system at the same time. As absurd as it sounds, a person can even take an oil-saturated mushroom cap and place it directly on the crown of the head, the top of the cap against the skin, and leave it there for an indefinite period of time, occasionally rubbing in more oil or changing the mushroom. Perhaps there is a secret symbolism relating to this practice in the design of the *zuchetto,* the small skullcap worn on the crown of the head by Catholic bishops. These caps were originally used to cover the tonsured area of the head, in the same manner I have suggested for mushroom caps. Interestingly, the cap of the Cardinals is red, while that of the Pope is white.

This method can also be seen as a form of sympathetic magic that places the crown of the mushroom in direct contact with the crown of the head. It is from the top of the head that light appears during intoxication, so it may have seemed logical to think that this would be the best place for the drug to be absorbed. When possible drug-delivery systems are being considered, no possibly effective method, however bizarre, should be excluded. Urine-drinking, for example, is extremely bizarre; yet it seems perfectly natural and even wholesome to someone who knows how to turn that water into "wine." People used to believe that witches rode through the air on broomsticks, but now we know that witches were actually using their broomsticks and other devices to apply psychoactive ointments to their vulvas.

The text says that the people outside, who had been attracted by the ravings of the apostles, heard the preaching in their own native tongues. This appears to be a gloss added by the author in order to make the psychedelic babbling of the apostles more acceptable for the text. Some who witnessed their ecstatic behavior and preaching would have thought them possessed by a spirit, while others, as the story points out, would have thought them to be merely drunk: precisely the way bemushroomed Siberian natives were described by some early European witnesses. The story of drunken behavior by the apostles must have been well-known at the time or the author wouldn't have included it and apologized for it.

Adding that people from all over the known world just happened to stroll by and hear God's glories being preached in their own languages may have seemed like a judicious move to the author, but to the modern mind it is a transparent fabrication. Writing earlier than Acts, Paul more accurately describes the phenomenon of spiritual babbling, noting that the one with the gift to speak in tongues talks to God and not to humans, "because nobody understands him when he talks in the spirit about mysterious things." In high psychedelic states this sort of "talking" can occur involuntarily and is often more of a side effect than a condition. The aforementioned waves of energy that are felt in this state can affect the jaw and breath, causing the jaw to chatter or move very rapidly in waves of frequency. If any vocalizing is added at this point the resulting sound is otherworldly and sometimes strangely beautiful; it sounds like the speech of angels, and perhaps it is.

The conversion and baptism of three thousand people brings to mind the mass feedings with which Jesus was credited. If he passed on his fly agaric secrets at the time of his death, he also would have passed on information about ergot and its use (I can almost hear the disciples exclaiming, "So *that's* how he did it!"). The disciples, for reasons of megalomania or whatever, became obsessed with the idea of converting the whole world to Christianity. It is possible that drug-inspired preaching about the God-man could have won over some converts on its own, especially among the poor and disenfranchised, but it is unlikely that such conversions, on the scale talked about by the early Church, happened without the use of an "incentive."

It is doubtful that the fly agaric was ever used on a large scale by the Christians. Perhaps it was used only among the inner circle of devotees, due to its relative scarcity and difficulty of procurement, while ergot was used, especially after Jesus' death, for the wholesale conversion of large groups of people, similar to what was done at Eleusis, once for all. Preaching to the crowds about the glory of after-death heaven never carries quite the persuasive power of offering them a *taste* of it while they're still alive. The preaching method might not produce much enthusiasm among a repressed underclass, but the ergot method surely would. Enthusiasm *and* conversions.

If Jesus offered ergot-bread at his two recorded "miraculous" mass feedings, then the disciples must surely have used it after his death in a similar manner. Jesus was dead, but those who joined the new cult were offered, as an inducement or a bonus, a bite of the cult's dead savior and a drink of his blood, both of which were claimed to have magical, transformative properties. The first eucharistic meal offered to the public in the name of Jesus may well have been, due to easy availability and sheer chemical strength, ergot-infused bread and wine.

The original "bread come down from heaven," the fly agaric mushroom, became for the masses an actual loaf of ergot-spiked bread. Later the two were combined: the bread of the host was reduced in size and baked in a shape resembling a dried mushroom cap, but with neither fly agaric nor ergot in the recipe. From that point forward the only intoxicant offered to members was "unmingled wine"; much later, as we shall see, even that was taken away.

What Happened to Paul?

After Jesus, the person most responsible for the creation of Christianity was Paul, a Jew who had never even met Jesus; Paul was such an ardent proselytizer that he probably could have created Christianity without Jesus. Some scholars believe he did. Known as Saul until sometime after his conversion, his name struck fear into the hearts of Christians because he was actively involved in persecuting the new Christian cult, avidly pursuing his goal of total destruction of the religion. His job, authorized by the Jewish high priest, was to round up cult members and send them to prison.

One day while travelling to Damascus with an arrest warrant he saw a bright light that seemed to come from heaven; he was completely engulfed in light. He fell off his horse and heard a voice that said, "Why are you persecuting me?" Saul asked who it was and the voice said, "Jesus." Paul was then told to go into the city where he would receive further instructions, but when he stood up he couldn't see; with his eyes wide open he saw nothing. His companions led him the rest of the way to Damascus, where for three days he remained without his normal eyesight, and during this time he neither ate nor drank. Then one of the disciples came to Saul saying that he, the disciple, had been sent by Jesus, and Saul's sight returned to normal. He immediately converted to the religion of Jesus.

In the 1960s and 1970s, some people who had taken LSD used to fantasize about putting it in the water supply or secretly "dosing" the President; not on a whim, but in order to stop the Vietnam war, and ideally warfare in general. It was believed, however naively, that no one who took a dose of LSD could support a war that was so clearly wrong. This may be what happened to Saul, only with fly agaric rather than LSD.

The cult members knew about Saul and must have hated him for causing the deaths of their members and trying to destroy the cult. They could have killed him, but this probably would have made things worse: the cult would have been seen as murderous rather than pacifist, as they claimed to be, and they would have been quickly wiped out. Things were bad enough as they were without making them worse. Far better to slip Saul a powerful dose of their own medicine and see what happened. A large dose of ergot could have produced similar results, but the story points more toward *Amanita muscaria*.

Let us assume that through collusion they were able to do so, that unbeknownst to him Saul consumed the equivalent of as many as eight or ten mushrooms. He would have been able to begin his journey to Damascus as though nothing had happened, but somewhere along the way it would have hit him like a sledgehammer. He might have found himself suddenly enveloped in brilliant white light that seemed to stream down from heaven, causing him to lose body consciousness and fall off his horse. He may well have heard heavenly voices, his own buried conscience perhaps, telling him to stop harming innocent people. And when he finally returned to body consciousness he may have been stone blind; not in the sense of everything being black, but in not being able to focus his eyes. Large doses of fly agaric can cause this kind of blindness, and it is very disconcerting. It is a real blindness, even though light and color can be seen; with extreme dosages this state can last a long time. Along with his blindness Saul also experienced anorexia, a common psychedelic side effect. He ate and drank nothing.

The disciples would have arranged for one of their members to be in Damascus and locate Saul sometime after he arrived. The disciple would tell Saul that this was the doing of the lord Jesus; Jesus was angry because Saul was persecuting the new cult, and perhaps Saul had better repent and embrace Christianity if he ever wanted to see again. The disciple, of course, knew that the blindness would soon end without anyone's help. Saul took the bait, converted, and lo! his sight returned. He soon applied the same unthinking, overweaning zeal he had used to round up Christians to rounding up new converts.

It probably would have been best for the disciples never to tell Saul/Paul what had really occurred and risk losing their best proselytizer, and possibly their lives, in the bargain. He seems only to have had the one "heavenly" experience, so this may be what happened. The relevant expression is, "Let sleeping dogs lie."

Revelation

The Book of Revelation hearkens back to the older Hebrew prophets with its vivid images of fiery angels and terrible punishments and plagues, and it is filled with some of the same fly agaric correspondences found in earlier works. Its author identifies himself as "John," though he probably wasn't the same person who wrote the other Johannine works. "Revelation" is a translation of the Greek *apokalypsis,* which means "an uncovering." Some modern (and earlier) Christian writers have made their fortunes "deciphering" the predictions in the book, which are extremely obtuse.

One thing that can be said about the terribly obscure and open-ended predictions of Revelation is that they have supplied abundant material for every Christian doomsayer that has come down the pike for the last nineteen hundred years; the horrid calamities forecast in the book, as well as the return of Jesus, have always been "just around the corner." Yet what good are predictions that never come true, or that become true only with the most tortuous interpretations? What may be more important in the book of Revelation than the prediction of future events is the "uncovering of something hidden" referred to in the title; this discovery might occur not in the future, but in the present, whenever the book is read.

Proof that Revelation should not be taken seriously as a book of predictions is the author's statement in the prologue: "Happy the man who reads this prophecy, and happy those who listen to him, if they treasure all that it says, *because the Time is close*" [Italics mine]. Well, the time wasn't close; everyone is still waiting nineteen hundred years later, and preachers are still crying, "The time is near!" Once again the power of prophecy takes a back seat to the power of suggestion, which has always been the real driver of religious prediction. While we may not wish to wager money on the likely occurrence of the events that are "soon to come," there is some gold to be gleaned from the text.

Shortly after saying "the time is close," the author reminds us that the one who has washed away our sins with his "blood" is soon coming back on the clouds, and with that the listing of fly agaric correspondences has begun. John goes on to state that while on the island of Patmos he was possessed by the Spirit. He heard behind him the sound of horns, and turning to see what was making the sound, he saw seven golden lampstands. A temple lampstand of the time consisted of a short tripod with a single metal rod rising from its apex; on top of the rod was an alabaster bowl that held the fire, making it in overall shape as well as metaphor quite similar to a mature fly agaric.

Standing in the midst of these lampstands was a "figure like a son of man." "Son of man" is either a banal way of signifying a person of the male gender or it means something else. Perhaps it is calling attention to maleness in particular, rather than simply informing us that the figure looked like a man; in other words it could be referring to the male sex organ, a major player in other stories we've seen. Stumbling upon a stand of mature, upturned and golden fly agaric "lampstands" is a beautiful and compelling sight, and it is not at all unusual to see among them a younger mushroom in its phallic stage, a "male" standing among the feminine bowls of the "lampstands" (see plate 3). Also it should be pointed out that it was a "figure *like* a son of man," which seems to say that it was *not* a son of man, a person, but somehow like one.

Here is what the figure looked like: "he" was ". . . dressed in a long robe tied at the waist with a golden girdle. His head and his hair were as white as white wool or as snow, his eyes like a burning flame [plate 31] . . ." After this we are told that his "voice" was like the ocean, a psychedelic sound explained earlier. He also holds "stars," similar to the fly agaric's having on its cap the sometimes starlike veil fragments. His face "was like the sun shining with all its force." When John saw this figure he "fell in a dead faint," one of the more common reactions to ingesting a large dose of fly agaric. The figure reassures John that he is not going to die by saying, "I am the one who has life in himself. I was dead and now I live for ever and ever, and I hold the keys of death and the underworld." The fly agaric can seem to kill people and carry them to the underworld; but the "one who was dead" has life within itself, not death; it resurrects those it kills, it lifts them out of purgatory and takes them to heaven.

The next section of the text consists of letters written to the seven churches, most of which receive a tongue-lashing; but woven into the letters are a number of significant mushroom correspondences:

> those who prove victorious I will feed from the tree of life set in God's paradise.
>
> I will give you the crown of life for your prize .
>
> . . . for those who prove victorious there is nothing to be afraid of in the second death [that is, physical death, having already "died" and come back to life with the mushroom].
>
> I will give the hidden manna [the dried mushroom] and a white stone [the unopened mushroom]—a stone with a new name written on it, known only to the man who receives it [a correspondence to the veil fragments which, as they separate, often form shapes that resemble letters—plate 32].

> . . . buy from me the gold that has been tested in the fire [the dried mushroom] to make you really rich . . . and eye ointment to put on your eyes so that you are able to see.
>
> If one . . . opens the door, I will come in to share his meal . . . I will allow [him] to share my throne.

The rest of the book is comprised of John's visions. These were primarily intended, at least on the surface, to scare everyone into submission to the faith, the idea being that since these things were all going to come to pass in a very short time there was no time to waste or waver: the reader must immediately repent and convert or else face the many unending tortures so colorfully described in the book. The section begins with more mushroom parallels:

> I saw a throne standing in heaven, and the one who was sitting on the throne . . . looked like a diamond and a ruby [veil "diamonds" on the ruby-red cap]. There was a rainbow encircling the throne, and this looked like an emerald [the new grasses that often grow with the mushroom]. Round the throne . . . were twenty-four thrones, and on them twenty-four elders . . . dressed in white robes with golden crowns on their heads [mature mushrooms, the same as the golden lampstands]. Flashes of lightning were coming from the throne, and the sound of peals of thunder [the requisite rainstorms for mushroom growth], and in front of the throne there were seven flaming lamps burning [the lampstands again], the seven angels of the presence [the presence of God experienced by the consumer: the "angels" contain it].

Next John describes four "animals" that surround the throne, all of them covered with "eyes." These creatures are nearly identical to the fiery beings described by Ezekiel, whose "wheels" had eyes all around.

Afterwards he saw a standing lamb "that seemed to have been sacrificed"; this presents the same image of white wool and red blood we saw earlier in plate 29. A sacrificed lamb could not be "standing" as the text says, but a mushroom would be. The young fly agaric may resemble a woolly little lamb, but once the veil separates the lamb's "blood" becomes visible, as though the lamb had been sacrificed, which it will be when it is harvested and consumed. The lamb had seven "horns" and seven "eyes," both of which correspond to the veil fragments, as in plate 26. The lamb received a scroll from the one on the throne and began to open its seals, which produced many terrible catastrophes for the inhabitants of earth.

After six seals were opened many people dressed in white robes appeared in front of the lamb. John was told that these people had washed their robes white again in the blood of the lamb, which makes no sense whatsoever except as still another red and white mushroom reference; now they would never hunger or thirst again because the "lamb" would lead them to "springs of living water."

After the seventh seal was broken an angel filled a censer with fire from the altar and threw it onto the earth, which caused peals of thunder and flashes of lightning; in other words, burning coals fell from heaven in a thunderstorm, or phrased differently, fly agaric mushrooms appeared after rainstorms.[55]

Following another series of imminent disaster predictions comes a rather startling passage, knowing what we do about eating the fly agaric. John saw a "powerful angel" descending from heaven surrounded with mushroom symbols: it was wrapped in a cloud; a rainbow (signifying ended rainstorms) was over its head; its face was like the sun; its legs were pillars of fire. In its hand it held a small scroll that was unrolled. The angel shouted like a lion and then seven thunderclaps were heard. John started to write but was told to keep the "words" of the thunderclaps a secret and not write them down, another clear allusion to the fact that the cult had unwritten secrets; here the secret is the identity of the "words" of the rainstorm.

As we saw earlier, the "words" of a thunderstorm, made flesh, are mushrooms. The author makes a play on these secret "thunder words" by connecting them to the scroll, which also contains the "word" of God; they represent the same thing. A voice told John to take the scroll from the angel; when he approached, the angel said, "Take it and eat it; it will turn your stomach sour, but in your mouth it will taste as sweet as honey." So John took the scroll and ate it, and it was just as the angel said: it tasted as sweet as honey, but after he ate it his stomach turned sour.

This "scroll-eating" is the same as in Ezekiel, a metaphor for the dried cap of a fly agaric mushroom. Dried caps are as pliable as leather and have a sweet, honey-like smell, unlike the fresh mushroom, yet eating them often causes an upset stomach, especially if they are chewed. The veil remnants on the cap often look like obscure writing of some kind, while the cap itself contains, and can reveal, the "Word of God," a word that can be seen as well as heard through the secret door of the mind. The medium, the mushroom, becomes the living Word after being in the belly of the human beast. Not surprisingly, after eating the scroll John was able to prophesy again.

John makes a few more predictions of the terrors to come and then describes a new vision: "Then the sanctuary of God in heaven opened, and the ark of the covenant could be seen inside it. Then came flashes of lightning, peals of thunder and an earthquake, and violent hail." After hearing once more of the ark and yet another thunderstorm, one might expect a description of the fly agaric to follow. Here is what John writes next:

> Now a great sign appeared in heaven: a woman, adorned with the sun, standing on the moon, and with twelve stars on her head for a crown. She was pregnant, and in labour . . . The woman brought a male child into the world . . .

The young mushroom with its swollen base looks as if it were pregnant. The base upon which it stands looks like the moon, while the cap is like the sun crowned with stars. The mushroom will soon "give birth" to a "male," that is, it will soon resemble a phallus (see plate 1).

Toward the end John discloses an important vision. First he says he saw heaven open, and then a white horse appeared with a rider whose name was Faithful and True; his eyes were fires; his head was adorned with many small crowns. "The name written on him was known only to himself, his cloak was soaked in blood. He is known by the name, 'The Word of God.'" So far the images are familiar. The "white horse" carries the god in the same way the white bull carries Shiva. The "eyes" are fiery red and the head is covered with small "crowns." Curiously, the rider's name is "written" upon his body, and it is unique to him, just as the "writing" on every fly agaric cap is unique to that specimen. The "cloak soaked in blood" sounds like a sure reference to the scarlet cap. Regardless of the rider's real name, he is known as The Word of God.

To make sure this point has been taken the author gives us one more clue: "On his cloak and on his thigh there was a name written: The king of kings and the lord of lords." We know why there is "writing" on the blood-red "cloak," but why on the thigh? Because cloak and thigh both represent the cap. "Thigh" is a well-known euphemism for "penis" in a number of cultures, and I think it applies here; if it does, then the writing on the rider's "penis" alludes to the same writing that was on the bloody cloak and on the scroll: the veil fragments on the fly agaric's cap.

Another long listing of plagues and torments follows, until finally the one on the throne speaks again:

> What I am saying is sure and will come true. It is already done . . . I will give water from
> the well of life free to anybody who is thirsty; it is the rightful inheritance of the one
> who proves victorious; and I will be his God and he a son to me.

Shortly after this the revealing angel makes the same kind of exclusionary statement made earlier by Jesus: "let the sinner go on sinning, and the unclean continue to be unclean." These will remain outside heaven to be thrown in the lake of burning fire. The elect, however, "will have the right to feed on the tree of life."

The epilogue contains a few more interesting statements. Jesus is speaking now, once again giving out his contradictory invitation to the whole world, most of which earlier has already been consigned to unending torture: "Then let all who are thirsty come: all who want it may have the water of life, and have it free." He then issues a stern warning not to add anything to what has been written, or else that person will face all the plagues enumerated in the book. Similarly, anyone deleting anything from the book will not get a share of the fruit of the tree of life. These two statements lead to the conclusion that the plagues were never meant as predictions except in the sense just mentioned: they were intended to frighten people so they wouldn't alter the text willy-nilly and inadvertently change or delete the important mushroom references salted throughout.

Jesus leaves the reader with one last prediction: "The one who guarantees these revelations repeats his promise: I shall indeed be with you soon." Jesus may not show up, but the fly agaric will.

10

The Knowers of God

Then I opened my mouth, and lo! there was reached unto me a full cup, which was
full as it were with water, but the color of it was like fire. And I took it and
drank; and when I had drunk, my heart poured forth understanding,
wisdom grew in my breast, and my spirit retained its memory.

IV Esdras 14:39–40

ALTHOUGH IT USED TO BE REGARDED AS little more than a bothersome Christian heresy, the recent discovery of ancient Gnostic writings unseen for over fifteen hundred years has shown Gnosticism to be a religion with its own distinctive system of beliefs. The term "Gnostic" derives from the Greek *gnosis,* which means "knowledge," referring to the knowledge of God; *gnosis* is cognate with and has the same meaning as the Sanskrit *Gnana.* One who has attained such knowledge is a Gnostic, a "knower." That Gnosticism also shares many characteristics with Christianity is due largely to the syncretism out of which nearly all the religions of the Middle East arose; there were so many religious traditions intermixing that it becomes impossible to isolate a pure strain.

Christian philosophy draws heavily on Gnostic philosophy. Gnosticism, like Christianity, has roots in the Egyptian and Greek mystery traditions, especially Hermeticism. While Hermeticism and its quest for gnosis is essentially a Hellenistic philosophy, it is thought to derive directly from the Egyptian mystery schools and is considered to be the "parent" philosophy of both Gnosticism and alchemy, with which it shares many of its concepts and principles. A small body of writings attributed to the Thrice-Great Hermes, the Greek form of the Egyptian god Thoth, forms the basis of what is known today about Hermeticism; how Hermetic gnosis was viewed historically is reflected and traced in the works of the Gnostics and alchemists.

While it is not always easy to distinguish between these various religious forms, Gnosticism differs from Christianity in several ways, such as its depreciation of the cosmos and rejection of the Christian doctrine of atonement. It posits an eternal duality comprised of the forces of light in conflict with the forces of dark matter, from which the individual strives to free its light-soul after which the soul will merge with the Father of Light in its true home, the pleroma. Judaism and Christianity both came into contact with Gnosticism and from this mingling Gnostic branches developed within, or alongside, both religions; there were pagan Gnostic sects as well, primarily Hellenistic Gnostics steeped in the Hermetic tradition.

In the Gnostic view the universe as we know it is something of a mistake. Due to the error and blindness of the Demiurge and his evil creation, the otherwise pure light-body of humankind became enmeshed in matter, or the physical world. This light-body is a part of the vast light-body of God, the pleroma, the fullness of the divine being, the Father of Light; light is trapped in matter by the physical body and its appetites, and therein lies the whole problem of human existence. It is only through revelation and the immediate experience of the transcendent light that the individual soul awakens to its true identity. When all the things of this world, including every thought and desire, are dissolved in the superabundant and blissful light of the divine, what is left to desire or despise? In that blissful state the question does not arise, because all clinging has ceased; there is nothing more to grasp, and no one to do the grasping. To enter into this light before physical death was the stated goal of Gnostic philosophy; how this was to be accomplished was, and remains, Gnosticism's biggest secret.

Christians seized upon the concept of the divine spark within every individual and appropriated it to their putative savior, Jesus, as so often happens in messianic movements. The spark of divine individuality, the *atman* of the Hindus, the imperishable divine in every human being and an individual's only true possession, became in Christianity the property of either Jesus or Satan. In the Christian view there was no other choice: a person either submitted to the authority of Jesus or automatically fell under the sway of Satan. No longer would individual effort count for anything in the scheme of salvation from a cruel and incomprehensible world; humanity had no recourse but to accept that Jesus was the only savior for all times and places or face unending torment in the fires of hell.

The Gnostics, on the other hand, even the Christian Gnostics, favored the old-time religion in which those with enough desire could upgrade their status in creation through individual effort because all individuals carried within themselves the *spinther,* or spark, of the divine. The Gnostics claimed to have the means to experience the knowledge of God while yet in the human body, a knowledge that saved them from the thraldom of dark matter. Christianity said that such union could only be achieved through Jesus, and then only after death and in a subordinate fashion, the individual remaining always unworthy and forever praising the divine rather than fully participating in the Godhead, or, God forbid, uniting with it as the Gnostics claimed to do.

Our knowledge of Gnosticism has been until recently very incomplete, so much so that it was usually considered as peripheral to the "real" religions of the time, but the discovery of buried Gnostic texts at Nag Hammadi in upper Egypt has changed all that. Even though many of the texts are badly damaged there is enough readable material to change the way we think of Gnosticism and its role in the ancient world. It is now accepted that Gnosticism threatened for a time to engulf Judaism and Christianity, until it was declared a heresy and persecuted by both religions.

The still-in-translation Dead Sea scrolls, for example, are revealing that the ascetic Essene sect broke away from orthodox Judaism and taught a form of apocalyptic Jewish Gnosticism that may have been more influential and threatening to Judaism than previously thought. Certainly many of the tenets of the sect seem to have been "borrowed" by Jesus, and it is possible that Jesus himself was an Essene. An Essene leader, a messiah-like figure reverently referred to in the scrolls as the Teacher of Righteousness, was crucified in 88 B.C.E. for leading an ill-conceived revolt; it was the first time the Jews had seen this gruesome foreign method of execution.

Gnosticism would probably be alive and flourishing today had it organized under some sort of central authority as the Christian Church did, but there were so many individual and different sects that it resembled modern Christendom in its disarray and virtually died out after the third century B.C.E. The exception to this is Manichaean Gnosticism, which due to its organization along the lines of the Christian Church became a growing and major religion in western Asia and eastern Europe from its inception in the third century until its violent suppression by Rome in the sixth. It "broke out" again in southern France from the eleventh to the thirteenth centuries until the antithetically named Pope Innocent III decided to launch a crusade against this neo-Manichaean "scourge" (the Bogomils, Cathari, and other sects). Manachaeism also existed in China from the eighth to the fourteenth centuries but was unaffected by the Christian church.

An example of the unbridgeable gulf between Gnosticism and the beliefs of Judaism and Christianity is found in the way these religions regarded the creator-god. For Jews and Christians this god was the one and only God, God of infinite goodness and compassion; lacking those qualities, he was a powerful, capricious, and punishing god who was more feared than loved by most, judging from the accounts of ancient Hebrew authors. To the Gnostics this same creator-god was the ignorant and self-deluded Demiurge, who through arrogance and blindness created a material world with the inherent ability to ensnare and imprison in bodies the imperishable light of the Father of Light. For them Adam and Eve represented not the first sinners, whose disobedience cursed all humanity forever, but rather heroic pioneers who ignored the jealous and duplicitous command of the evil Demiurge in order to gain knowledge for themselves.

Among the Naasenes (from the Hebrew *naas,* "serpent") and some other Gnostic sects it was believed that the serpent "pusher" of the Garden was actually Jesus, briefly incarnated for the purpose of getting our first parents to disobey the Dark One, and prefiguring the role he would later play in his own cult as the revealer of mysteries. It was, after all, Jesus' own disobedience to Jewish law that set him apart among the other claimants to the title of Messiah; like the disobedience of Eve and Adam, it was also what got him into so much trouble.

What was it about Gnosticism that made it such a threat to Judaism and Christianity? Why did the Gnostics claim to be the only true Jews or, especially after Jesus' death, true Christians? What was the knowledge they claimed to have, and how did they get it? Is there any reason to suspect that they too may have been using the fly agaric?

It is known from their own writings as well as from writings about and against them that sacred meals, taken in private, were central to most Gnostic practice. This was called the *Agape,* the love feast. The identity of the food and drink taken at these holy meals is unknown and open to conjecture. Apart from such "feasting," rumors also abounded that the Gnostics were given to "drinking parties" that usually included nudity and sexual activities. What was consumed at these events, and why was the mere consumption of food and drink given spiritual, even mystical, importance? Once again it is the texts themselves that supply the best clues for answering these questions.

The Nag Hammadi Texts

These amazing writings have opened a door into a hidden world that was secret even when the books were buried some fifteen hundred years ago. They are filled with mysteries and myths that reveal to the modern world a sophisticated religion based on the personal experience of God. The writings were collected and hidden by a Coptic Christian Gnostic sect. The content of the material indicates that more was happening in these cults than sipping wine and eating consecrated toast. Many of the Gnostic writings are lacking neither clues to the secret practice nor enthusiasm for it, as we shall see. (Missing portions of damaged texts are indicated by [. . .].)

> This is the prayer that they spoke: "We give thanks to You! Every soul and heart is lifted up to You, undisturbed name, honored with the name 'God' and praised with the name 'Father,' for to everyone and everything comes the fatherly kindness and affection and love, and any teaching there may be that is sweet and plain, giving us mind, speech, and knowledge: mind, so that we may understand You, speech, so that we may expound You, knowledge, so that we may know You. We rejoice, having been illuminated by

Your knowledge. We rejoice because You have shown us Yourself. *We rejoice because while we were in the body, You have made us divine through Your knowledge.*

"The thanksgiving of the man who attains to You is one thing: that we know You. We have known You, intellectual light. Life of life, we have known You. Womb of every creature, we have known You. Womb pregnant with the nature of the Father, we have known You. Eternal permanence of the begetting Father, thus have we worshipped Your goodness. There is one petition that we ask: we would be preserved in knowledge. And there is one protection that we desire: that we not stumble in this kind of life."

When they had said these things in prayer, they embraced each other and they went to eat their holy food, which has no blood in it[56] [Italics mine].

This quotation from the Nag Hammadi texts is called the "Prayer of Thanksgiving," and is considered to be Hermetic in origin; its inclusion among the codices of the Nag Hammadi library shows how well Gnosticism and Hermeticism harmonized. More important, though, are the prayer's content and the enthusiasm it conveys. "Enthusiasm" literally means "god within," in the sense of being inspired or possessed by a divinity; such possession results in the kind of bubbling fervor we have come to associate with the word. The prayer is enthusiastic in the extreme, and its joyous and knowing tone amply demonstrates why the established religions feared the breakaway sects: their members were going directly to the source to experience the blissful light of God. ". . . while we were in the body, You have made us divine through Your knowledge . . . We have known You, intellectual light."

This kind of language did not sit well with orthodox Jews and Christians back then, and it still doesn't today. The difference is that in ancient times a person could be killed for saying such things; on second thought, maybe there is no difference.

After the effusive and specific prayer is finished, we are told that the participants embraced each other and went to eat their "holy food." We are also informed, rather curiously, that the food had no blood in it. This could mean any of several things. Some of the more ascetic sects were vegetarian, and the reference may simply be to this practice, though it seems doubtful that this restriction would be mentioned. Rumors of the time abounded with accusations that the Gnostics regularly sacrificed and ate babies, so perhaps the "no blood" reference is a reaction to such charges. It may be that the "holy food" was personified within the cult in the same way it is today in the cult of Jesus, where participants eat and drink their savior verbally and mentally, but physically eat something less provocative; actual flesh-eating and blood-drinking would be denied among Christians, as it was among the reputed "baby-eaters" of Gnosticism. Of course Jewish law demands that animals slain for food be drained of blood before eating, so this law could be the intended reference, although this too seems unlikely because it is unnecessary; the author probably wasn't Jewish, nor was the cult concerned with Jewish law.

If the holy food was the fly agaric mushroom then all the references make sense. This prayer is liturgical; it was recited, as the text indicates, before the holy food was eaten and was intended to create an anticipation, based on past experience, for what was to come: the holy meal, the consumption of which would bring about the very knowledge so eloquently praised in the prayer. To someone who felt trapped in heavy matter the mushroom could be a literal savior by causing that person to ascend to the light-realms, and it contained and released what looked like blood. A personified discussion of these matters overheard or read about by a noninitiate might, and did, seem like a description of necrophiliac cannibalism, so it may have been deemed important to include the "no blood" disclaimer in the prayer.

In the Nag Hammadi codices the Prayer of Thanksgiving is bound directly behind another text that is probably Hermetic in origin and may have been used ritually in conjunction with it. Where the prayer gives ecstatic thanks for gifts received from God, the Discourse on the Eighth and Ninth, which precedes the prayer, is clearly an initiatory text in the form of a dialogue between hierophant ("my father") and initiate ("my son"). It begins with the initiate asking to be brought mentally to the "eighth" and "ninth," referring to the heavenly spheres outside the seven material spheres, all of which, it was believed, encircled the earth concentrically. The hierophant answers that it is not an automatic process; each step must be firmly held in mind. He then makes a very telling statement:

> After I received the spirit through the power, I set forth the action for you. Indeed the
> understanding dwells in you; in me it is as though the power were pregnant. For when
> I conceived from the fountain that flowed to me, I gave birth . . . I gave birth to it as
> children are born.

This "pregnancy" caused by the power of God sounds very much like the pregnancy of the gods that occurred when Agni and all the other gods consumed Shiva's semen. The hierophant says he became "pregnant" by drinking, we assume, from the "fountain" that flowed to him, after which he "gave birth" to the power "as children are born."

The hierophant's "fountain" may refer to the prepared "juice" of the mushroom or to his having received the pregnancy-causing "fountain of god's seed" from another. The "birth of the power" has a double meaning. It can refer to the "birth" of higher consciousness in the mind, and also to the "impregnated" urine that has been created by drinking from the fountain, which afterwards exits the body through the genitals as children do when they are born. This "child of the power of God" has all the power of the "father" after it is born. We should recall that the drinking of Shiva's seed, aside from causing numerous pregnancies, also caused a "child" to be born.

The rest of the short text is filled with ecstatic prayer and advice to the initiate on how to keep ascending. Another parallel to the light-bringing fly agaric comes in the initiate's prayer: "I call upon you, who rules over the kingdom of power, whose word comes as a birth of light." Toward the end of the prayer he says, "For from you, the unbegotten one, the begotten one came into being. The birth of the self-begotten one is through you, the birth of all begotten things that exist." "Unbegotten" is God, "begotten" is humanity and all creatures, and "self-begotten" fits the mushroom perfectly.

The instructor and then the student both eventually have the experience of light: "Rejoice over this! For already from them the power, which is light, is coming to us. For I see! I see indescribable depths! How shall I tell you, my son?" The son rejoices to see his father smiling and recites another prayer, ending with, "And by a spirit he gives rain upon everyone. What do you say to me, my father, Hermes?" He answers, "Concerning these things I do not say anything, my son. For it is right before God that we keep silent about what is hidden." The text concludes with "Hermes" demanding that whoever reads the book must swear to guard what has been written; those who do will be reconciled with God, but those who don't will face God's wrath.

The Apocryphon of James

The Apocryphon (secret book) of James also contains some intriguing passages:

> [Jesus] said, "Verily I say unto you, no one will ever enter the kingdom of heaven at my bidding, but only because you yourselves are full. Leave James and Peter to me that I may fill them." . . . And having called these two, he drew them aside.

Once again reaching heaven seems to have something, or everything, to do with a secret initiation and eating or drinking.

This next passage appears to be an enigmatic reference to the cap or "head" of the fly agaric. After James worriedly tells Jesus that people are beginning to ask the disciples to prophesy, Jesus says, "Do you not know that the head of prophecy was cut off with John?" James replies, "Lord, can it be possible to remove the head of prophecy?" At this Jesus poses a riddle:

> When you come to know what "head" means, and that prophecy issues from the head, then understand the meaning of "Its head was removed." At first I spoke to you in parables and you did not understand; now I speak to you openly, and you still do not perceive . . . be eager of your own accord and, if possible, arrive even before me.

As Jesus says, he is speaking openly.

Jesus next compares the kingdom of heaven to a palm tree whose fruit has dropped to the ground beneath it. A fly agaric mushroom has the same dome-on-a-pillar configuration as a palm tree, and it appears beneath a host tree (though not a palm) as though it were fruit fallen to the ground. Jesus says,

So it is also with the fruit which had grown from this single root; when it had been picked, fruit was borne by many. It was certainly good, and if it were possible for you to produce the new plants now, you would find it [heaven].

A little later "Jesus" says something that may indicate that the Gnostics were also using ergot:

For this cause I tell you this, that you may know yourselves. For the kingdom of heaven is like an ear of grain after it sprouted in a field. And when it had ripened, it scattered its fruit and again filled the field with ears for another year. You also, hasten to reap an ear of life for yourselves that you may be filled with the kingdom!

It may only be a simple metaphor, but an ergot-infected ear of grain could literally do this.

The Gospel of Truth

The Gospel of Truth contains mushroom correspondences similar to those we've seen earlier, including this allusion to a "hunt," a tree, and fruit:

Through this, the gospel of the one who is searched for, which was revealed to those who are perfect through the mercies of the Father, the hidden mystery, Jesus, the Christ, enlightened those who were in darkness through oblivion . . . *He was nailed to a tree and he became a fruit of the knowledge of the Father. It did not, however, cause destruction because it was eaten, but to those who ate it it gave cause to become glad in the discovery, and he discovered them in himself, and they discovered him in themselves.* [Italics mine.]

It seems quite unnecessary for the author to point out that eating fruit did not bring destruction to the eaters, unless the fruit in question was under a "poison" taboo as is the fly agaric. Even today most people who have heard of the mushroom regard it as a deadly poison.

We saw earlier how the Aryans called the fly agaric the Tongue of the Way. Consider this passage from The Gospel of Truth:

For, as for everyone who loves the truth—because truth is the mouth of the Father; his tongue is the holy spirit—he who is joined to the truth is joined to the Father's mouth by his tongue, whenever he is to receive the holy spirit, since this is the manifestation of the Father and his revelation.

A few paragraphs later the tongue metaphor is expanded to include tasting:

He gave them the means of knowing the knowledge of the Father and the revelation of his Son. For, when they had seen him and had heard him, he granted them to taste him and to smell him and to touch the beloved Son.

The author tells his readers that Jesus came to anoint the lost ones with the ointment, and then says, "[The Father] is good. He knows his plantings, because it is he who planted them in his paradise. Now his paradise is his place of rest." Toward the end of the text comes this statement regarding Jesus, "who came forth from the depth . . . and to the region where he received his establishment he will hasten to return again and to take from that place—the place where he stood—receiving a taste from that place and receiving nourishment, receiving growth." This could easily be a reference to the mushrooms' yearly return to the place where, after coming forth from the depths, they receive nourishment and growth; it is to this same region that the seeker must also return, both physically and spiritually.

One final passage in this text is worth noting. It seems to have a connection with the "head of prophecy":

> For the place to which they send their thought, that place, their root, is what takes them up in all the heights to the Father. They possess his head, which is rest for them, and they are supported, approaching him, as though to say they have participated in his face by means of kisses.

Joined, no doubt, to the Father's mouth by his "tongue."

The Gospel of Thomas

The Gospel of Thomas may be the oldest text in the Nag Hammadi collection, written perhaps as early as the middle of the first century. It is a mystery document containing 114 barebones sayings that the author claims are the "secret sayings" of Jesus. These sayings, though "secret" or concealed, were meant to be deciphered. The series begins with Jesus' saying, "Whoever finds the interpretation of these sayings will not experience death." Several of the sayings have relevance to our subject.

After asking his disciples to tell him whom he is like, one disciple answers, calling Jesus "Master." Jesus replies, "I am not your master. Because you have drunk, you have become intoxicated from the bubbling spring which I have measured out." The fly agaric correspondence here is obvious, but less so in the following. After saying this Jesus took Thomas aside and told him three things. When the other disciples asked what was said, Thomas refused to answer, saying, "If I tell you one of the things which he told me, you will pick up stones and throw them at me; a fire will come out of the stones and burn you up." This suggests several things, one of which is that Jesus had a secret teaching or initiation, as we have seen previously; Jeasus says so openly in saying number sixty-two: "It is to those who are worthy of my mysteries that I tell my mysteries." The stoning reference also suggests that there is something shocking or scandalous about the secret, or at least one specific part of it. The prior mention of the bubbling spring "measured out" by Jesus may not be incidental in this regard. The final clue is the image of fire emerging from a stone, which is a metaphorical way of describing the mushroom's fiery cap emerging from the "stone" or "egg" stage.

A few sayings later rocks are again mentioned in an initiatory context: "If you become my disciples and listen to my words, these stones will minister to you." The image of "ministering stones" is as odd as stones that sprout fire, but once again corresponds to the fly agaric. Jesus continues, "For there are five trees for you in Paradise which remain undisturbed summer and winter and whose leaves do not fall. Whoever becomes acquainted with them will not experience death." This may have an esoteric meaning, such as referring to subtle energy centers similar to the Hindu chakras, or it could be meant literally. Conifers of various kinds make up the majority of the trees that grow at higher elevations in the Middle East, and conifers are a favored host of *Amanita* species. Their leaves do not fall: they are evergreens. In any given area in which the mushrooms grow a user must become acquainted with the host species. Once this host is determined and the locations of the groves are known, the plant of immortality can be found.

I speculated earlier that the older Jewish mushroom cult was probably kept secret among a very few people. The following saying appears to verify this hypothesis:

> Jesus said: "The Pharisees and the scribes have taken the keys of knowledge and hidden
> them. They themselves have not entered, nor have they allowed to enter those who
> wish to. You, however, be as wise as serpents and as innocent as doves."

Is it another convenient coincidence, after mentioning the hidden keys of knowledge, that serpents and doves are mentioned? Both are fly agaric metaphors.

Later on Jesus makes a similar reference, only this time it involves eating: "Woe to the Pharisees, for they are like a dog sleeping in the manger of oxen, for neither does he eat nor does he let the oxen eat." The author is saying quite clearly in these two examples that known methods of attaining spiritual knowledge were being withheld by the religious establishment.

This is very similar to a verse of the Rig Veda apparently composed after the use of the sacred mushroom had ended, though the priests still knew about it. It says, in effect, that those who perform the Soma sacrifice think they are drinking Soma, but that the Soma known to the Brahmins no one drinks. Critics of Wasson's Soma theory have taken this to mean that perhaps there never was an actual Soma plant; that it existed only as an ideal in the minds of the priests, and every plant used in the sacrifice through the centuries was nothing more than a surrogate for the "imagined" Soma. This is a good example of the cart preceding the horse. A person does not write ecstatic poetry about the realms of light and the supernal bliss experienced from taking a drug unless that person has taken the drug, just as someone lacking these experiences will not fully comprehend what is written about them.

One of the strangest images presented in these sayings comes near the end: "He who will drink from my mouth will become like me. I myself shall become he, and the things that are hidden will be revealed to him." It may be only a poetic way of describing a follower who listens to Jesus' words, but I think it means more than this. If Jesus is a personified drug of some kind in this reference, or is speaking about a drug, then the mystical union described after drinking from his mouth makes more sense. But what does "drink from my mouth" mean? Would Jesus or the hierophant take a drink of the sacred potion, hold it in his mouth, and transfer it to a cup or to the mouth of an initiate with a kiss, thereby imparting to the liquid some imputed personal virtue? We do know that one outward sign of being a Christian (even among the ostracized Gnostic Christians) was the public practice of greeting other members of the cult with a kiss on the lips, a practice that led to further allegations and accusations: not only were the Gnostics eaters of babies, they were *homosexual* eaters of babies. There is another possibility. It is well known (and sometimes joked about) that the flattened opening of the urethra on the head of a penis resembles and is figuratively called a "mouth," and it may be that this is the mouth being referred to here.

A passage from a legend of the Native American Anishinaubeg tribe in which a mushroom-shaman is singing to a group of people shows that this interpretation might not be as farfetched as it seems on the surface:

> Because of my supernatural experience in the Land of Miskwedo [the fly agaric], I have
> a cure to alleviate your ills, to take away all your unhappiness. If only you will come to
> my penis and take the quickening waters flowing from it you too can be forever happy.

The legend goes on to state that the people catch his urine in birchbark containers and drink it, considering it to be a great boon given by the fly agaric spirits. They call it *Kesuabo,* the liquid Power of the Sun. One must admit that the two passages are similar in content and tone, although mushroom use in the Gnostic passage is decidedly circumspect. In the Native American myth the mushroom stands revealed—or should I say "circumcised"?

The Gospel of Philip

The Gospel of Philip follows Thomas in Codex II and is filled with the kind of fly agaric correspondences with which the reader is now more or less familiar. I will quote a number of the more significant parallels, but first I want to call attention to an explanatory statement early in the treatise which seems to be saying that there are secrets hidden in the words of the text:

> Names given to the worldly are very deceptive, for they divert our thoughts from what
> is correct to what is incorrect. Thus one who hears the word "God" does not perceive
> what is correct, but perceives what is incorrect. So also with "the father" and "the son"

and "the holy spirit" and "life" and "light" and "resurrection" and "the church" and all the rest—people do not perceive what is correct but they perceive what is incorrect, unless they have come to know what is correct. The names which are heard are in the world [. . .] deceive.

We will read more of such statements later in the writings of the alchemists.

It is through water and fire that the whole place is purified—the visible by visible, the hidden by the hidden. There are some things hidden through those visible. There is water in water, there is fire in chrism.

This enigmatic statement seems to allude to potentized urine—water in water—as well as to fly agaric-infused oil, the "fire in chrism."

Do not despise the lamb, for without it it is not possible to see the king.

As we have seen, the lamb can be a metaphor for the mushroom, which allows one to see the "king," or God. Note also that the author refers to the lamb as "it" rather than "he."

Echmoth is Wisdom simply, but Echamoth is the wisdom of death which is the one which knows death, which is called "the little Wisdom."

This text parallels the two poles of fly agaric experience and their fruits: the light of God, which produces wisdom, and the darkness of death, which produces its own less desirable form of wisdom.

It is from water and fire and light that the son of the bridal chamber came into being. The fire is the chrism, the light is the fire. I am not referring to that fire which has no form, but to the other fire whose form is white, which is bright and beautiful, and which gives beauty.

The "fiery chrism" produces the beautiful white light of higher consciousness.

The following statement is very mysterious:

Joseph the carpenter planted a garden because he needed wood for his trade. It was he who made the cross from the trees he planted. His own offspring hung on that which was planted. His offspring was Jesus and the planting was the cross.

Joseph, not truly a father, acts as one here. In my own experience I have found that it is possible to "plant" the fly agaric by sowing spores beneath a known host tree species, and this could be what the whole passage is about, remembering that the host tree indirectly produces the "cross" of the mushroom. The author continues, "But the tree of life is in the middle of the garden," implying Joseph's cross-growing garden, not the Garden of Eden. Now he tells the reader what to do with the fruit: "However, it is from the olive tree that we get the chrism, and from the chrism, resurrection."

> In the place where I will eat all things is the tree of knowledge. That one killed Adam,
> but here the tree of knowledge made men alive. The law was the tree. It has power to
> give the knowledge of good and evil.

The Gnostics knew that eating the fruit of knowledge would not kill them, but rather
bring them into the light of union. They knew also that they should strive for such union
in the here-and-now or risk missing it entirely in the hereafter:

> If anyone becomes a son of the bridal chamber, he will receive the light. If anyone does
> not receive it while he is here, he will not be able to receive it in the other place . . . [To
> the one who receives light] The world has become the eternal realm, for the eternal
> realm is fullness for him. This is the way it is: It is revealed to him alone, not hidden in
> the darkness and the night, but hidden in a perfect day and a holy light.

On the Origin of the World

The treatise On the Origin of the World, a non-Christian Gnostic text, contains many similar themes:

> When [Pronoia] was unable to satisfy her love, she poured out her light upon the earth.
> Since that day, that emissary [personified light from the eighth heaven] has been called
> "Adam of light," whose rendering is "the luminous man of blood," and the earth
> spread over him . . .

This bloody Adam of light also might be the bloody mushroom of light which also begins
its life with the earth spread over it, as shown in plate 2.

> And the tree of eternal life is as it appeared by God's will, to the north of paradise, so
> that it might make eternal the souls of the pure . . . Now the color of the tree of life is
> like the sun . . . And next to it is the tree of gnosis, having the strength of God. Its glory
> is like the moon when fully radiant [full moon] . . . And this tree is to the north of Par-
> adise, so that it might arouse the souls from the torpor of the demons, in order that they
> might approach the tree of life and eat of its fruit and so condemn the authorities and
> their angels.

This passage previews an idea developed at length by the alchemists in their concept of the
philosophical tree with sun and moon fruits.

> And the first soul loved Eros, who was with her, and poured her blood upon him and
> upon the earth. And out of that blood the first rose sprouted up, out of the earth, out of
> the thorn bush, to be a source of joy for the light that was to appear in the bush.

The fly agaric is a "thorn bush" like the rose because of its white "thorns" and its color; it "sprouts up" out of the earth like a large drop of blood which then turns into a "flower" on a stalk. The light appears "in the bush" when it is consumed.

> When Eve saw her male counterpart prostrate she had pity upon him, and she said, "Adam! Become alive! Arise upon the earth!" Immediately her word became accomplished fact.

Adam (Red Earth), previously covered with earth, arises immediately; the red mushroom, covered with earth, arises quickly after the living "word" of the thunderstorm speaks it into existence.

After a lacuna the text is rejoined in the midst of a digression on the mythical phoenix, a bird known for feeding its young with blood, consuming itself in flames, and regenerating itself endlessly from its own ashes or from a worm that emerges from them:

> [. . .] so that in their world it might pass a thousand years in paradise—a soul-endowed living creature called "phoenix." It kills itself and brings itself to life . . . [About the earthly phoenix] it is written in the *Sacred Book* that it is consumed . . . the phoenix appears as a witness concerning the angels . . . And the worm that has been born out of the phoenix is a human being as well. It is written (Ps. 91:13 LXX) concerning it, "the just man will blossom like a phoenix." And the phoenix first appears in a living state, and dies, and rises again.

The fly agaric likewise "kills" itself and brings itself to life. It is consumed by nature in a short time if it is not harvested, and it is also consumed by the harvester. The phoenix (from the Greek *phoinios*, "blood-red") with its burning wings is like an angel and both correspond to the mushroom. The "worm of the phoenix" corresponds to the fly larvae that often infest the mushroom. "The just man will blossom like a phoenix" can be restated, since we know that birds don't "blossom," as The phallus-mushroom will blossom and resemble a self-regenerating bird with fiery wings. It appears as a living thing that grows, dies, and reproduces itself in the same areas year after year from the "ashes" of its spores, just as the phoenix is said to do (see plates 10 and 12). The concept of the phoenix was also developed by the alchemists, who identified it with their stone and with Jesus.

The Apocalypse of Adam

The non-Christian Apocalypse of Adam contains a fascinating list of fly agaric parallels:

> He was nourished in the heavens. He received the glory of that one and the power. He came to the bosom of his mother. And thus he came to the water.
>
> And a bird came, took the child who was born and brought him onto a high mountain.

And he was nourished by the bird of heaven. An angel came forth there. He said to him, "Arise! God has given glory to you." He received glory and strength. And thus he came to the water.

[A heavenly being went down] to the aeon which is below, in order to gather flowers. *She became pregnant from the desire of the flowers.* She gave birth to him in that place. The angels of the flower garden nourished him. He received glory there and power. And thus he came to the water.

. . . he is a drop. It came from heaven to earth. Dragons brought him down to caves. He became a child . . . And thus he came to the water.

A cloud came upon the earth and enveloped a rock. He came from it. The angels who were above the cloud nourished him . . . And thus he came to the water.

[One of the nine Muses] came to a high mountain and spent some time seated there, so that she desired herself alone in order to become androgynous. *She fulfilled her desire and became pregnant from her desire.* He was born. The angels . . . nourished him. And thus he came to the water.

. . . his god loved a cloud of desire. He begot him in his hand and cast upon the cloud above him some of the drop, and he was born. He received glory and power there. And thus he came to the water [Italics mine].

The many correspondences in these passages to the stories of Shiva, Agni, and Soma should be easy to discern. The text ends with a statement of the work's secret nature: "This is the hidden knowledge of Adam . . . which is the holy baptism of those who know the eternal knowledge . . . who came from the holy seed: . . . the Living Water."

A few more significant citations from the Nag Hammadi texts are worth noting before looking at other Gnostic works.

From Authoritative Teaching:

Secretly her bridegroom fetched it. He presented it to her mouth to make her eat it like food, and he applied the word to her eyes as a medicine to make her see with her mind and perceive her kinsmen and learn about her root.

[Because the soul has been blinded by matter] she pursues the word and applies it to her eyes as a medicine, opening them.

[The soul] looks for those foods that will take her into life, and leaves behind those deceitful foods. And she learns about her light.

[The soul] learned about God . . . She ate of the banquet for which she had hungered. She partook of the immortal food. She found what she had sought after.

From The Concept of Our Great Power:

> Wake up and return, taste and eat the true food! Hand out the word and the water of life.

From Zostrianos:

> . . . therefore [. . .] waters are the perfect ones. It is the water of life that belongs to Vital-
> ity in which you now have been baptized in the Autogenes (Self-generating One). It is
> the water of Blessedness which belongs to Knowledge . . . It is the water of Existence,
> which belongs to divinity.

From The Interpretation of Knowledge:

> And we see that it is her water that the supreme authority granted to the one in whom
> there is a sign. This is that water of immortality which the great powers will grant to
> him while he is below in the likeness of her young son.

Finally, from Asclepius, we are treated to a metaphor designed for the person who is trying, but failing, to comprehend the mysteries that are covertly being discussed in the texts.
The author makes comparison to the act of sexual intercourse, performed in secret so that
the two people involved might not embarrass themselves in front of others who have not
experienced the same thing: "For if it happens in the presence of those who do not understand the reality, it is laughable and unbelievable." This is precisely the problem I faced in
writing this book.

In the anti-heresy writings of the fourth-century Church father Epiphanius is found a startling quotation from a Gnostic work entitled Interrogationes maiores Mariae. It is
remarkable for its content as well as for its verbatim inclusion in Epiphanius' work. Gnosticism with its strange and "sinful" practices held a place of inordinate importance in the
minds of some Church fathers, just as witchcraft would later.

In this work Jesus took a woman named Mary with him to a mountaintop. When they
arrived he produced a woman from his side and proceeded to have sexual intercourse with
her in front of the stunned Mary, who watched as Jesus pulled out of the woman and
caught his semen in his hand. Then Jesus ". . . partaking of his flowing semen, showed that
this was to be done, that we might have life."[57] Mary swooned and fell to the ground from
the shock of witnessing the event. When she revived Jesus chided her, saying, "Why do
you doubt me, you of little faith?"

We would suppose that Mary's doubt was regarding the spiritual motive behind Jesus'
somewhat bizarre and rather worldly actions with his recently manufactured sex partner.
Jesus' calling into question Mary's faith is probably meant to refer to John 3:12, where
Jesus tells Nicodemus that in order to enter the kingdom of God a person must be born

through "water" and the Spirit, an assertion Nicodemus doesn't understand. Jesus says, "If you do not believe me when I speak about things in this world, how are you going to believe me when I speak about heavenly things?" He ends his next sentence with a statement discussed earlier: ". . . and the son of man must be lifted up as Moses lifted up the serpent in the desert, so that everyone who believes in him may receive eternal life."

Although some Gnostic circles did practice ritual intercourse that included the consumption of semen, doing so today will not produce the heavenly results claimed by the Gnostics; at least no one has come forward to say so. One possibility, of course, is that the semen referred to represents fly agaric urine, here identified with the "seed" of the hierophant as it was in the Shiva myths. The seed-drinking in this story is done in front of a "Mary," who may be representative of one who is being initiated into the mysteries, since the act is performed before a witness and has the stated intention that if she wants to have "life," she must do the same thing; yet the act is so unbelievable and shocking to the witness that she faints dead away.

Ordinary semen becomes in the story "living semen," a doorway to life itself when consumed. Surely this must refer instead to "living urine," the consumption of which can actually do something to a person's consciousness. This fly agaric "living water" symbolically becomes the seed of the male god because it exits through the penis and has the capacity to generate God .

At this writing (1993) photocopies of the Dead Sea scrolls have recently been released to the public for the first time and are being examined as never before. The sect at Qumran practiced a form of Jewish Gnosticism but they were also political; they wanted to establish their kingdom on earth with their Teacher of Righteousness as king. The messianic politics of the group provided an irresistible target for the authorities, as did the cult of Jesus a century later. Their teachings on how to attain divine knowledge were kept a strict secret and it is only now that outsiders can get a glimpse of their life and beliefs. From the Thanksgiving Psalms, possibly written by the Teacher of Righteousness himself, comes a poem whose elements we have come to recognize:

> You placed me among cypresses and pine, among cedars like your glory. There concealed among the trees drinking the water are other springs of life near springs of mystery, which issue shoots of an eternal Plant, and before they flower they expose their roots to the waters of life and become the eternal fountain [see plate 25]. All beasts . . . feed on the leafy branches of the Plant, wanderers trample its trunk . . . But that tree planted in truth, destined to flower in branches of holiness, is sealed and secret, unesteemed and unknown. O God, you hedged its fruit with enormous angels and walls of fire so no stranger might come near the fountain, nor drink its water like the eternal tree, nor bear fruit from the rain of heaven. The stranger saw but did not believe in the fountain of life . . . But you, God, placed morning rain in my mouth . . . and living waters which will not fail . . . the rich Plant near the eternal fountain is a park of glory, is Eden.[58]

Some of the most beautiful sacred poetry ever composed is found in the Odes of Solomon, a Gnostic hymnbook from the second century.[59] The soaring imagery again sings of knowing God in the flesh and in the present. This combined with many unusual and striking metaphors arouses suspicion that the Odes were plant-inspired.

> The Lord is on my head like a crown . . . You live and blossom on my head. Your fruits are full and perfect and filled with salvation.

> Your seal is known. Creatures know it. Hosts possess it. Archangels are robed in it . . . Distill your dews upon us and open your rich fountains that pour forth milk and honey . . . And you knew the end and gave freely so you might withdraw and give again . . .

> The drink came from the highest one. Blessed are the ministers of that drink, who guard his water. They assuage dry lips. They raise up those who have fainted. Souls that were about to depart they have drawn back from death . . . They gave strength to our feebleness and light to our eyes. Everyone knew them in the Lord and by the water they lived forever.

> Joy moves over the beloved and floods us with fruit . . . His way is knowledge . . . over it are the traces of his light.

> My heart was cloven and there appeared a flower, and grace sprung up and fruit from the Lord . . . I received his knowledge and sat on the rock of truth where he placed me. Speaking waters came near my lip from the vast fountain of the Lord, and I drank and was drunk with the living water that never dies, and my drunkenness gave me knowledge. I threw off the madness of the earth . . . and the lord renewed me in his raiment and held me in his light. From above he gave me uncorrupt ease . . . dew was on my face, and my nostrils enjoyed the aroma of the Lord. He took me to Paradise where I knew joy and worshipped his glory. Blessed are they planted in your land, in Paradise, who grow in the growth of your trees and change from gloom into light . . . There is much space in Paradise but no wasteland. All is fruit. Glory Lord, and eternal delight of Paradise.

> Like the flow of waters truth flows from my mouth, and my lips reveal its harvest, and it gives me the gold of knowledge for the mouth of the Lord is the true word and the door of his light.

> I was crowned by God, by a crown alive . . . He became my certain salvation . . . I spread my knowledge and love and sowed my fruits in hearts and transformed them . . . They lived. I gathered them and saved them.

> A cup of milk I was offered and I drank its sweetness as the delight of the Lord [plate 33]. The son is the cup and he who was milked is the Father and he who milked him is

the Holy Ghost. His breasts were full and his milk should not drip out wastefully [see plate 24]. The holy ghost opened the Father's raiment and mingled the milk from the Father's two breasts and gave that mingling to the world, which was unknowing. Those who drink it are near his right hand. The spirit opened the virgin's womb and she received the milk. The virgin became a mother of great mercy; she labored, but not in pain, and bore a son. No midwife came. She bore him as if she were a man, openly . . . She loved him, and swaddled him, and revealed his majesty.

Drink deeply from the living fountain of the Lord. It is yours. Come, all who are thirsty, and drink, and rest by the fountain of the Lord. How beautiful and pure. It rests the soul. That water is sweeter than honey . . . It flows from the lips of the Lord. Its name is from the Lord's heart . . . and was unknown until it was set in our midst. They who drink are blessed and they rest.

The dew of the Lord rinsed me with silence and a cloud of peace rose over my head . . . It became my salvation . . . He gave me milk, his dew, and I grew in his bounty, rested in his perfection. I spread my hands out as my soul pointed to the firmament and I slipped upward to him.

The first "dew" reference corresponds to the intense perspiration that literally rinses a person who has consumed fly agaric; it then becomes a metaphor for the liquid or seed of God that is milked out and drunk.

I went up to the light of truth as into a chariot . . . It was my haven and my salvation and put me in the arms of immortal life . . .

All who see me will be astonished for I am an alien among you. The father of truth remembered me. He possessed me from the beginning. Through his riches and the thought in his heart he engendered me . . . Light found daybreak in the word . . . The Messiah is one, known before the foundation of the world. He saves souls in his truth . . .

I stretched out my hands and came near my Lord. It is my sign, stretching my hands as spread on a tree. That was my way up to the Good One. I became useless to those who did not take hold of me. I hide from those who do not love me, but I am with them who love me . . . I rose up and am with them and speak through their mouths . . . like the groom over the bride, so is my love over those who believe in me.

11

The Mysterious Grail

Hear now how those called to the Grail are made known.
On the stone, around the edge, appear letters inscribed,
giving the name and lineage of each one, maid or boy,
who is to take the blessed journey.

Wolfram von Eschenbach

LIKE THE PHILOSOPHERS' STONE and the unicorn, the Holy Grail is regarded by most people as a complete fiction. I intend to show that it did and does exist, though in a hidden fashion; in the next chapter I will state the case for the existence of the philosophers' stone and the unicorn as well.

The word "grail" comes from the Old French *graal*, meaning a dish or bowl and has come to be identified in the popular mind with the cup used by Jesus at the Last Supper. According to legend this cup came into the possession of Joseph of Arimathea, in whose tomb Jesus was buried. The story in which Joseph stands beneath the cross to catch the blood of Jesus in the cup we know; another version states that the blood-catching came later, when Joseph was preparing Jesus' body for burial. In either case it is the blood in the cup that is the key element in the story and gives the cup the strange powers attributed to it; without the blood it is only an empty cup and would not be so celebrated or sought after. We do not, for example, inquire overmuch about the bowl in which Jesus washed everyone's feet that same night. No, the cup is holy only because it holds the blood of God.

The stories of the Grail are many and varied; my retelling here incorporates details from several sources. After the reputed resurrection of Jesus, Joseph was imprisoned, accused of stealing Jesus' body. He was given nothing to eat, but a dove flew into his window every day and put a wafer in the cup, and these morsels kept him alive until his release. After this point the stories vary considerably, but most agree that he sailed away with his sister, her husband Bron, and the cup of Jesus. They settled somewhere in Europe and established the Grail Table, a ritualized representation of the Last Supper table with one seat, representing Judas; left vacant and dubbed the Siege or Seat Perilous because of its tendency to swallow up anyone who sat there. Some versions say Joseph later sailed to England where he established the first Christian church at Glastonbury and instituted the Mass of the Grail, using the cup to hold whatever it was they drank as symbolic blood during the services. Others say that Joseph never left continental Europe and passed on custodianship of the Grail cup to Bron; after performing a feeding miracle with a fish à la Jesus, Bron became known as the "Rich Fisher."

The Grail-keepers built a castle in which to house the Grail and established a second Grail Table and an Order of Grail Knights (who, according to Wolfram, were modeled after the Knights Templar, themselves often accused of being closet Gnostics). The Grail-keeper became a hereditary position known as the Grail King, and he served as priest to the rest of the company. They celebrated some form of Mass, again using the Grail as the chalice of the sacred drink, and had regular feasts, the Grail producing whatever foods were desired. It was a cornucopia: all foods were present before it.

All was well until the King suffered a genital amputation by a pagan knight, after which the land surrounding the castle fell to waste in a terrible drought. The King's wounds would not heal, even though the King was the Grail-keeper and the Grail was known to possess magical powers, nor was the land restored. For this restoration to occur a certain question relating to the Grail would first have to be asked. Along with the Grail were kept the other hallowed objects of the cult: a bleeding lance, two ten-branched candlesticks, and a silver platter, said to be the one that once held the head of John the Baptizer.

King Arthur and his knights were also associated with the Grail. Merlin is said to have established the Round Table as the third Grail Table, complete with a Seat Perilous. It is ironic that these rough warriors became the champions of the cult of chivalry, the chief tenets of which were fairness, courage, helping the poor, and utter respect for women, including (and especially) their protection. The knights sitting together one day witnessed a vision of the Grail, seen as if behind a veil and floating in light; this sent the knights off in all directions to find it. Their search often led them deep into great forests. Only a few had varying degrees of success.

Lancelot got very close to the Grail but was temporarily blinded; Perceval, Bors and Galahad all reached the Grail castle and received a vision: there stood Jesus, first celebrating the Mass with the Grail, then appearing as a child (sometimes *in the chalice*), and finally appearing in the host in his crucified form; Galahad was the only one pure enough to be allowed to look inside the Grail and attain the fullness of its ecstatic mystery. Perceval was finally able to ask the correct question, which broke the drought and restored the wounded King, who thereafter died in peace, having been kept alive by the mere presence of the Grail. Perceval became the new Grail King in his place. Bors returned to Camelot with a report of their success. Galahad died at the peak of his divine experience, rising up to heaven with a host between his lips.

Stories dealing with mysterious spiritual objects and foods almost always exist in differing versions or at least have some elements that don't appear elsewhere. Here are some other variations of the Grail myth:

> Different stories depict the Grail variously as a chalice, a broad-mouthed dish, a jewel, or a stone. As a chalice it holds the blood and water of Jesus and provides food as well. As a dish it is made of gold and studded with gems; it holds the sacrificial lamb of the Last Supper. As a jewel it once was set in the crown of Lucifer, but during the war in heaven it was dislodged and carried to earth by angels. As a stone it is sometimes the stone of exile, the stone of no worth, or the stone fallen from heaven; its power is said to derive from the same source by which the phoenix is able to burn in its own flames and be reborn from its own ashes.
>
> One version of the myth allegedly came from a book written in Arabic by a Jewish astrologer from Toledo, who in turn had heard it from a singer of Provence, home of the Gnostic Cathars.
>
> Another says the story came from a red book written by Abraham the Jew. It was written on paper made from tree bark.
>
> The Grail was called the Sangreal, which contains the words "Saint Grail" and "Sang Real," Royal Blood.
>
> The Grail was a chalice, made "not of stone, not of bone, not of metal."
>
> The Grail was the fruit of Paradise, still available because Eve took a branch from the tree of knowledge and planted it. The branch grew into a white tree that turned green after Eve gave birth. When Cain murdered Abel the tree turned red and would bleed when it was cut. Without the branch there would have been no fruit and therefore no Grail, so the Grail-fruit was considered to be both fruit and branch.
>
> The Grail knights were wont to dress in red, with accents of ermine.

The first time I saw a fly agaric in full spore-releasing mode I thought immediately of the Holy Grail legend, about which I knew little at the time. The graceful cup-shape resembled a chalice carved in white marble or bone, and the red interior of the cup contained a small pool of rainwater tinted red from the mushroom. Subsequent reading about the Grail convinced me that my reaction was the correct one; a review of the story elements presented above will demonstrate why.

The central image the myth deals with is of course the vessel itself, whether chalice or dish, which also supplies the most obvious fly agaric correspondence: the fully mature mushroom becomes a literal cup (if it is deep) or dish (if it is shallow). If the cap gets wet at this stage rivulets of red run down the cup's interior and pool at the bottom. It looks like a chalice of blood mixed with water. Even without water the mushroom gives the impression of being a cup of blood, as in plates 12 and 33. Joseph survived in prison by eating a "host" placed in the cup by a dove. The dove and the cup both correspond to a mature fly agaric specimen, and the host corresponds to a dried mushroom cap. Putting it in the cup as the dove did symbolizes that the host becomes a liquid and is drunk.

Joseph left the Middle East and went to Europe, where the fly agaric is found in abundance. Once there he started a cult centered around the mysterious cup of blood, taking great pains to identify it with the story of Jesus. The details of the mystical "mass" celebrated by the participants were kept secret; an empty seat representing Judas was kept to remind everyone what happens when the cult secrets are made public or revealed to the authorities. The images of the Rich Fisher and Fisher King are a clear tie to Jesus but may also represent dried fly agarics bobbing in the water like so many fish. With these mushrooms one person can feed many.

The Grail was considered a source of food and with good reason. Actual cups or chalices never produce food or drink on their own, and certainly no one would ever consider eating a cup or chalice. The mushroom-cup, however, contains both food and drink and is itself edible. Not only this, but when it is eaten one becomes "full," that is to say one becomes temporarily anorexic, full physically as well as spiritually, and perfectly content with the food afforded by the mushroom.

Everything went along smoothly with the new cult until the King had his amputation. I say "amputation" rather than "castration" because the nature of the King's wound "across the thighs" is never fully explained, even though it seems clear that it is a euphemism for a wound to the genitals. Castration refers only to losing the testicles, while amputation can refer to both the testicles and the penis. Since the myth already abounds in fly agaric imagery we might assume that penis amputation is being referred to, which would put the Fisher King in the illustrious company of Rudra, Attis, Osiris, and Uranus, penis amputees all.

Coincident with the King's amputation is a terrible drought, which brings to mind Elijah and his drought dilemma. During a severe drought there will be no mushrooms produced. If the drought continues for a sufficient length of time it will kill the mushroom mycelia and create a real supply problem. Just as Elijah would not have been able to initiate a successor until the rains came, the wounded King could not reproduce until he got back his "penis," which wouldn't happen unless it rained again.

Another interpretation of the amputation episode is voluntary suppression of mushroom use by the Grail King, just as the Jewish priests seem to have done in Jesus' time. We note also that the King was unmanned by a pagan, which may represent "unauthorized" use of the mushroom by non-Christians. Still, the amputation and the drought occur at the same time, just as the King's "healing" and the end of the drought happen together, so a drought-caused shortage is more likely being represented.

Many of the Grail stories were well-known by C.E. 1200, around which time the Church by papal decree withdrew the chalice of the Mass from use by the laity. Thenceforth the Church's policy would be Wafers Only—No Wine. Since its inception the Christian Church had waxed eloquent over the importance—nay, the necessity—of eating the flesh of Jesus (the bread) and drinking his blood (the wine), and all worshippers consumed both during the ritual. Then all of a sudden, after 1,200 years of drinking, the Church said, "No more wine for the laity." What could have caused such a radical change in the sacrosanct ritual of the Lord's Supper, instituted by Jesus himself? The reaction among the rank and file must have been one of bewilderment and resentment. There were, after all, only two foods in the Supper, bread and wine; for the Church to take away the best of the two must have seemed cruel and unnecessary.

Perhaps the Church's decision to deprive worshippers of their sip of blood from the chalice reflects a reaction to the underground Grail cults and the stories about them that were springing up all over Europe. If these heretical cults were going to persist in using the sacred chalice in their debauched rituals, then let them, said the Church; there was no stopping them anyway. The Grail cults were drinking Jesus' blood from their chalices and claiming to have divine visions after they drank. But Church authorities didn't want the laity to begin thinking that anything truly divine or supernatural could happen to *them* by drinking mere wine from the Church's chalice, which of course was also said to contain the blood of Jesus.

One sure way the Church could put a stop to such expectations from the laity would be to stop the drinking of "Christ's blood" altogether, and that is what they did. This hypothesis is strengthened by the fact that the Church instituted the transubstantiation dogma in 1215; this decree stated that during the Mass, the wine and bread become the actual blood and body of Jesus and that Jesus is fully present in either or both. The dogma served as the justification for withdrawing wine from the Church's menu, although "pretext" may be a better word than "justification." The Grail cults were based on personal experience of the divine, while the Church of the time said that faith alone was needed. Perhaps something more than faith was required to believe that a little round cracker was the actual flesh and blood of Jesus.

In the mysterious ritual called the Procession of the Grail several objects were paraded.

PLATE 28 *above left:* The fly agaric's first appearance is in a manger, wrapped in swaddling cloths (p. 115). Other references: The newborn baby is already anointed (p. 116).

PLATE 29 *below:* The blood and wool of the Lamb of God (p. 117). Other references: The slain lamb of Revelation (p. 132).

PLATE 30 *above right:* The shriveled body of the crucified savior. The same mushroom, dried, as that shown in plate 17 (p. 125).

PLATE 31 *above left:* "His head and his hair were as white as white wool or as snow, his eyes like a burning flame . . ." (p. 131).

PLATE 32 *below:* "I will give the hidden manna and a white stone—a stone with a new name on it, known only to the man who receives it . . ." (p. 131).

PLATE 33 *above right:* "The son is the cup and he who was milked is the Father and he who milked him is the Holy Ghost." (p. 152). Other references: The Grail chalice (p. 157). The cup of serpents' poison (p. 175).

PLATE 34 *above:* The Holy
Grail, filled by Nature
(p. 161).

PLATE 35 *right:* The red and
white headed sacrifice
becomes the sacred drink
(p. 161).

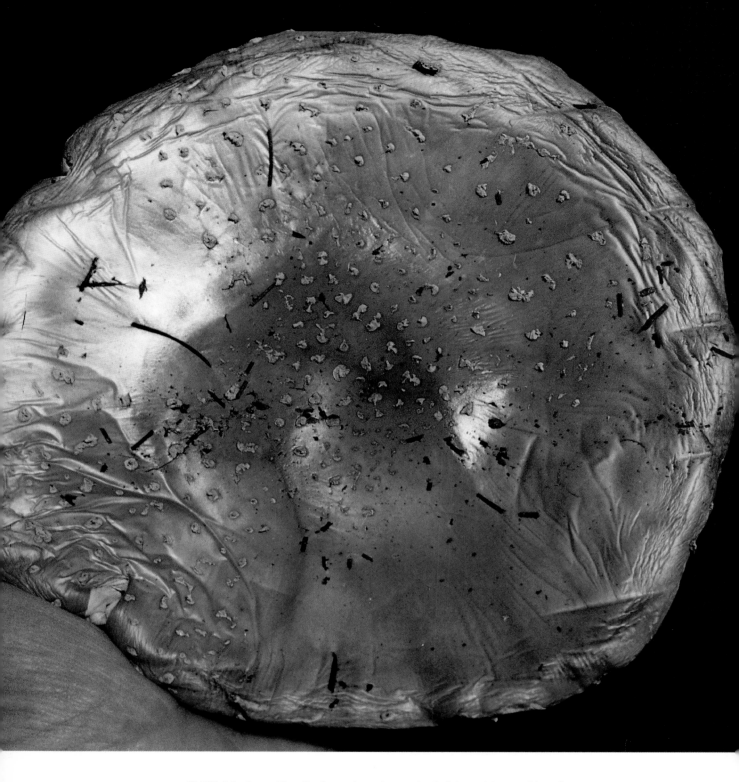

PLATE 36 *above:* The Grail as a broad-mouthed dish, golden and jewel-studded, upon which rests the sacrificed lamb (p. 162). Other references: The Grail looks like it is made of metal but is not (p. 163). His blood runs from the margins and pools in the center (p. 199).

PLATE 37 *facing page:* Lucifer's crown jewel, highly polished and unfaceted (p. 162).

PLATE 38 *facing page:* The divine sun-moon hermaphrodite of alchemy (p. 172).

PLATE 39 *above left:* The egg of the philosophers (p. 173).

PLATE 40 *above right:* The heads of Sol and Luna side by side, the union of the sun and moon (p. 173).

PLATE 41 *below left:* The wings and golden belt of the hermaphrodite (p. 173).

PLATE 42 *below right:* The philosophical gold, goal of the hermaphrodite's transformation (p. 174).

PLATE 43 *above left:* "He who drinks and does not drink again, does not know what drinking is." (p. 198).

PLATE 44 *detail below left:* Gabriel's arm and shield (p. 198).

PLATE 45 *detail above right:* Jesus lying in a mushroomlike manger (p. 198).

PLATE 46 *below right:* "Behold the lamb of God." X marks the spot (p. 199).

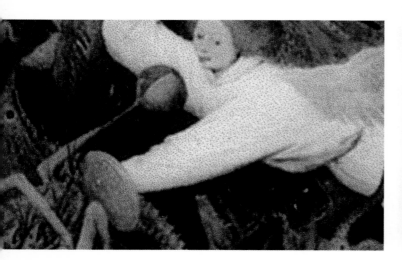

The first was a bleeding lance said to be the lance that pierced Jesus and/or the lance that performed the King's amputation. A lance, even more than a sword, is a phallic symbol, and in this regard it is the perfect weapon to use to cut off a penis. Blood flowing from the tip of the lance makes it correspond to the fly agaric. The second objects in the procession were two golden candlesticks set with flaming candles, another fly agaric correspondence and a favorite image of the author of Revelation. These columns topped with fire can also be seen as phallic, depending on their length and thickness, such as the large Paschal candle used in the Catholic Easter Mass.

After being lit the Paschal candle is carried to the baptismal font while the choir sings, "As the deer pants after the fountains of water, so longs my soul after you, O God. My soul has thirsted for the living God: when shall I come and appear before the face of God?" After prayers praising the wonderful way in which water is turned to wine and living water, the candle is thrust into the water three times with the prayer, "May the power of the Holy Spirit descend into the fullness of this font. And make the whole substance of this water fruitful for the effecting of regeneration." Though the font is ostensibly for baptism, most of the language is about drinking the water, not bathing in it. Could this rite be a remnant of the secret practices of the original Jesus cult? The burning candle immersed repeatedly in water could easily be a surrogate for the fiery candle of the fly agaric, perhaps the only "candle" that could benefit from repeated immersion in water.

The Paschal candle is the candle of the sacrificed lamb, thrust into the font as the penis of God to transform the water through his fiery seed into "living" water, the drink of immortality. The fly agaric/candle/bloody lamb/phallus is likewise sacrificed and immersed in water, where it releases its "blood" and its "seed," impregnating the waters with salvation as surely as the Paschal candle does not.

Third position in the Grail parade was held by the light-giving Grail itself, which symbolizes the fully mature mushroom as well as the experience of light it provides. The silver platter, the fourth object, represents the head of John the Baptizer: the bloody, severed "head of prophecy" enigmatically described by the Gnostic Jesus. It corresponds to the harvested fly agaric cap severed from the stalk.

Jessie Weston felt that the Grail myths were artifacts of earlier fertility religions that were grafted onto the Christian myth, and she may be right, though she was puzzled about some of the recurring details of the Grail legends.[60] She notes, for example, that the first visit to the Grail castle always connoted failure, and only after this initial failure did each knight's quest for the Grail begin in earnest. This may be an allusion to the difficulties many people encounter when they take the fly agaric. Often, as stated earlier, the mysteries of the mushroom are not revealed on the first "visit"; it takes determination to press on and find the "real" Grail experience.

What really intrigued Wesson were the drops of blood that dripped continually from the tip of the lance, usually onto a sparkling white tablecloth or white snow. Staring at the brilliant red drops against the white background would somehow cause the seekers to fall asleep or into a trance and thereby miss seeing the vision, hearing the crucial information, or asking the right question. She thought that the blood itself was somehow the "operating cause" of the sleep or trance and suggested that the constantly recurring theme of falling asleep at the crucial moment and its connection with the drops of blood must have a rational explanation. I agree.

We can see an allusion to the fly agaric in the striking contrast provided by drops of bright red blood on white backgrounds, but why would these drops be associated with falling asleep? If the blood does represent the fly agaric then the story is saying that consumption of the mushroom can cause drowsiness and sleep, which if not resisted can turn into quite ordinary sleep, and the user awakens many hours later refreshed but no wiser. The chance to see the vision, hear the crucial information, and ask the essential question has by the morning vanished like the Grail castle, leaving the seeker to start again from the beginning; or, as is often the case with fly agaric novices, cease trying altogether.

In my experience the onset of drowsiness is a wake-up call that is easily put on hold. It may sound oxymoronic but sleeping through a psychedelic experience is definitely possible, both literally and figuratively. All levels of mystical practice, whether self- or drug-induced, have one thing in common: for there to be success in the endeavor one must pay attention, and to pay attention one must above all remain awake. The story seems to be saying that even finding and consuming the mushroom is not enough if the user sleeps through the experience. Yet the same drops that cause sleep on one occasion can, on another occasion, cause heaven.

The Round Table appears to have been a real novelty when it was "invented" by the crafty magician Merlin. The ostensible reason the table was made in a circle was to assure that no one who sat there could claim pride of place, something that was becoming a real problem when knights were seated together at traditional rectangular tables. Today we are used to the idea of round tables, but before Merlin's table appeared they seem to have been unknown in Europe. Its novelty turned the Round Table into an instant symbol of the search for the Grail. If the Grail is the fly agaric then the symbol becomes more literal, since a mature mushroom has the same shape and orientation to the ground as a round table; the mushroom is just smaller. This similarly might seem incidental were it not for the fact that the fly agaric in particular is named the *toadstool,* though it could just as easily be called the toads' table.[61] We saw that Vishnu was called an altar for the same reason: he looked like one. The mushrooms are often big enough to sit upon or use as a small table, though of course they're not strong enough; the point is that they *resemble* both stools and tables.

Chivalry, like the word cavalry, originally meant "fully armed and mounted warriors," but due to the often gallant and honorable behavior of some of these men the term soon came to signify the qualities themselves and was used to designate the type of behavior that was expected of a knight. Later in general usage "chivalry" came to mean "courtesy." Why such a noble ideal would develop in the midst of the barbarism and cruelty of the times is something of an anomaly, especially among such fierce warriors, yet the virtues they expressed were similar to those expressed by Jesus when he preached love and compassion to a similarly barbaric and benighted society. The original disciples may not have been warriors but they did carry weapons, proved by Peter's swordplay at Gethsemene.

Jesus obtained a glimpse of heaven and the higher life of humanity, possibly through the use of certain drugs, and felt compelled to spread his message among the downtrodden. The good knights seem to have been similarly inspired; their obsessive devotion to the Grail parallels that of the early Christians to the eucharist, as well it should: the Grail *contains* the same bloody eucharist.

I mentioned earlier that the fly agaric can be so difficult of access that many people think it is ineffective as a consciousness raiser, and this fact is also reflected in the Grail myth. Even though all the knights (and many non-knights) were in some way acquainted with the Grail, very few received the supreme vision of light it offered. This was something that took a great deal of determination, persistence, patience, and courage, even after the Grail had been found. The same holds true for the fly agaric and its use.

Arthur's knights had a vision of a shining chalice bathed in heavenly light, a chalice filled with the blood of the slain savior: the same blood that when drunk will transport a person to heaven according to Jesus. The Grail of their vision is described as being behind a veil, which suggests that veiled imagery is being used; for example, "a chalice behind a veil" might refer to the mushroom that first hides behind a veil and then turns itself inside-out to become a chalice (plate 34). A veiled reference indeed.

The "vision" reads more like a description of the Grail and its effects than an actual vision. Perhaps like Hanuman the knights had the sacred plant described to them and then were sent out into the forests to search for it, wearing their red clothing decorated with white puffs of fur as sympathetic magic to help them in their quest. Lancelot appears to have attained the "blindness" stage of fly agaric intoxication and nothing more, which can happen (at least Paul had a vision of light before he was blinded).

The shared vision of the three knights at the Grail castle is also suggestive of the fly agaric. Jesus first appeared before them at the altar, celebrating mass with the Grail. Then he appeared smaller than a baby and sitting in the Grail (plate 35). These two forms of Jesus bear a striking resemblance to the two forms of Vishnu, who could expand to the size of an altar or become a tiny dwarf beneath the ground, and who, as the sacrificial victim, also ended up in someone's cup. The main implication is that Jesus is meant to be drunk.

Finally Jesus appeared in the host as a crucified man, which means that he is to be eaten as well as drunk. If the "host" of the vision represents the dried discs of the fly agaric then the phrase "crucified man in the host" makes sense in fly agaric terms: the "man," the phallus-mushroom, will become cruciform at maturity, after which time the mushroom's body (or only the bloody head) should be taken away and preserved. Careful drying can take from one to three days, after which, now shrunken and resembling a round, unleavened loaf, it is ready for resurrection in the body of the believer: the body and blood of the savior being fully present in each and every little loaf.

Galahad represents not only the highest experience offered by the Grail but the culmination of the spiritual search as well. He became so absorbed in his vision that he was "taken to heaven." In the state of perfect union described in the Yoga Sutras one is by definition in a nondual state wherein even the subtlest of differences disappear entirely. Even the I-sense is absorbed in the pure light of consciousness itself, so there is no longer an enjoyer or a thing enjoyed; there is no individualized reflector at all. The fact that this state can't even be experienced in the way we normally understand experience makes it rather difficult to write about, but this appears to be what happened to Galahad. Yoga theory states that one can remain in this delicate condition (in which one has lost all body-consciousness) for up to twenty-one days, but after that time the body, deprived of food, drink, and oxygen more or less forgets what it is doing and dies, leaving the consciousness of the former individual still merged, one hopes, in the light. Galahad's departure with a host wafer between his lips may allude to a particular sect's belief that the solid as well as the liquid form of the mushroom should be consumed in order to achieve the maximum effects or may be simply another allusion to the dried mushroom cap.

Eventually Perceval came up with the right question to heal the King and restore his penis, which meant that the drought was over. But did the drought end when the King grew his penis or did the "penis" (mushroom) grow when the drought ended? The question must have been, "Just what is this Grail anyway, and what does it have to do with blood, penises, and the drought?" Getting the correct answer made Perceval the new Keeper of the Grail, and of its secrets.

The four main ways in which the Grail was described—chalice, dish, jewel, and stone—all have direct mushroom correspondences. The chalice corresponds to the mature mushroom's shape, as we have seen, and the blood and water it contains. As a broad-mouthed dish, "golden and jewel-studded," it is said to carry the sacrificed lamb, another mushroom analogy. A "broad-mouthed dish" is an apt description of a mature fly agaric cap as well (plate 36). The jewel form of the Grail parallels the early, unexpanded stage of the mushroom, which sometimes shines like a polished, unfaceted jewel (plate 37) and brings to mind the red jewel produced from the Soma-churning. Lucifer is drawn into the tale because he is an exile from heaven and because his name means "Light-bringer," both characteristics which also apply to the fly agaric, certainly an exiled jewel in its own right.

The reason the crown jewel was said to be "carried to earth by angels" is because the mushroom's "jewel" phase will transform into its angel or bird phase. In "stone of exile" and "stone of no worth" we hear echoes of the ancient fly agaric taboos, yet the Grail-stone was said to contain the same power as that by which the phoenix burns and regenerates itself. With clues like these it's easy to see why the secret of the Grail has remained a secret for so long. The Grail and the phoenix have the same power because in spite of their apparent dissimilarity they both correspond to the same red and white mushroom.

The story of the legend's origin in Provence ties the tale to the Cathar Gnostics; that it was carried by a Jew connects it with the ancient Jewish mushroom cult. The second story of origin says that the legend was found in a red book written by Abraham the Jew; the book's paper was made of tree bark. Once again a connection to Jews is made and specifically to Abraham, the possible founder of a Jewish mushroom cult. The red cover of the book corresponds to the fly agaric, as does the white paper. "Paper made from tree bark" quite possibly refers to the birch tree, a favored host for the mushroom. Anyone familiar enough with birch trees to make paper from their bark would surely know about the fly agaric as well.

A very clever clue to the Grail's identity comes in the saying "not of stone, not of bone, not of metal," first of all by its implication that the plant kingdom must be involved. But the real clues lie in what is denied about the stone: everything denied is a metaphor for the fly agaric. The mushroom is not of stone, though it can appear both as a rough white stone in the ground or a polished round stone on the ground; it is not of bone, though the base and stem look like bone (see plate 4); it is not of metal even though the drying cap can look as though it is made of metal, as in plate 36.

The legend that the Grail is the fruit of Paradise ties back nicely to the Garden of Eden episode, stating as it does in no uncertain terms that the Grail is a fruit. As fly agaric metaphor, the story goes like this: Eve took a branch from the tree of Paradise and planted it. This could refer to the planting of known host trees or cuttings by someone who wants to establish a personal fly agaric colony in the backyard (or elsewhere). Eve's tree turned white when it took root, like a birch tree in winter, when it is white only, having lost its leaves. After the birth of Eve's first son the tree turned green; the son of heaven and earth, the mushroom, is born just before the birch puts on its new greenery. After Cain killed Abel the tree turned red and would flow with blood when cut, which means metaphorically that the fruit of the tree is "blood," Sang Real, the royal blood that is both fruit and Grail.

Those who used this metaphor said also that the Grail was both fruit and branch, ostensibly referring to the branch purloined by Eve. We can see, however, that the fly agaric too is both fruit and branch: it grows out of the ground on a solitary white "branch," on top of which sits the shiny red fruit, in much the same way that Shiva appeared as "fruit on a post." A second implication of the Grail's being both fruit and branch is the mushroom's need for a host tree, without which it cannot be born. The symbiosis that takes place between the mushroom mycelia and the rootlets of trees means that nutrients are exchanged between the two plants, making the mushroom both fruit and branch in a very literal way; the author seems at least aware that the mushroom will grow only beneath certain trees and nowhere else.

As the need for chivalrous knights came to be supplanted by the forces of law and order, such as they were, knighthood as a vocation became obsolete. The knights' peculiar preoccupation with the vessel of God's blood faded away along with knighthood. Consciously or not the Grail image of the exiled stone was taken up by the alchemists and transmuted into the stone of the philosophers.

Some of the first collateral victims of the end of the age of chivalry were the turned-out blacksmiths and sorcerers of the bankrupt Old World defense industry, forced into new occupations by the changing times. An armor-maker, already skilled in metallurgy and the use of fire, could have converted rather easily to the occupation of "puffer," so-called because these early alchemists were forever puffing at their numerous fires with bellows. Subtler perhaps than their former masters, their own preoccupation was not with the Grail so much as with its contents. Like their alchemical contemporaries their true quest was for the elixir, the philosophical water, the drinkable gold, the liquid and fiery stone.

12

Elixir: The Secret Stone of Alchemy

Our Water

An aching heart
A king starts to waken
Harken back to olden days
An alchemist beckons again
What's old is new, he says
and everything is shaken
Retort, vial and vas are broken
Even earth is quaking
A shaking hand betakes the potion
—this is not the time to weaken—
puts the chalice to his lips
and pours the liquor down
He cries "Elixir!
Rosy blood of God!
Living waters truly!
Holy tincture of my Art
lift me up to heaven's door—
Cleanse my mind and heal my heart!"
Then having drunk he drinks once more

Our Stone is life to him who knows it and how it is made, and he who knows not and has not made it and to whom no assurance is given when it will be born, or who thinks it another stone has already prepared himself for death.[62]

> For there is one stone, one medicine, to which nothing from outside is added, nor is it diminished, save that the superfluities are removed.[63]
>
> For the stone is the self-same permanent water; and while it is water it is not the stone.[64]

If a prize were offered for the most obscure and intentionally baffling philosophy in history it would surely be awarded to alchemy, the much maligned parent of chemistry and, by extension, Jungians. Alchemy has from its inception suffered from an image problem, primarily because its practitioners claimed to be able to turn base metals such as iron or lead into gold; it wasn't so much the claim that tarnished their reputation as the fact that they were unable to do so.

On the surface the alchemist often appeared to be a more or less enlightened quack, dabbling and experimenting at the frontiers of physical and metaphysical science. Sometimes, or perhaps often, he was a complete fraud, making claim after false claim about what he could do; yet within the alchemical literature can be found gems of philosophic insight demonstrating that there were some alchemists of a different order, and that the stone of the philosophers, the elixir, was not mere fantasy. Yet as in the Grail quest the right questions must be asked if the puzzle is to be solved. What were the alchemists really up to? What is the elixir they tried so hard to create and took such pains to conceal? These are simple questions, but even the alchemists themselves couldn't agree on the answers, and those they gave are enough to confound even the most dogged investigator—because this was their avowed intention:

> This science transmits its worth by mixing the false with the true and the true with the false . . . and it endeavors to transmit the work obscurely and to hide it as much as possible.[65]

> They tell the truth in regard to all things but men do not understand their words . . . whence through their assumption they falsify the verities and verify the falsities . . . The error springs from ignorance of the writers' meaning, when they heard divers words unknown to their understanding, *since these have a hidden meaning* . . . For this belongs to him who subtly perceives and is cognizant of the inner meaning.[66] [Italics mine.]

Uncovering the truth in alchemical writings and illustrations can be extremely daunting, as the two quotations illustrate. The alchemists' method of explanation was *"obscurum per obscurius, ignotum per ignotius"* (the obscure by the more obscure, the unknown by the more unknown), making many of them masters of obfuscation if nothing else: a person could sound like a real alchemist by making up nonsense shrouded in mystery because the real alchemists were saying similar sounding things that didn't make obvious sense either. Since one of the stated goals of alchemy was to make gold there was no shortage of lesser minds trying to accomplish that hopeless task, just as there were wealthy patrons hoping to become even wealthier by supporting these fakers. Meanwhile the true alchemists stated over and over in their writings that the gold of which they spoke was not the "common" gold.

If attempted gold-making was the pastime of the false alchemist, what then was the real alchemist doing? If the symbols of alchemy don't always refer to chemical operations, to what do they refer? At least with alchemy, as opposed to most of the other systems we have examined, the fact that there were hidden secrets was well-known; what was not known, and has remained unknown to this day, is what the secrets were.

Carl Jung did an admirable job of putting a respectable face on alchemy, rescuing it from the trash heap of human ideas to which it had been consigned by history. Jung constructed an elaborate rationale for alchemy's existence, a system of psychological renewal and completion based on the images of the collective unconscious. He believed that the often bizarre and contradictory symbols of alchemy had erupted spontaneously in the alchemical mind due to the intense concentration and isolation required of the alchemists by their experimentation. Many of the same motifs appeared in the dreams and drawings of Jung's psychiatric patients (as well as in his own dreams and visions), and the striking similarities he observed led him to speculate that the alchemists had unknowingly been performing a kind of self-therapy as they dealt with a flood of mental images brought on by the practice of their "chymical art."

In both situations Jung attributed this upwelling of images to be a consequence of the collective dominants of society having fallen into decay, especially the religious dominants. When a person in such a situation is overwhelmed by the numinous images pouring forth from the unconscious to form new dominants, a kind of possession of the individual takes place, proportional to the extent to which a person identifies with the images; it is this kind of possession that Jung assigns to the alchemists and anyone else, for that matter, in whom the religious dominants have decayed. "For this reason," he says,

> there have always been people who, not satisfied with the dominants of conscious life,
> set forth—under cover and by devious paths, to their destruction or salvation—to seek
> direct experience of the eternal roots, and, following the lure of the restless unconscious
> psyche, find themselves in the wilderness.[67]

Embracing and redefining Hermetic philosophy, this "direct experience" is exactly what the alchemists sought, and some of them became enlightened as a result or as a by-product of their efforts, yet Jung states flatly that the stone of the philosophers, the goal of their work, never existed physically.[68]

I will not deny that much of the imagery of alchemy derives from the collective unconscious; it is why and how the imagery was generated that is problematic. Intense concentration is sometimes its own reward, it is true; much of meditation theory is based on this premise and, rarely, a level of enlightenment can be gained in this way. Even allowing for this possibility there is more in alchemical symbolism than beached archetypes of the unconscious. The images of alchemy, due to their obscure and often bizarre content, have become something of a Rorschach test for investigators, who project their own meanings onto them; but unlike those suggestive ink blots many of the alchemical images have real and hidden meanings apart from their correspondence to the images of the collective unconscious. These secrets constitute the *arcanum,* the secret substance of the work that no one was supposed to reveal directly, though everybody and his *soror mystica* seems to have taken a turn at describing it cryptically. It's as if the alchemists vied amongst themselves to see who could create the most obscure yet accurate description of the material. It is the very strangeness and contrariness of these images, and their correspondence to similar images already encountered, that arouse suspicion about the *arcanum's* identity and suggest an answer.

It is not my intention here to give a lengthy exegesis of alchemy and its processes, especially since much of the material is designed solely to confuse the uninitiated. The success of their obfuscatory attempts is perhaps proven by the abundance of new books about alchemy that seem to be appearing almost daily; one finds in these nearly as many "correct" interpretations of alchemical symbolism as there are authors. Yet with all this new scrutiny and deconstruction still no one has ventured a guess as to the physical identity of the secret substance that the alchemists swore was real, and which remains the key for unlocking alchemy's mysteries; most investigators seem content assuming with Jung that the stone was only a psychic experience.

The alchemists themselves said repeatedly that their stone was both physical and spiritual, which is a good general description of an entheogenic substance (one that "generates God" within a person). Perhaps one crucial piece of the puzzle has been missing, and only that piece will create order out of the alchemical chaos. As the alchemist Michael Maier wrote, "He who wants to enter the philosophers' rose garden without a key is like unto a man who wants to walk without feet."[69] That is, there will be such a conspicuous lack of "understanding" that the task will prove impossible.

To arrive at the hidden truth the alchemists advised the seeker to read not one book but many books, and to read them again and again until the seeker can see the places where the authors are in agreement; therein, alchemists say, will the secret be found:

> *For greatly doubted evermore all such,*
> *That of this science they may write too much:*
> *Every each of them taught but one point or twain,*
> *Whereby each of his fellows were made certain:*
> *How that he was to them a brother,*
> *For every of them understood each other;*
> *Also they wrote not every man to teach,*
> *But to show themselves by a secret speech:*
> *Trust not therefore to reading of one book,*
> *But in many authors works you may look;*
> *One book opens another says Arnold the great cleric.*[70]

This practice is similar to the way Jesus and his inner circle shared secrets that were for them alone, and not for those "who have not."

Among the scores of names given by the alchemists to the various substances and processes of their work are several names that are used repeatedly by most of the authors and artists, and it is these names that are of primary interest. There is not much coherent order or logic apparent in the alchemical writings as a whole, save the logic secretly encoded; authors often contradict each other or name and arrange the processes of the work differently. In spite of this tendency there are certain characteristics of the Art that rise above the muddle of false leads that surrounds them, and these characteristics bear an uncanny similarity to various aspects of the fly agaric and its use. I have found so many parallels that they could be the subject of a whole book rather than just one chapter, but I have selected some of the best examples to include here.

Secrecy was paramount among alchemists. If they were using drugs they had good reason not to reveal their secrets, given the social and political tenor of the times, governed as it was by the dogmas and attitudes of the Christian Church. To say that the Church would have been unsympathetic to the aberrant practices of a mushroom cult takes understatement to new depths. Imprisonment, torture, and death were powerful inducements for the alchemists to do one thing and say another. They were fortunate to have found expression for their consciousness experiments not only in the chemical terms they devised but also in the language and symbols of the very institution that would have condemned their activity had it been known: the Church. It was one thing to pretend to be eating the flesh and blood of a dead claimant to God's throne; almost everyone did that. It would have been something else entirely to have outsiders discover that a certain group was consuming preparations of fly agaric and perhaps rubbing ointments into their naked bodies or drinking their urine in the process, while claiming to know God by doing so.

Simply stated, the alchemical work begins with a secret raw material called the *prima materia,* or prime matter, a single substance absolutely essential to the work but never identified except by the most unusual terms. It is called the radical moisture, the round body from the center, the hermaphroditic monster, Adam's tree of paradise with many flowers, the water, the sperm of the world, the empress of all honor, the dragon, and many other names. Once in hand the *prima materia* must be transformed through the alchemical operations into the philosophers' stone, although some authors maintain that the *prima materia* is the stone. In any case, the next step is to extract from the secret stone, through the torment of fire, the miraculous water: the *aqua permanens* or *aqua divina,* also known as that strangest of liquids, drinkable gold.

When the divine water is thus tinctured from the secret substance success is at hand, but how does an alchemist know if the liquid produced is the *correct* liquid, or if it is supposed to be a liquid at all? It is called the divine water, yes, and the living fount, the tincture, the elixir, and the panacea; but it was also called the philosophical stone, Adam, fruit, father, son, king, light, and so on. The list is long. Both the *prima materia* and the elixir produced from it were said to have a thousand names, many of which were shared by both; this abundance of names only adds to the already considerable confusion surrounding the art.

Yet the confusion is only apparent, not real, because all the names are merely different ways of describing the same secret matter in different stages: "There can be no doubt that the arcane substance, whether in neuter or personified form, rises from the earth, unites the opposites, and then returns to earth, thereby achieving its own transformation into the elixir."[71] In this statement Jung is paraphrasing a work popular in the Middle Ages called the *Tabula smaragdina,* putatively authored by Hermes Trismegistus, which describes the secret substance in enigmatic terms. It says in part:

> Its father is the sun, its mother the moon; the wind has carried it in his belly; its nurse is the earth. Its power is complete when it is turned toward the earth. It ascends from earth to heaven, and descends again to the earth, and receives the power of the higher and lower things. So will you have the glory of the whole world.[72]

If we take the alchemists at their word, that everything they wrote or drew had a hidden and specific meaning, then all of alchemy becomes a vast puzzle whose solution has gone begging these many years. With outrageous metaphors they concealed and revealed their secrets at the same time, challenging those with enough wit to figure out what they were talking about. Assuming the requisite intelligence, we would be remiss not to try; the astute reader will already have noted most of the fly agaric parallels in the quotations above.

Read as a fly agaric metaphor the *Tabula* quotation reveals a hidden meaning: the secret substance's father is the sunlike mature mushroom, whose "seed" falls from his body to bring about the birth of his offspring. Its mother is the white, rough-textured "moon" of the mushroom embryo, which seems to give birth to the solar cap. The wind carries the mushroom spores as well as the rainstorms that cause the mushroom's birth.[73] The earth "nurses" the mushroom from egg to cup as the mushroom draws water from it. "When it turns toward the earth" corresponds to the end of sporulation, when the upturned cap begins to dry out and turn back toward the ground; this is the optimal harvest time, because fully mature mushrooms have the highest concentrations of muscimol, the main active ingredient. Drying converts ibotenic acid to muscimol as well; once completely dry "its power is complete." The last statement of the quotation recapitulates the whole process, adding that the substance receives the power of higher *and* lower things. The "higher and lower things" refer to the powers of heaven and earth, but also warn the initiate to be aware that the same mushroom can lead to both heaven and hell. The final promise is that the glory (bliss) of all creation awaits the person who likewise receives the powers of the secret substance.

The alchemists were just as obtuse in their visual representations of the work. It was noted above that one name of the *prima materia* was "Adam's tree of paradise with many flowers," another name for the tree of the philosophers or tree of life. The *Miscellanea d'alchimia*[74] portrays this in a most unusual fashion (fig. 7). Apparently poor Adam's penis has turned into a tree, and he is pinned to the ground by the arrow of Mercurius, about whom we'll hear more below. What could this possibly mean? We know that the tree represents the secret substance, but here it is also Adam's penis. There should be a real penis at the base of the tree, apparently an upright one, and it should be red because Adam was red. Here is one way to interpret the scene: the secret material is a plant that will be found on the ground, beneath a certain type of tree only, and it will look like an erect red phallus rising up from the ground; as it grows it will turn into a "flower of paradise." It will not be found away from the tree because it is stuck to the ground beneath the tree as if by an arrow, and it will die beneath the tree; but the tree will remain and produce many more phallus-flowers.

FIGURE 7: A tree grows where Adam's red phallus should be found.

The tendency to personify the *prima materia* was widespread among the alchemists. It is the same tendency we observed in the stories that personified a sacred plant as Soma, Agni, Shiva, and the rest. Soma was both plant and God; Yahweh was both plant and God; Jesus was both food and God. The alchemists named their God *Mercurius,* and he was both elixir and God. Never does Mercurius refer to the "crude" or "vulgar" metal mercury; he is always the god Hermes, renamed and reinterpreted for the times. Mercurius had a devilish dark side to his nature, a tangible shadow similar to the Rudra and Bhairava forms of Shiva and the Old Testament Yahweh. Jesus had a table-tipping dark side too, but it was projected and personified as his evil twin, Lucifer. Lucifer was considered by the alchemists to be the light-bringer his name declares and was yet another name for Mercurius and the *prima materia*.

So unpredictable and dangerous was this dark side of Mercurius that he was often called "serpent" and "dragon"; so deeply duplicitous was his nature that he was usually represented as a winged hermaphrodite. Khunrath says Mercurius is generated from the hermaphroditic seed of the macrocosm and experiences an immaculate birth from the hermaphroditic matter. He is also, according to various authors, the earth of paradise, the goal of his own transformation, the stone, the philosophic gold, the tincture, the king, the light of lights; he is the *alexipharmakon* (that which renders poison harmless, like Shiva) and the *medicina catholica* (universal medicine); he is the Mediator, the Preserver, and the Healer; he is self-generating, self-transforming, self-reproducing, and self-destroying; he is divinity itself (or a very close second).

In the light of all his other qualities it may seem insignificant that Mercurius, like Shiva, was hermaphroditic, but in terms of identification it is quite important. We saw the real reason Shiva is known as a hermaphrodite, and I believe the same applies to Mercurius. The fact that Mercurius also has wings, like Agni in the seed-drinking story as well as doves and angels elsewhere, makes the similarity to fly agaric even greater. Add to this the fact that Mercurius represents both the raw material and the transforming elixir that takes a person to heaven and the identification is complete: Mercurius, the revealing angel who is at once the beginning, middle, and end of the work, the winged hermaphrodite who begins life beneath the ground but lifts himself up, is a nearly perfect personification of the fly agaric mushroom.

Dorn calls Mercurius the true hermaphroditic Adam and Microcosm who contains the perfections, virtues, and powers of the sun, ". . . and in his regeneration has obtained the power of above and below, wherefore he is to be likened to their marriage, as is evident from the *white and the red* that are joined in him"[75] [Italics mine]. There is a colorful painting of the divine hermaphrodite in Trismosin's *Splendor solis* which illustrates these descriptions and others (plate 38). The painting depicts the secret substance and all its transformations in the person of a two-headed angel standing beneath a tree. When the hermaphrodite Mercurius is shown with both male and female heads, as he is here, he is often called "rebis," a word that means "by things" and refers to a kind of riddle in which the secret is represented by pictoral clues. Puzzles and riddles by definition all have solutions, so there should be a solution to this rebis hidden in the painting.

> White-skinned lady, lovingly joined to her red-limbed husband, wrapped in each other's arms in the bliss of connubial union, merge and dissolve as they come to the goal of perfection: they that were two are made one, as though of one body.[76]

If the rebis does represent the fly agaric he is standing in the right place, beneath what looks like a type of fir tree. The creature's legs are painted in a way that suggests it is standing on only one leg, mushroom-fashion.

The two heads of the rebis are Sol, who is red, and Luna, who is white, and they represent the union of the sun and moon, another important and strange alchemical conception. They are the brother-sister hermaphrodite, in perpetual sexual congress, that gives birth to the stone. In the painting both heads have their eyes fixed on what appears to be an egg, held in the "lunar" left hand. This is the egg of the philosophers which has hatched out the double-headed hermaphrodite that now holds it, and it has a direct correspondence to the egg stage of the fly agaric (plate 39).

FIGURE 8

The mushroom in the photograph has a yellow veil because it was rained upon while still underground and absorbed color from the cap; this made it resemble a hard-boiled egg, but an egg nonetheless. It is also similar in appearance and relative size to Vreeswyck's depiction of a hand-held baby Sol, newly hatched from its storm-borne egg (fig. 8). Coincidentally, though probably by design, if the visible area of the egg in Trismosin's painting is traced it reveals the distinctive fly agaric shape, as if to say that this is what the egg contains (fig. 9).

As the mushroom embryo continues to grow it delineates into two spherical segments, the cap and the base. The base is rough and white, like the moon; the cap, now showing red beneath the cloudlike veil, looks like the rising sun. Metaphorically the mushroom has become the union of the sun and moon. If a mushroom at this stage is tipped horizontally and compared with the painting one can see why Sol and Luna are represented as two heads next to one another on the same body (plate 40).

FIGURE 9

The next clue is in the red and white wings of the rebis. The color connection to fly agaric is apparent, but the subtler implications are not. The third stage of the mushroom occurs when the cap separates from the base; first the stalk is revealed and then the annulus veil. This is the stage personified as the coitus of the hermaphrodite. As the *Museum hermeticum* says, "Sun and moon must have intercourse like that of a man and woman . . ."[77] (see plate 11). When the annulus drops, the feathery white gills are seen for the first time. A mushroom at this stage, with a section removed from the cap to reveal the gills, bears a strong likeness to the wings of the rebis, and even to his golden belt (plate 41).

There will still be those people who attribute such correspondences to "mere" coincidence, however unlikely. Perhaps anticipating this criticism the artist included one more clue, held in the angel's "solar" right hand. Variously described by other commentators as a mirror or target, the object does not lend itself to easy identification; yet when its identity is revealed it will seem almost too obvious, and the real meaning of the term "open secret" will be understood.

We will recall that before a fly agaric can be put to beneficial human use it must first be dried; to expedite the drying process and forestall worm invasions the stalk is often cut or broken off at the cap by the harvester; when the cap dries its color changes from red to golden or reddish-gold and the outer rim of the cap curls under. What the rebis is holding in its right hand is a dried fly agaric cap, with the gill side facing the viewer (plate 42). The artist has correctly placed the dried cap next to the red solar head to imply that they are the same thing at different stages (just as Luna holds the egg by its "lunar" bottom), and directly in front of the red wing to show precisely the difference in color between fresh and dried caps. The "mirror" at the center is where the stalk joined the cap and where the base used to "mirror" the cap in the second stage. The dark circle represents the bruised remnant of the stalk wall, while the larger white ring represents the gills. The orange outer circle corresponds perfectly in color and proportion to the margin of a dried cap that has curled back over the gills to reveal its golden hue; the artist has even painted in the gill striations that show through on the skin of the dried cap.

Without the secret of the secret—that the mushroom must be dried—the identification of the rebis was not enough; it was only after the material underwent all of its transformations, including drying, that it could participate in the transformation of humans. The *Turba* says that once the philosophers see the dragon changed wholly into blood ". . . they leave him a few days in the sun, until his softness is consumed, and the blood dries, and they find that poison." [78]

The tree gives birth to the egg; the egg gives birth to the sun and moon in one body; the body has sex with itself (see plate 11) and sprouts red and white wings; Sol and Luna are transformed by fire into the elixir (the dried cap): it's all in the painting, and it all fits the fly agaric perfectly. The "moon" holds the beginning of the work, the *prima materia* "egg"; the "sun" holds the end of the work, the "gold" of the philosophers.

> His soul rises up from [the secret substance] and is exalted to the heavens, that is, to the spirit, and becomes the red rising sun, waxing in Luna into the nature of the sun. And then the lantern with two lights [red and white], which is the water of life, will return to its origin, that is, to earth. And it becomes of low estate, is humbled and decays, and is joined to its beloved, the terrestrial sulphur. [79]

A black and white representation of the rebis from the *Rosarium* uses some of the same symbols as the *Splendor solis* painting but adds a few others (fig. 10). The rebis is standing on the *rotundum,* another version of the philosophical egg, from which three vomiting serpents emerge; this image implies that the serpent is another name for the mushroom, that it rises snakelike from beneath the ground, and that it can cause vomiting, especially in its "emergent" phase. The two heads of the rebis still represent the red sun and the white moon in sexual union; in this rendition Sol and Luna share a single crown covered with points. There is only one crown because the mushroom has only one crown, the many-pointed veil on top. Instead of an egg Luna holds a serpent by the throat, indicating her identity with the portion below the head, just as in the painting she held the bottom of the egg. Red Sol holds the cup (plate 33), which is filled, we presume, with the liquid equivalent of three "serpent heads," thereby identifying himself with the "head" of the creatures and giving the dosage at the same time.

FIGURE 10

The upraised wings convey several meanings. They look like bat wings, implying both descent into the underworld and flight under the light of the moon (the mystical experience of white light); the underside is striated, with parallel lines that run to the margins, like mushroom gills; the wavy shape of the wing corresponds to the convolutions of a dried cap; and the outline of the entire figure, including the skirt and the rotundum, is homologous to a mature, uplifted fly agaric specimen. The rebis stands next to a tree bearing sun-fruits, which are the same as Sol's red head. But Sol stands *next* to the tree, which is where the red fruit of the sun is really found, not in the tree; still the tree is absolutely necessary. Behind the figure is the red lion, another synonym for the substance and the mushroom. In the nest is the red phoenix, feeding her chicks with blood.

There are many bird analogues for the arcane substance (see below) but none so perfectly matched to the life cycle of the mushroom as is the phoenix. It is the red firebird, hatched from an egg, which spends all its life in its nest. It feeds its young with drops of blood, meaning that young mushrooms will be round and the color of blood. It lifts its fiery wings and "consumes itself" in flames, leaving nothing but "ashes" in the nest (plate 10). Some versions of the myth say the bird becomes a worm after it burns, an allusion to the worm infestation that is likely to occur by the time the mushroom's "wings" are fully uplifted; when they finish their work in an unharvested specimen only worms and "ash" remain in the nest. From its own ashes the firebird will then be reborn, whether phoenix or fly agaric.

Two more examples of rebis art should suffice to show that the similarity between the rebis and the mushroom was meant to be visual as well as verbal; I've roughly traced out what the artists may have intended as the solution to the puzzle (figs. 11 and 12).

Unless more convincing evidence to the contrary is presented, I think the hidden rebis stands revealed.

Mercurius is also the winged dragon (or serpent), dual-natured and dangerous. One of his names is Pantopthalmos, "All Eyes," because his body is covered with eyes; he lies everwaking on a "certain mountain" with some eyes open, some eyes closed. This image

FIGURE 11

brings to mind Indra, who had a thousand "eyes" covering his body, as well as Ezekiel, who saw eyes all around the burning "wheels." A more common name of the dragon is Uroboros, "Tail-eater," who fertilizes and begets himself only to devour and then once again give birth to himself in a manner similar to the phoenix. He is at once metallic and liquid, matter and spirit, cold and fiery, poison and healing medicine; he combines the cthonic nature of the serpent with the aerial nature of the bird. "Uroboros" is also a pun, because the Greek word for tail, *oura,* and the word for urine, *ouron,* both share the combining form *uro-.* "Tail-eater" therefore suggests "urine eater."

We can already recognize the fly agaric in these written descriptions of the dragon, but viewing alchemical portraits of Uroboros helps even more in the identification. An engraving from *Pandora* depicts the dragon as some sort of plant on a thick stalk, coyly named the "tree" of the philosophers; it already bears a resemblance to the fly agaric in its outline (fig. 13). By biting its own tail the dragon becomes the philosophical egg that will hatch out, in this instance, the double-headed red and white eagle. Connecting lines

FIGURE 12

declare that the sun, moon, and stars are all part of the egg.

To decipher the image we can begin with the dragon. The egg it has created represents the fly agaric egg, which also has a "head" and a "tail." The dragon or serpent is said to bite its tail because at this early stage the head, the cap, is "biting" the tail, the mushroom's base; that is, the lip of the cap is wrapped like a mouth around the base of the stalk. As the cap expands it opens its "mouth," which corresponds to the dragon releasing its tail to open the egg and hatch out the bird. The eagle then spreads its red and white wings and transforms into the elixir. Sol and Luna are present throughout the process as the cap and base, while the "stars" are the veil remnants on the cap.

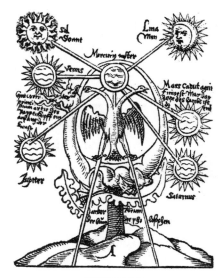

FIGURE 13

Another engraving from *Pandora* renders "our Mercurius" a little differently (fig. 14). Here the tail-eater is itself enclosed in a two-part egg, again similar to the fly agaric. Out of its lunar left foot, representing the base of the mushroom, arises a stalk that exfoliates in the manner characteristic of a fly agaric stalk. Once out of the egg the stalk divides into three different flowers, although since they stem from a single stalk they all must actually represent a single "flower." The three flowers shown are a red rose, a white rose, and a "flower of wisdom." In alchemy red and white roses are a code name for the fly agaric with its white "thorns," similar to the thorny flowers of the Song of Songs. "Flower of wisdom" describes the plant's effects.

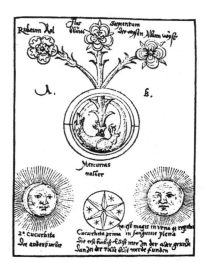

FIGURE 14

The way to slay the dragon and avoid his poison is described in the *Book of Lambspringk*;[80] substitute "mushroom" for "dragon" and the verse describes the fly agaric:

> A savage dragon lives in the forest, lacking not the strongest venom. When he sees the bright rays of the sun and its bright fire [after the rains], he scatters abroad his poison and flies upward so fiercely that no living creature can stand before him [a reference to the mushroom's amazing growing power], nor is even the basilisk equal to him. He who has skill to slay him wisely has escaped from all dangers [that is, the "slain" mushroom should be a fully mature specimen, and it must be dried before it is safe]. All his veins and colors are perceived in the hour of his death, *his venom becoming the greatest medicine* [because he has been "slain wisely"]. He quickly consumes his own venom [like Shiva], for he devours his own poisonous tail [as the whole mushroom dries, the "tail," the stalk, shrivels as if con-

sumed by the cap; first bitten, then consumed]. *All this is performed on his own body,* from which flows forth glorious balm, with all its miraculous virtues. Hereat all the sages do loudly rejoice. [Italics mine.]

Similarly, from the *Aurelia occulta:*[81]

I am the poison-dripping dragon, who is everywhere and can be cheaply had [due to its bad reputation]. That upon which I rest [the stalk], and that which rests upon me [the cap], will be found within me [in the egg] . . . My water and fire destroy and put together; *from my body you may extract* [the blood of] *the green lion and the red. But if you do not have exact knowledge of me, you will destroy your five senses with my fire.* From my snout [cap] there comes a spreading poison that has brought death to many [the taboo] . . . *I am the egg of nature,* known only to the wise . . . I am named Mercurius; my spouse is the gold; I am the old dragon . . . I come forth from heaven and earth . . . *I am the carbuncle* [a deep red stone] *of the sun,* the most noble purified earth. [Italics mine.]

FIGURE 15: The Tree of Life.

The secret dragon is imaginatively depicted in the *Opera chemica*[82] as a serpent wrapped around the tree of life (fig. 15). The tree grows through both a table and the white cup that rests upon it. Among clues that I believe are red herrings (or refer to obscure methodology) are several with strong correspondences to the fly agaric. The four figures at the corners "sprout from clouds" just as mushrooms indirectly do; they all should have two legs but stand on a single torso, making them in effect one-legged. The red and white clothing corresponds as well to the fly agaric.

The red-capped man in the chair declares, "I am the teacher of natural science." The man at the top left says, "Know that this dragon never dies except with his brother and sister," an allusion that identifies the dragon with red Sol and white Luna; when one dies they all die, because they are the same. Regarding this Maier says, "For whenever the heavenly sun and moon meet in conjunction, *this must take place in the head and tail of the dragon*; in this comes about the conjunction and uniting of sun and moon, when an eclipse takes place"[83] [Italics mine]. First the "moon" hides the "sun," then the sun overshadows the moon.

The man at the upper right says, "Know that this dragon kills himself with his own dart, by swallowing his own sweat." The "dart" is the stalk of the mushroom which "pierces" the cap; "swallowing his sweat" refers to the loss of liquid as the mushroom "kills itself" by drying out and shrivelling after sporulation. It also alludes to the sweat that pours from the consumer. The man at the lower left says, "I am the king, strong and powerful, and I fear nothing except that dragon." This represents the personified mushroom warning the reader that simply finding and eating the "king" mushroom does not guarantee a pleasant experience, even with dried specimens; a user must always watch out for that nasty dragon. The man at the lower right says, "I am the naked man and the subtle beggar, of a strong nature, for I bear arms and am made to kill the dragon." This may simply refer to the person strong enough to harvest and consume the mushroom.

The head of the dragon is shown as a white head with a white crown, which is analogous to the all-white egg phase of the mushroom (see plate 9). Directly below this head are three others, all of which are bleeding into the cup; these represent dried mushrooms being "bled" of their red juices. They are shown on the side of the cup in their former red color. Three heads on the cup indicate that three mushrooms is an average dosage; the red heads also imply that they *are* the cup. Every round, red mushroom "head" will become cup-shaped at full maturity, and the red that was on the outside will then be found inside the cup. The cup rests upon a flat, disc-shaped table, the table shape the cap assumes before it begins to form a cup. The artist seems intentionally to have created an analogue of the Round Table and the Grail cup filled with the blood of Jesus.

FIGURE 16

The bark of the tree above the cup is brown, while that below the table is white; this white bark is also distinguished from the brown roots that surround it. Tracing out the table and the white portions of the trunk (and the area just below it) renders an image remarkably similar to a fly agaric mushroom in its "table" phase, complete with dropped annulus (fig. 16).

The painting tells us in pictures that beneath the tree of life or knowledge, after a rain, can be found the white-crowned dragon, and blood-red "heads" that open up into round "tables"; each table in turn "holds" a cup of the sacred blood, because each table will itself *become* such a cup.

The circles are also quite suggestive, apart from the fact that we are seeing a red circle surrounded by white on a stalk. The outermost white circle says,

> Observe that at the end of the tenth month, the spouse is ready, who is then born, a
> most generous king, wearing a diadem on his head [since the mushroom season is

about two months long, a new season starts every ten months]. Therefore, take your king, coming from the fire, crowned with a diadem [the pointed veil remnants], and nourish him with his own milk [the white portion of the mushroom, where most of the liquid is], until he has attained his perfectly complete age and nature [a double reference: let the fiery mushroom reach full maturity before harvesting, and then dry it completely].

The second and third circles reveal still more:

And because he is prepared for begetting sons and creating daughters [he is "self-impregnating" and makes millions of spores], to replenish the earth and see his sons and daughters to the first, second, third, and fourth generation, know that these sons and daughters [new mushrooms] cannot perform remission except *by pressing out blood and sprinkling ash,* for there is no remission unless this is done. Pouring blood and sprinkling ash, this is the divine circle. [Italics mine.]

As important as it is to "press out the blood," it is also important to sprinkle "ash," creating a circle of use and propagation that ensures future generations.

The author has chosen his words well. "Pressing out blood" describes perfectly what was done to hydrated mushrooms in the Soma ceremony and elsewhere. "Sprinkling ash" is shaking and tapping a mushroom to release spores, something every conscientious forager does when harvesting.[84] "Remission," with its many shades of meaning, is a good word to describe what happens after the pressing, when the king and his children "perform." Remission is a relinquishing, a lessening of pain; it is pardon and healing; it is cessation and release.

The red circle, reminiscent of Soma's identity with Agni, says, "This is indeed the element of fire." The innermost golden circle says, "There will be a great question asked me by my friend, and he who has understood the great question clearly and well, shall have the philosophers' stone." If the right question isn't asked, no one understands anything.

Severed heads and the propagation motif appear again in another painting from *Splendor solis.* The gory dismemberment that is pictured is explained in a strange way:[85]

Rosinus relates of a vision he had of a man whose body was dead and yet beautiful and white like salt. The head had a fine golden appearance, but was cut off at the trunk, and so were all the limbs.

If "plant" is substituted for "man" in the above it describes a fly agaric harvest; this speculation is borne out by the rest of the passage:

. . . next to him stood an ugly man of black and cruel countenance [the harvester], with a blood-stained double-edged sword in his right hand, and he was the poor man's [plant's] murderer. In his left hand was a paper on which the following was written: "I have killed you, that you may receive a superabundant life, but *your head I will carefully hide,* that the world may not see you, and destroy you in the earth; *the body I will bury,* that it may putrefy and grow and bear innumerable fruit." [Italics mine.]

The author stresses the need to keep the harvested golden heads hidden so that the authorities won't discover the devilish practice and destroy the sacred mushroom groves and the alchemists along with them. One reason to bury the body is to hide the evidence: if no "bones" are found in the forest no one knows a murder [harvest] has taken place there (plate 13). The primary reason for burial is stated plainly: ". . . that it may putrefy and grow and bear innumerable fruit." The stalk of a fly agaric is somewhat sticky, a fact that causes innumerable spores to adhere to it during sporulation. If the stalk is buried beneath a fly agaric host species it will indeed putrefy, thereby releasing its many spores into the soil near the rootlets of the tree; if germination takes place a new mycelium can be established by a single spore. Cutting the "body" into pieces as the author suggests and burying them separately greatly increases the possibility of starting new mycelia, which in turn will "grow and bear innumerable fruit," just as the author says.

It is possible to induce fly agaric growth under the proper tree; I have done so myself by burying sporulating caps under a tree that had been a nonproducer for the first twelve years I had observed it. After two seasons of "burials" followed by abundant rains I was rewarded with a crop of five beautiful specimens; mushrooms have continued to sprout each year since then at an ever increasing rate. Ripley seems to be referring to propagation when he says the god Hermes (Mercurius) "watered his tree with that water and with his glass made the flowers grow high."[86] "That water" is the philosophical water or divine water that marks the end of the work of transformation. Dried mushrooms contain large numbers of viable spores, many of which pass into the drink that is made from them. Pouring some of this juice under the proper tree has the same effect as burying the mushroom and can cause the "flowers" to grow high if spores germinate and take hold. Mylius says, "The blood [juice] causes all unfruitful trees to bear fruit of the same nature as the apple [the red mushroom]."[87]

Some people in India must have also known about this method of propagation. In two different Puranas Parvati is described as missing her son Skanda so much that she sometimes poured pitchers of water beneath pine trees "as though feeding her son from her own breasts."[88] Skanda, we will recall, was the son with many identical heads, born without a mother on a mountainside from a white pot filled with Shiva's fiery seed.

Trees, fruits, and flowers as synonyms for the divine substance are commonplace. Since it was associated with or even *named* Adam, the secret fruit was sometimes called an apple, as above. Ventura says, "Sweet of smell is this apple, rich in color this little apple";[89] Figulus calls the divine fruit "the golden apple of the Hesperides, to be pluck't from the blest philosophic tree."[90] Dorn says the stone causes the most beautiful colors to appear when it flowers.

Likewise they have said that the fruit of their tree strives up to heaven, because out of the philosophic earth there arises a certain substance, like to the branches of a loathsome sponge . . . The point about which the whole art turns lies in the living things of nature . . . From a likeness not altogether remote they have called this material virgin's milk and blessed rose-colored blood . . . For in the blood of this stone is hidden its soul.[91]

A bleeding sponge? A hydrated fly agaric fits that description.

Blaise de Vigenere calls the *arcanum* the trunk of the tree of death that sends out a red death ray.[92] Pordage says, "Here I saw the fruit and herbs of paradise, whereof my eternal man should thenceforward eat, and live."[93] Pseudo-Aristotle speaks of the stone's double nature: "Gather the fruits, for the fruit of this tree has led us into the darkness and through the darkness."[94] The fruits of the tree are the sun and moon, the immortal fruits that have life and blood.

The *Rosarium* (Rose garden) says Mercurius is cold and moist; so is a fly agaric, as well as so many other things. The text becomes more specific:

> . . . he is the whole elixir of the whiteness and the redness, and the permanent water, and the water of life and death and the virgin's milk, the herb of ablution [a double meaning: a plant that "washes" one, and a plant upon which water must be poured] and a living fountain [Shiva; the urinating man offering "water" to Krishna's friend; Jesus; the Anishinaubeg mushroom shaman] of which who shall drink does not die [in spite of taboos to the contrary]. He [the elixir] takes on colors and is their medicine, causing them to acquire colors [as Moses did], and he is that which mortifies [makes as if dead], dessicates and moistens [two double meanings: the mushroom itself dries and is later moistened, and the consumer dries out internally by being "moistened" with floods of perspiration], makes warm and cool [sweating copiously while one has the chills, for example], and does contrary things . . . And when alive, he performs certain kinds of operations [growth, sporulation, etc.], and when dead, others [shrinking, changing color and chemical make-up]; and when in the state of sublimation, others again [sublimation means refinement or purification, i.e., drying or cooking; it also means being "lifted up"], and again others when in the state of solution. And he is the dragon who marries himself and impregnates himself, and brings to birth in due time, and slays all living things with his poison.[95]

We can see how easy it was for the alchemists to keep renaming and reinterpreting their secret substance; as long as a metaphor fitted it was considered worthy to keep in the lexicon, and each new name became a way to confuse even further the noninitiated. The *prima materia* is Mercurius is the dragon is the hermaphrodite is the stone is the tree is the fruit is the gold is the tincture is the elixir—the list goes on and on, and gets even stranger.

Mercurius was also called the salamander and the serpent, especially the brazen or metallic serpent. The latter was often depicted hanging from a cross to show its identity with the metallic serpent of Moses and with Jesus (fig. 17). I believe these serpents represent the same thing they do in the Moses story: the twisting, metallic, serpentine caps of dried fly agaric shown in plate 19. Other artists were just as imaginative in their depictions of the drying process; though some of these are more literal renderings than those of the crucified serpents, they are still quite hidden from profane understanding. In one work an alchemist is drying his "salamander" next to a roaring fire (fig. 18); the salamander's body is similar to a dried cap without its stalk (fig. 19). The serpent in another illustration is also drying over a fire; the naked figures represent water (and perhaps poison) leaving the serpent as it dries (fig. 20). One alchemist described the process this way: "Only dissolve and coagulate me long, wash and cook me, then you won't go wrong. *And so by roasting draw the foulness,* as many a philosopher has been advised."[96] [Italics mine.]

FIGURE 17

Birds play a central role in many alchemical metaphors, as we might expect if the fly agaric was being used; we have already seen winged creatures and red and white eagles. Lambspringk's engraving of a forest tree with two nesting birds carries the following inscription:

> A nest is found in the forest, in which Hermes [Mercurius] has his birds; one always strives to fly upward, while the other rejoices to sit quietly in the nest; yet neither can get away from the other. *The one that is below holds the one that is above, and will not let it get away from the nest, as a husband in a house with his wife, bound together in closest bonds of wedlock.*[97] [Italics mine.]

FIGURE 18

The "nest" is where the mushroom "egg" is found and where the "birds" hatch; the cap strives upward and lifts its "wings" but can't escape because it remains attached to "the one below." The author says they are bound together in a way that resembles the sexual intercourse of humans, "the closest bonds of wedlock," a most strange analogy unless both refer to the fly agaric (see plates 11 and 12).

Lambspringk expresses the same image in a slightly different way in the text of another engraving: "In India is found a beautiful wood in which two birds are bound together. *One is white as snow, the other red,* and they bite each other dead. As one devours the other, both are changed into a white dove."[98] When seen in profile the fully mature mushroom appears

FIGURE 19

FIGURE 20

FIGURE 21

completely white; the red on the top of the "wings" is hidden from sight.

An alchemist named Senior had a vision of these same birds (fig. 21). An old alchemist is holding in his lap a book entitled *The Book of Secrets,* which he holds open for all to see even though it is secret. Senior says the whole science of alchemy is hidden in this open book, and I have to agree with him. At the bottom of the left-hand page sits the philosophical egg in its all-white moon phase. As we know, this egg hatches and becomes the tail-eating dragon, sometimes depicted as two dragons or, as here, a wingless dragon on the bottom and a bird on top. By placing the moon and sun above the bird the artist signifies that this tail-eating is the same as the union of white Luna and red Sol; like the bird releasing the dragon, the sun sprouts wings when it lets go of the moon.

On the right-hand page of the book the moon is again at the bottom, this time surrounded by two concentric circles. Senior says it is the circle of the moon surrounded by a sexual embrace called "two in one"; the outer circle he calls the "single sun." These three circles taken together are another representation of the sexual union of Sol and Luna and are an accurate rendering of a fly agaric as viewed from the bottom, very similar to the depiction in the rebis painting and the corresponding photograph (see plates 38 and 42). The moon represents either the bottom of the base of the mushroom or the white circle left after removing the stalk; the moon's white rays are the white gills with the annulus veil removed; and the wide outer ring, the "single sun," is the downturned red cap. The sexual union Senior mentions, the "two in one," we recognize as the "coitus" of the stalk and the cap.

The two suns at top right both have descending lines (called "rays" by Senior) that touch the circle below them to establish their identity with the cap of the mushroom and perhaps to suggest that the harvested mushroom should be put in the sun to dry. Three suns are on this page, again corresponding to dosage.

An engraving from *Atalanta fugiens* shows an alchemist holding a sword above an egg sitting upright on its larger end. The motto says to cut the egg with a fiery sword, but the text later declares that no sword is necessary. After explaining the transformation of the four elements the text continues:

> and while all [earth, water, fire, and air] are copulating, a specific form originating from
> the stars produces an individual, a certain species of bird, namely that to which the egg
> belongs *and in which the semen is infused* [cf. Agni, the semen-infused dove] . . . I also tell you
> that no instrument [for cutting the egg] will be produced except for our white powder,

star-like, splendid, and deriving from the white stone; and this powder will constitute the appropriate instrument for cutting the egg. However, they have never named the egg nor revealed the bird of that egg.[99]

The white stone and the white egg are the same thing; the "cutting by the white powder" is accomplished when the white "powder" of the universal veil tears apart; no fiery sword is needed, but the "cutting" exposes the fiery cap and releases it; the veil remnants dotting the cap are the "star-like" portion of the white "powder."

More eggs and birds appear throughout the illustrations of *Speculum veritatis,* a poorly drawn but highly suggestive work. In the first drawing the alchemist holds two upright eggs in one hand and the sun in the other, held by a stalk-sized ray; he is showing the viewer what will come from the eggs, and how big it will be (fig. 22). One-legged Vulcan, a mushroom personification, sits beneath a tree that is also a furnace for refining the "gold." The alchemist is entrusting his egg to Vulcan and his tree, so that the sun can hatch. If the handheld sun is placed on top of each of the vessels in the furnace they become homologues of the mushroom.

FIGURE 22

The second illustration has Vulcan standing before a strange mushroom-shaped apparatus; the tower is banded like an exfoliated fly agaric stalk and the "cap" is filled with birds, indicating that this is the birdlike portion of the mushroom (fig. 23). Two hens brood over their eggs while Mercurius watches over all. Vulcan is applying heat to the collecting vessels to show that juice of the fresh mushroom can be heated to bring about the desired chemical changes; this is a variation on drying the mushroom and accomplishes the same thing. The fiery devices Vulcan is using are more clearly shown in another illustration from the same work (fig. 24). We can now see that the device is a sword handle and hilt; the top of the hilt is in flames. His left hand holds the splitting philosophical egg; his right holds a fiery fly agaric by the stalk, the cap shown in cross-section.

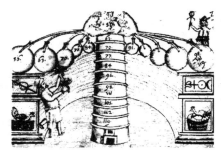

FIGURE 23

In the fourth illustration the "chicken of the wise" nests in the tree of the philosophers, telling us that this is where such eggs are to be found (fig. 25). Mercurius drives a sword through the king, pinning him to the tree; the philosopher does the same with a serpent. The king and serpent are both the fly agaric; being pinned to the tree means that the mushroom will be found only near certain trees. The mushrooms

FIGURE 24

FIGURE 25

can't escape, and they meet their deaths there. Mercurius holds his caduceus towards the ground at the king's feet to indicate where to look for him. The alchemist holds in his left hand the "arrow of Mercurius," which is another fly agaric homologue: the point is the mushroom's base; the shaft is its stalk; the cross-piece is the annulus; and the flaming triangle is the fiery cap.

Another surprising animal found masquerading as the secret substance is the unicorn, which for the alchemists was both their stone and their savior Jesus; this animal too has correspondences to the fly agaric. The horn of the unicorn was considered to possess magical qualities; powdered horn would cure any ailment when eaten and immersing the horn in water rendered any poison safe to drink. Because of the latter quality cups made of unicorn horn were in great demand by those who had enemies.

The unicorn's having only one horn is analogous to the mushroom standing on only one foot or leg, as in Soma's epithet "Not-born Single-foot." Soma as the red bull was known for sharpening his horns in the ground (one at a time) and churning up the soil, and so was the unicorn. When seen in profile at maturity the upturned cap can be seen as the horns of a bull, a ready metaphor for the cattle-raising Aryans. On closer examination, however, it is seen that what looked like two horns is actually only one "horn," in the shape of a cup. The fly agaric is a horn that becomes a cup, as is the unicorn horn, and it too has "magical" powers. It is a "poison" that through heating becomes nonpoisonous. The mushroom gained a reputation for being able to render any poison harmless, the same as unicorn horn. By the time the mushroom reaches its maximum cup-shape at the end of sporulation its poison is already converting to a more enlightening chemical, and the cup soon becomes salutary.

The fly agaric has long been known and used for its curative properties; today in Germany we can find in almost any pharmacy bottles of *Amanita muscaria* tincture *(Agaricus muscarius)*, available by prescription. It has been used for many years without any patient experiencing negative side effects; on the contrary, most report a positive effect on mood as well as improved mental and physical well-being. Among other things it is used for the treatment of depression, nervous tics, paresis of the bladder, epileptiform ailments, menopausal flushing, hyperhydrosis, melancholy, mental weakness, Parkinson's disease, and as a tonic. *Heating the tincture to boiling increases the effects* by converting ibotenic acid into muscimol, which is five to ten times stronger than the former.[100] Maybe the alchemists were close to accurate when they called the horn of the unicorn a panacea.

The unicorn is known for its fierceness and wildness and for its inability to be domesticated; though it has, they say, an unusual fondness for virgin maids. Spying a virgin in the forest the unicorn will approach and lay its horn in her lap, at which time hunters can rush in and saw off the horn. This is a metaphor for the mushroom growing only in virgin earth and for its phallic appearance when poking its head out of the virgin's "lap." The horn is aggressively masculine while the cup is receptively feminine, paralleling the dual sexuality of the hermaphrodite.

Since the unicorn and the lion are the bitterest of enemies another method of capture was devised. A man wearing the skin of a lion will go to the haunts of the unicorn and stand before a tree. When the unicorn sees the ersatz animal it will charge with its horn; the man steps aside at the last moment and causes the horn to stick fast to the tree, and then he saws it off. This image is the same motif seen above when the king and serpent were similarly stuck to a tree, and it means the same thing: the fly agaric is bound to its host tree. In a variation of the theme, tapestries and other artworks often portrayed the unicorn lying next to the tree of life, with a fence encircling both.

A clever poem from *Theatrum chemicum* describes another quality the unicorn and the fly agaric have in common:

> *I am the right true unicorn.*
> *What man can cleave me hoof [base] from horn [cap]*
> *And join my body up again*
> *So that it no longer falls in twain?*[101]

As we have seen, the alchemists sometimes called their stone a carbuncle, a deep red stone; Khunrath calls it a "shimmering carbuncle light" and "the carbuncle stone shining in the firelight," for example. Legend held that this carbuncle stone could be found under the horn of the unicorn. The Grail author Wolfram von Eschenbach writes:

> *We caught the beast called unicorn*
> *That knows and loves a maiden best*
> *And falls asleep upon her breast;*
> *We took from underneath his horn*
> *The splendid* male *carbuncle stone*
> *Sparkling against the white skull-bone.*[102] *[Roman emphasis mine.]*

There are two ways in which the mushroom can be seen as a horn digging up the ground. First, the young mushroom with its many white "horns" breaks up the earth like a horned beast and then forms its single horn, as described above. Wolfram describes the second way in his poem, where the stone is found *under* the horn. This apparent contradiction is easily resolved by picturing a mature specimen with upturned cap and then inverting the specimen. Now the base and stalk of the mushroom become the single horn, which the unicorn sticks into the ground or "into" a tree; the stalk joining the now inverted bowl-shaped white gills corresponds to the horn joining the animal's skull. Underneath the horn, sparkling against the white "skull," is found the beautiful red stone.

Could this identity of unicorn horn and fly agaric be what the alchemist Scaliger

FIGURE 26

FIGURE 27

FIGURE 28

intended to portray in his strange depiction of a unicorn at the ear of the pope, who wears an elaborate stacked crown surmounted by a phoenix? (figs. 26 and 27.)

Breasts should have nothing at all to do with alchemy, yet they play a prominent part in the literature and artwork. In an engraving by Schwan a woman stands in the Red Sea; like Vulcan she stands on only one leg (fig. 28). She represents the secret substance, which she is expressing from her breasts as virgin's milk and blood, indicating the colors of the mushroom as well as its breastlike shape, as in plate 24. The dragon in the sea represents the dried mushroom, which even when fully saturated will float on water. The two streams issuing from the dragon's head are the two liquid forms of the mushroom.

"Its father is the sun, its mother the moon . . . its nurse is the earth." How would the alchemists illustrate these central tenets of their Art? A literal rendering of the famous saying, again by Schwan, is typical of the genre (fig. 29). The baby's parentage is obvious: he is the image of his father the sun, only in miniature, for "as above, so below"; the baby's head with its pointed rays is homologous to a young fly agaric cap. His mother the moon nurses the secret baby while standing in an underground stream, where her feet appear to be bound; in fly agaric symbolism this means that the mushroom's base is bound to one spot in the earth, and it draws its moisture from beneath the ground. Superimposed on her body is an image of the whole earth; looking carefully below her right breast we see that she has actually penetrated the earth from beneath, like a mushroom; her lower portion is underground. Even though the baby nurses directly from the moon's white breast (the mushroom's base) he indirectly nurses from the earth through her.

At the right is the nest of the red and white birds, representing the next stage of the mushroom's growth. The bottom bird corresponds to the moon, bound to the bottom of the nest; the top bird is the upraised solar cap, bound to the bottom "bird." At the left a salamander with "stars" on its back frolics in the fire as it is transformed into the philosophical gold. Additionally, the dark, round earth with its patchy continents and white legs is homologous to a fly agaric in its "fruit on a post" phase.

FIGURE 29

A similar image is found in an illustration accompanying Melchior's famous alchemical paraphrase of the Mass (fig. 30).[103] The alchemist-as-priest is shown offering praise to Mary, the mother of Jesus, who is shown at the left nursing her son. This engraving exemplifies the way some alchemists Christianized the Work; we can see that Luna has become Mary, who sits in the cusp of the moon. Sol has become Jesus, symbolized by the solar flares surrounding Mary; tracing the lunar and solar portions yields an image strikingly similar to a "nursing" mushroom (fig. 31; compare to plate 1).

The Mass begins by identifying Jesus as the inspiration for the sacred art and as the stone itself, descending

FIGURE 30

> like rain upon the fleece, and as showers falling gently upon the earth . . . O salutary medicine for men, that cures every weakness of the body: O sublime fount whence gushes forth truly the true water of life into the garden of your faithful.

Following the gospel the *Ave praeclara,* an alchemical hymn to Mary, is to be sung. The hymn begins with praise of the woman who bears God, she who is

FIGURE 31 (tracing of fig. 30)

> divinely born for the enlightenment of nations . . . Virgin, ornament of the world, queen of heaven, elect above all *like the sun, lovely* as *the light of the* moon . . . *Let us drink in steadfast faith* [you won't die] of the sweet stream that flowed from the rock in the desert, and . . . *gaze upon the crucified brazen serpent.* O Virgin, who has been made mother by the sacred fire [because she "gives birth" to the fiery cap] and the Father's word [lightning and thunder], which you bore *like the Burning Bush,* let us, *as cattle ringstreaked, speckled and spotted* [milkable fly agaric caps], draw near with our feet [Take off your shoes!], with pure lips [with which to eat] and heart. [Italics mine.]

FIGURE 32

Melchior ends by saying that the hymn must be sung: "it shall be called the "testament of the art," *since the whole chemical art is concealed therein,* and blessed is he that understands this sequence" [Italics mine].

Sol and Jesus aren't the only heroes to nurse at Alchymia's breasts; the occasional toad horns its way to the breast as well, an occurrence depicted in *Atalanta fugiens.* The motto describes the ostensible action: "Lay a toad on the breast of the woman so that she, suckling it, may die as the toad grows big with her milk."[104] The ancient European toad deity lent his name to only one fungus: the wart-backed fly agaric, known throughout Europe and elsewhere by one of its oldest names, toadstool. In this instance the toad is another name for baby Sol, the recently born secret substance. Instead of solar rays the segmented veil is depicted as warts, and the cap as the body of a toad; the white "breast" of the round base remains the same in both cases. This is a picturesque way of admonishing foragers to let the cap keep "nursing" until the base shrivels and the cap reaches its full size.

The *Symbola aurea* presents an image of breasts that is perhaps even more obscure than that of the nursing toad (fig. 32). The motto reads "By the ignited art the shadow is bereft of a thick body."[105] Behind the naked woman Vulcan holds fire next to her shadow as if trying to shrink it; but is he? The alchemist is pointing directly at the flaming heart held by the woman, but he also points directly at her breasts, leaving the viewer to infer the connection between them; both breasts and heart correspond to the mushroom. The woman's shadow looks nothing at all like her body; it does, however, approximate the shape of an inverted fly agaric stalk, indicating that the drying process is being discussed. The handle of the adze upon which Vulcan is leaning has the same shape as the woman's shadow; in fact, except for the head's snubbed end, the adze is the shape and size of a large fly agaric specimen. As Vulcan ostensibly applies heat to the shadow he is really heating the adze, thereby depriving it of a "thick body." The last clue is the flaming heart itself, analogous to a fully upturned mushroom that has its "fire" inside the cup; this is also the best time to harvest and dry such a specimen.

Drinkable Gold

No discussion of alchemy would be complete without mentioning the liquid forms of the stone, variously called the philosophical water, our water, permanent water, divine water, red tincture, drinkable gold, rose-colored blood, poison, vinegar, sea water, urine, and many other names; not surprisingly this "blessed water" is sometimes named Mercurius, dragon, serpent, and stone. As confusing as these names appear there was general agreement that the water, by whatever name, must be extracted from the *prima materia* or the stone; the water represented the perfection of the art, the tinctured stone, while the serpent and dragon usually referred to the raw, unrefined material. Also relevant to the liquid stone are the many references to the ageing king (the mature mushroom) drowning in water or drinking so much water that he dissolves, in both instances only to be reborn later young and healthy.

As we know, the fly agaric has two liquid forms: a water extract of the dried caps (or the heated juice of fresh caps), and the urine of a bemushroomed person. References to extracting the divine water abound in the literature, as well as in an unsettling number of visual representations of little men urinating into containers.

A woodcut from the *Rosarium* depicts a fountain of philosophical water, over which are poised a double-headed dragon and Sol and Luna, who explain their identities to the reader:

> We are the metals' first nature and only source, the highest tincture of the art is made through us. No fountain and no water has my like. I make both rich and poor men whole or sick, for deadly can I be and poisonous.[106]

In his allegory of the waters Lambspringk does his confusing best to explain how the waters are extracted.[107] The last three engravings of the series portray the king, first about to eat his son; then lying in bed; and finally seated on his throne opposite his son, with a winged Mercurius between them. In the accompanying verses the king can be seen as both the secret substance and the experimenting philosopher. In the first verse the king is the alchemist and his son is the renewed substance. Seeing his son coming, the king became extremely happy. "But when the son entered the father's house, the father took him to his heart and swallowed him out of joy, and that with his own mouth."

The engraving of the king in bed has this verse: "Now the father sweated on account of his son [because he had just eaten the secret substance], and earnestly beseeched God . . . *to bring forth his only son from his body* [a double intention, referring both to the urine of the alchemist and to propagation of the mushroom], and restore him to his former life [now as impregnated urine, and later as a new mushroom]." God answers by having the father lie down and sleep, and then sends a great rain, a "fertilizing, silvery rain, *which bedewed and softened the father's body*" [Italics mine]. Here the king represents the mushroom once again. In order to bring back the king's son, the body of the king (a mushroom) is buried ("he sleeps") beneath the appropriate tree; after "great rains," spores from the decomposing king form a new mycelium.

In the last verse the propagation is complete; even though the king was "changed entirely into limpid water" by the rain, he's back:

> And there is now a strong and beautiful father, and he brings forth a new son, which forever remains in the father [as spores], and the father in the son [as spores] . . . *they produce untold fruit* that can never perish anymore, and can, nevermore die any death

[because mycelia can live for hundreds of years]. By the grace of God they abide for-ever, the father and the son, triumphing gloriously. Upon one throne they sit [the same mushroom], and the face of the ancient master is straightaway seen between them. *He is arrayed in a crimson robe.* Laud and glory to God alone. [Italics mine.]

The softening of the king's body with water also describes the hydration process for dried mushrooms. Basil Valentine seems to have understood the whole process quite well:

The king imparts great strength and potency to his water and tinges it with his own color, that thereby he may be consumed [swallowed] . . . and in its essence it must have an abundance of blood like the pelican [phoenix], which . . . rears up many young ones with its blood. This tincture is the rose of our masters, of purple hue, called also the red blood of the dragon, or the purple cloak of the Supreme Lord of our art [the crimson robe cited above], with which the Queen of Salvation is covered [red Sol covering Luna] . . . *Carefully preserve this mantle of glory* together with the astral salt [the universal veil] which is joined to this heavenly sulfur [the cap] and screens it from harm [pre-cisely what the veil on the cap does][108] [Italics mine].

In the *Crowne of Nature* Luna joins Sol in the water after they have been heated and pow-dered (calcined): "Thus Sol and Luna are philosophically calcined with the first water, *and their bodies are made spongious* and subtle that the *second water* may have the better ingression to work his effort"[109] [Italics mine].

FIGURE 33

The bath of Sol and Luna is given a rather lurid twist, even for alchemy, in Eleazar's rendition (fig. 33). The bath is combined with the "slaughter of the innocents" motif, one of alchemy's more unusual metaphors for the *arcanum*. All the action takes place near a tree; next to the tree is a well into which Sol and Luna are about to immerse themselves. Sol-diers busy themselves killing children. In the short text[110] the author uses all the metaphors he can think of for the secret substance:

Dissolve the king or the queen in this red blood of chil-dren, then the sun and moon will take their bath in it . . . A king stands with a naked sword while his soldiers slay the innocent children and gather their blood. They throw them into the well in order to color it still more, the well being already filled with blood.

Next the author mixes metaphors even more, further confounding the ignorant while elu-cidating the meaning for the initiate:

Therefore they have poured these volatile birds with solar and lunar feathers over the python [serpent]; then the python has again melted into these birds. Then they have poured out the clear solution and once more thrown it over a new python and so obtained a fat and heavy liquor. Then they have united the king and queen and poured them together.

The philosophical fountain is nowhere more curiously illustrated than in Michalspacher's *Cabala* (fig. 34). The artist must have thought he was putting up a good front by having Jesus squatting in the fountain of life, even though he is surrounded by the symbols of a heretical mystery cult. Fortunately the cult of Jesus had nearly as many strange symbols as alchemy. Jesus was, after all, the water of life, and for the alchemists he was a personification of their stone, as in the *Aquarium sapientum*:

> Thus we have briefly and simply considered the unique and heavenly foundation and cornerstone Jesus Christ, that is to say how he is compared and united with the earthly philosophical stone of the sages, whose material and preparation, as we have heard, is an outstanding type and image of the incarnation of Christ.[111]

The engraving renders this quotation rather literally, as we shall see.

The fountain sits within the philosopher's protected garden; usually depicted as a garden of white and red roses, this one is nothing but trees, suggesting it is a sacred grove. Surrounding the garden is a grape arbor, symbolizing the need to press out the savior's blood like wine from grapes. The porticoes on either side with their pillars and caps are homologous to the fly agaric.

The three round basins of the fountain are connected visually with Jesus' crowned head, so we might suspect that they also represent the mushroom; certainly they do resemble upturned mushrooms, although the design is typical of the time. Yet there are three basins, an average dose if they represent mushrooms, and each one is filled with blood; all the standing figures are mushroom analogues, not the least of which is Mercurius at the top, standing one-legged on a round-bottomed pillar.

The entire garden is surrounded by a rainbow and clouds, indicating that all of the symbols arise after rain has fallen. A bird flies from God through the clouds and into the basin at Jesus' head; it represents both the holy spirit and the mushroom. Another bird flies back to God (through Mercurius' heart) from the wine press where a cross-carrying Jesus is having his blood squeezed out by a winged angel. This bird represents the spirit of the mushroom returning to the heavens to await rebirth by way of the rainclouds.

The stream of blood flows under the grape arbor, touches the large basin, and then seemingly enters Jesus and flows out of his side, creating an identity between all these features. Jesus offers cups of his blood to Sol and Luna, signifying that this is what these "cups" contain. Pointed crowns are on the ground next to the pair, indicating where such crowns are found. Below the scene the planets, portrayed as practicing alchemists, point

FIGURE 34

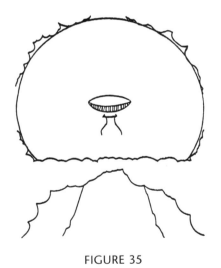

FIGURE 35

their bellows at the flaming swords that block their way; this illustrates the need to subject the stone to fire before trying to enter paradise, as well as the "trial by fire" the mushroom experience represents.

In what may be only a fortuitous coincidence, a tracing of certain elements of the engraving produces a fairly accurate rendering of a young, unopened mushroom, the clouds suggesting rain as well as the cloudlike veil (fig. 35). The image is mirrored by Jesus and the basin at his head, except that this second image represents the same mushroom at maturity, with cap upturned and annulus dropped, and now we see why he is squatting with his knees out. Both images are cut off at the same place on the bottom to show that they represent the same specimen at different times and also to show how much of the base is usually found in soil. These hidden images could be intentional, and not merely coincidental, because Michalspacher prefaces his engravings with this clearly stated challenge to the viewer: "Cabala and Alchemy give you the highest medicine as well as the Stone of the Wise in which alone the foundation rests, *as can be seen to this day in these figures by anyone who has eyes*"[112] [Italics mine].

With so many strange synonyms for the substance and the work of the alchemist, calling the water of life "urine" probably didn't seem any more odd to an uncomprehending public than all the talk of blood, dragons, and the rest, but in this case "urine" was meant literally. When everyone outside of alchemy believed that all names were only synonyms for an unnamed substance, it became possible to refer openly to a real substance used in the work. Who on earth (save Brahmins and Parsis) would believe that the urine referred to by the alchemists actually referred to urine?

The *Speculum veritatis* contains two quite graphic depictions of Our Water. "Water," as is well-known, is used around the world as a euphemism for urine. In the first example the philosopher symbolizing Mercurius stands by a furnace holding two objects (fig. 36). His right hand holds a bunch of grapes wrapped by a speckled serpent, both of which are fly agaric metaphors. In his left hand is the caduceus of Mercurius, consisting of a stalk wrapped by a rising serpent; the serpent's head merges with a bird from whose head issues fire. These again are all mushroom metaphors. From a cloud above, the *homunculus* (the mysterious "little man" of alchemy) urinates into the heating vessels of the arcane substance.

In the second example Adam stands at the left holding a serpent and pointing to a bird; he also points to the alchemist's kettle to show where the snake and bird are to go (fig. 37). Above Adam a red rooster mounts a white hen in a familiar image that is echoed on the right by the two stacked balls above the vomiting fountain; above these is a caged bird representing the harvested mushroom. The alchemist standing on the right holds in his left hand a stylized egg surmounted by a cross and elevates a mushroom-sized Mercurius with his right. From the clouds the *homunculus* relieves himself into the alchemical brew.

FIGURE 36

The author of *Gloria mundi* describes a procedure similar to the pictured urination: "The spirit which is extracted from the metals *is the urine of children and of the sages, for it is the seed* and the primal matter of metals. Without this seed there is no consummation in our art"[113] [Italics mine]. Notice that the author identifies urine with seed, a confusion we have seen before.

A painting from *Splendor solis* depicts the philosophical fountain as two conjoined basins, each with its own pissing manikin standing on top of stacked mushrooms (fig. 38). The alchemist stands astride the two basins dressed for battle; in one basin is white water, in the other red. Taken together they form a stylized representation of a young fly agaric on its side, with cap, stalk, and base. The fountain is next to what appear to be fir trees. The text on the man's shield advises first to make one water out of two, then to give the sun and moon to drink of the "inimical wine." The "two waters" are the prepared mushroom juice and ordinary urine; after the juice is drunk the two become one in the now potentiated urine. Since Sol and Luna are already in the body as juice or consumed caps, drinking the recycled water "gives them to drink." Thus will the alchemist "obtain vision at their death."

FIGURE 37

FIGURE 38: The red and white alchemical fountain.

Urine-drinking is portrayed in an unusual fashion in Valentine's eleventh *Key* (fig. 39). Two figures ride lions, symbols of the secret substance and hold "hearts" into

FIGURE 39

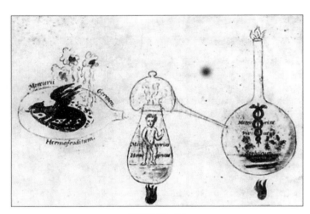

FIGURE 40

which are pouring the contents of the sun and moon. The lion on the right is urinating, and her children are greedily drinking up the flood. Valentine says the engraving depicts the "multiplication" of the red tincture.

A final visual example of this theme comes from the *Cabala mineralis,* which illustrates the transformations of Mercurius (fig. 40). The figure on the left is the "germinating hermaphrodite" biting its tail within the philosophical egg, upon which rain is showering; rain is, of course, the very thing that germinates the fly agaric egg. The middle figure depicts an alchemical vessel being heated. The alchemists did use vessels shaped like this object, but may have copied nature to get the design; we have to see that the figure is almost identical to a separating fly agaric.

Mercurius personifies the phallic mushroom as he stands upon one leg and urinates into the vessel. Written directly across his urination is *"Mercurius Homogenens,"* "Mercurius generated from identical parents"; that is, the urine has the same "parents" as little Mercurius and the dragon: the sun-moon hermaphrodite mushroom, which produces offspring identical to itself.

On the right is *"Mercurius vivus sophorum,"* "Mercurius of living wisdom," a round-bottomed vessel with a long cylindrical neck; the vessel is open at the top and flames issue from it. The figure is a homologue of a mature mushroom, except for one thing: where the fiery cap should be, or the outspread wings of the dragon, only flames remain. The alchemist, like Moses before him, has succeeded in making water from the fiery stone. The secret substance has been completely transformed into the conjoined liquids within the flask: it has become the elixir, the drinkable gold, the water of living wisdom. The top is open to symbolize the release from bodily bondage already attained by Mercurius and awaiting the thirsty philosopher.

Certain alchemists were philosophers in the purest sense of the word; wisdom, beauty, and love had arisen in them through the instrumentality of the secret stone and the powerful experiences it engendered. Some of them died only to come back to life; others were for a time rapt in the mystical coupling of the soul and God, bathed and made whole by the blissful light that streamed over them. When they spoke of the higher art of alchemy they knew whereof they spoke, and some of them did so beautifully. The true philosopher's devotion to the art is eloquently given voice below in an alchemical paraphrase of a well-known passage from the book of Proverbs. Yet even in the midst of lavish praises the author felt compelled to mention that in the use of the stone a person must be prepared to work hard and persevere:

> She it is that Solomon chose to have instead of light, and above all beauty and health; in comparison of her he compared not unto her the virtue of any precious stone . . . to gain her is better than the merchandise of silver and the most pure gold. And her fruit is more precious than all the riches of this world, and all the things that are desired are not to be compared with her. Length of days and health are in her right hand, and in her left hand glory and infinite riches. Her ways are beautiful and praiseworthy, not unsightly nor ill-favored, and her paths are measured and not hasty, but are bound up with stubborn and day-long toil. She is a tree of life to them that lay hold on her, and an unfailing light. Blessed shall they be who retain her, for the science of God shall never perish, as Alphidius bears witness, for he says: He who has found this science, it shall be his rightful food forever.[114]

Was there a true and physical philosophers' stone? It appears that there was. Did some of these phrase-making lovers of wisdom really drink the red tincture and the water of life, as they so insistently claimed? Evidently they did, and it opened for them the light of heaven.

> Hermes the prince. After so many wounds inflicted on mankind, here by God's counsel and the help of the art flow I, a healing medicine. Let him drink me who can: let him wash who will: let him trouble me who dare: drink, brethren, and live.[115]

13

An Artistic Conspiracy?

ARTISTS AND POETS HAVE ALWAYS BEEN the avant-garde of society, venturing into uncharted territories to break new ground and the taboos of the timid. Sometimes, however, discretion is the better part of valorous art and artists are forced by intolerance to be more circumspect than they might otherwise be. The discovery of what I believed were intentionally hidden images in the alchemical art led me to look with the same eye at other European artwork of the time to see if artists outside alchemy were indulging in this type of artistic subterfuge. Some of the results of this nonexhaustive search have already been shown, and several more works are presented here, if only for the purpose of piling even more unlikely coincidences on top of an already tall stack.

The alchemical motif of the pissing boy appears in Titian's *Bacchanal of the Andrians* (plate 43). In the foreground a young Dionysian figure lifts his gown and urinates into the stream of "wine" that is flowing by. A man downstream, fully aware of what is happening, fills his jug with the mixture. Everyone is in varying states of ecstasy or torpor. A note in the foreground reads "He who drinks and does not drink again, does not know what drinking is."

In Bruegel's *Fall of the Rebel Angels* a white-robed angel is doing battle with horrible demons (detail, plate 44). Isolating the arm and shield of the angel creates a remarkably literal depiction of a white-stalked fly agaric, its red cap fading to golden at the margin.

Petrus Christus was a close follower of Jan van Eyck, whose painting *The Adoration of the Lamb* is also suspect. In a painting titled *The Nativity* Christus has painted the baby Jesus lying on the ground in or on the strangest manger ever seen (detail, plate 45). Directly above the baby is an angel dressed like a fly agaric, with only one white leg visible. Jesus himself appears to be lying on a dried or drying fly agaric cap that is perfectly colored, red in the center fading to gold. His "blood" seems to be running from the golden margin and pooling where he lies, like the mushroom in plate 36. On the ground surrounding the "cap" and on Mary's gown striations have been painted; these do not match the red lines on the cap, so they look as though they are radiating out from underneath the "manger." In between the more visible lines are still others, perfectly spaced and virtually identical in proportion to the gill structure or white spore print of a mushroom that size.[116]

Andrea del Verrocchio was the teacher of Leonardo da Vinci, who himself did some of the painting of *The Baptism of Christ* (fig. 41 and plate 46). It appears innocent until the fly agaric key is put to the lock. A tracing of the dove at the top produces a quite respectable likeness of a fly agaric cap and a portion of the stalk in cross-section (fig. 42). The bird's red beak may have been meant to stand for the red skin of the cap, but even so the golden rays issuing from the beak touch and create an identity with John's red-gold dish and Jesus' head, especially his red and white nimbus. Jesus, who told John that Jesus must be immersed, is standing on only one leg.

FIGURE 41: "Behold the Lamb of God."

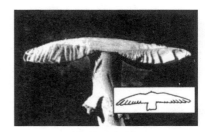

FIGURE 42

All attention in the painting should be on the Lord of the Universe, but the angel closest to Jesus is distracted; he is staring at the other angel's nimbus as if to call our attention to it. Both haloes, and John's also, have the shape, relative size and coloration of mature fly agaric discs.

There is one more distracting element in the painting: the black bird pointing like an arrow to the grove of trees on the hilltop. These trees have been carefully painted to reveal to the viewer that they are a species of pine or other conifer. John is holding a staff in his left hand with a banner that says "Behold the lamb of God," the putative words he spoke when he saw Jesus. Mounted on the top of the staff is a cross of red-gold; the horizontal and vertical axes cross precisely at the base of the trees pointed out by the bird, X marks the spot. It is here beneath the trees that we may behold the lamb of God who sheds his blood for many; here it is that the cross of death is transformed into the golden cross of life. The fruit of that cross is the body of the savior, by which we have salvation only if we eat its flesh and drink its rosy blood. Hallelujah.

14

Heaven and Hell

Heaven

My own experience with the capricious mushroom is long and varied, but I will briefly relate the two most impressive events, both of which occurred in 1977. My friend Michael and I had decided to give the mushroom a good test. After a few nauseating yet somehow uplifting experiences with fresh specimens we discovered that the mushroom should not be eaten raw; this discovery was fortunate, since Michael seemed near death the first time he ate some raw fly agaric and I became extremely nauseous every time I tried it. After harvesting and drying a sufficient quantity of specimens we embarked on what was to become a thirty-one-day trial period.

We ate mushrooms every day; usually not very many per day, but every day. We lost interest in food. We lost interest in work. We were rapidly losing interest in the whole world, and our wives were beginning to think of losing us, as in "getting rid of." I was reminded of the Siberian folk tale related by Wasson, in which the men leave their wives during the mushroom season and go off to live with the "*Amanita* girls." Even so, we continued; the longer we persisted the more we felt divinely inspired to go on. If Soma really was the fly agaric, and every day we were more convinced that it was, then a breakthrough experience might be just around the metaphysical corner. We weren't at all certain we wouldn't die trying, but in our growing dispassion we soon stopped worrying. After all, this was important research, science at its most basic and best. Death by accidental overdose would be a noble way to die, we rationalized, and as a bonus we would avoid old age. We considered it a fair trade-off. Besides, we felt divinely inspired. What could go wrong?

For thirty days in varying degrees we experienced many of the effects described in the present work. We felt immense energy, strength, spirituality, occasional sickness, and frequent euphoria but being taken up into the blissful light eluded us.

The thirty-first day was a full moon. We fasted all day and began nibbling on mushrooms early in the evening. Later I performed a traditional Vedic fire ceremony, putting a piece of a mushroom cap into the fire as I sang the ancient offertory mantras to Agni, Soma, Prajapati, and Indra. Afterward we drove to a nearby bluff and consumed between us about ten dried caps of different sizes (I lost track of the exact number; bad science). We tore each cap in half in an effort to have the same experience, knowing that potency varied from cap to cap. At the time I wasn't aware that mature specimens develop more muscimol than immature specimens. The mushrooms we ate were the most mature that we had collected, saved for last because they were the least attractive and, we thought, the least potent; for this reason we ate more than we would have otherwise. They were indeed less virulent than immature mushrooms, but as we were about to find out, far more potent in the qualities for which we had been searching.

We were getting cold, so we went to Michael's house and built a fire. Neither of us had urinated since before we started eating mushrooms. This abstention was intentional, as we wanted to test the urine's effects, but now both of us were ready to burst. Michael got out two bowls and handed one to me. We looked at each other, laughed nervously, and retired to opposite corners of the room where we filled our respective containers. I stress *respective* containers; even seminal research has its limits. We returned to the center of the room and looked at the tinctured water we had wrought: it was glowing with a fiery orange cast. Since we were about to drink it we first smelled it to see what we were in for, and were surprised at its pleasant odor, or rather, its fragrance.

The phrase "water into wine" redefined itself in my mind as we drank what we were truly hoping would do something extraordinary to us; if our experiment didn't work would be more embarrassed than disappointed. We might even be angry, but at least we would know where the phrase "pissed off" originated.

Even before we drank the urine we were feeling good. Very good. Extremely good. But within minutes after drinking something amazing started to happen. My body began to feel very light, as though I weighed almost nothing. It felt as if the molecules that comprised my body were separating and allowing air to pass between them, or that I could feel the space between the atoms. I became aware of tremendous energy at my feet that rose up through my body in wave after wave. "Feeling good" was rapidly changing into the most blissful feeling I had ever experienced. I looked at Michael and he was radiant. We started laughing and exclaiming in disbelief as the bliss kept increasing. My mind and entire body were in the throes of a kind of meta-orgasm that wouldn't stop—not that I wanted it to.

I picked up a Bible from the bookshelf, opened to the Book of John, and started reading aloud. What I had before considered ridiculously partisan prose and poetry (fiction really) was now revealed in a whole new light. It became for us a fly agaric initiation document, speaking the living truth directly to us through the mists of the centuries, uncovering layer after layer of meaning artfully hidden in the text. We understood it all; all the references, all the metaphors, all the hidden wisdom. We were completely delirious, of course, but in our delirium we were being initiated into the ancient cult of the personified fly agaric. It was as though God had manifested from the book and was addressing us directly. And we couldn't have been happier.

I would read a passage and Michael would exclaim in joy and recognition as we both careened in excitement about the room. After a short while I became so engrossed in the text that I stopped reading aloud, but Michael, who wasn't looking at me, kept responding at the appropriate times. I silently read another line and watched him respond to it. When I realized what was happening I thought "Michael" and he turned his grinning head and looked at me, and we experienced simultaneous amazement. At first we tested ourselves, still without speaking, by mentally requesting a gesture of some kind from the other. It worked. Then for the next short period of time we carried on the most unusual and effortless conversation of our lives, which wasn't a conversation at all, really, because regardless of who was having a thought it instantly became the thought of the other. It sounds confusing but it wasn't; far from it. As this silent communication was happening the bliss we were experiencing increased still more, which I hadn't thought was possible. Of course, it didn't matter what I thought; I was on a juggernaut, having the ride of my life.

At an unspoken signal we turned out the light and positioned ourselves on the floor at opposite ends of the room. I closed my eyes and became very still. The few thoughts that arose in my mind drifted through like enlightening holograms; I was thinking at the pre-verbal level. I was *seeing*. I had the subtle apprehension that only a few thoughts remained in my mind; these were in the process of passing through and, it seemed, out of my mind, not to return or be replaced. The last picture to appear was that of a Middle Eastern woman walking down an ancient road, carrying on her head an earthen jar filled with seeds; the seeds were leaking out of a hole in the bottom.

I saw this image because I had been troubling over the meaning of a saying attributed to Jesus in the Gospel of Thomas from the Nag Hammadi texts, one of many writings in which he is answering the question of the unenlightened everywhere: "What is the kingdom of heaven like?" Jesus explained that heaven is like the woman described above, who doesn't know her jar is leaking and continues to walk home. When she arrives at her home, she sets down the jar and it is empty. End of answer.

We can see Jesus' audience scratching their heads at this "description" of the heavenly kingdom, just as I did. But in the instant of revelation that was my thought, I understood. The jar is like the head, filled with the seeds of thought and future actions. The woman's only concern is to get home. She is so one-pointed she doesn't even realize she is losing her cargo, and consequently the journey becomes easier the closer she gets to home because her burden keeps lightening. She realizes the jar is empty at the same moment she arrives home, and this, says Jesus, is the kingdom of heaven. As Patanjali said, stopping the flow of thoughts while still retaining awareness causes the individual soul to be absorbed momentarily into the light of the Godhead, and this is the sense in which the parable explained itself to me in that brief vision. The main method prescribed for attaining this state is one-pointed concentration, symbolized by the woman's single-mindedness.

The final part of the seamless vision was that it was *my* last seed, and then there was nothing. Before another thought could arise in my mind, in the midst of a great darkness and a great silence, the heavens opened above my head. In an instant I was flooded with light from above, light of the utmost whiteness and splendor, that quickly dissolved everything in its glory. The bliss I had experienced prior to this new revelation now paled to insignificance in an immensity of light that was also the purest love. As the truth of the situation dawned on me the word "FATHER" resounded in this heaven of light and I was taken up and absorbed by the unspeakable Godhead. No longer separate, there was neither an enjoyer nor a thing enjoyed; there was union.

This is a big claim to make, I know, and the reader may wish to add "suffers from delusions of grandeur" to my other sins. Yet even if this experience existed nowhere but within my own mind and has no reality outside of it, still it remains the single most important event of my life. Nothing at all can be compared to it, just as Alphidius said; yet in assessing the validity of the experience I am forced to answer with a comparison. Next to this state ordinary reality is like a bad imitation, a cheap parlor trick in a grimy hotel, an eternally baited trap for the mind and senses. The Gnostics had this much right: we're trapped in bodies and we can't see our way out. The day-to-day world we create with our perceptions has no independent reality; it's all done with mirrors.

I have no idea how long I was in that glorious state because time does not exist there, just as there is no "there" there. I came back to my senses in the morning as I awoke to find myself flat on my back on the hard wood floor. In utter amazement I reviewed the events of the night. Nearly as incredible as the experience I'd had was the fact that I was still on earth in a human body; even though I had experienced something for which countless others had spent their whole lives searching and not often finding, in my immaturity I felt cheated. What kind of God would lift a person to a state like that only to drop him right back into the dark and cruel world, without so much as a farewell? I resolved then and there to try again in several days, and next time I would hold on to the experience.

Hell

It was a beautiful, clear day, and it was going to be hot. I hiked to the top of a hill, sat down, and took out the large, special mushroom I had been saving for just such an occasion.

I had harvested and dried the cap while it was quite immature, and even now it was a deep crimson color. I knew it was a powerful specimen; I just didn't know what powers it was about to unleash.

I was impatient to return to the heaven I had so recently experienced, so I ate the whole cap in less than five minutes and waited nervously for it to take effect. I didn't have to wait long. After fifteen or twenty minutes I began to sweat and salivate excessively. In a very short time I was soaking wet; water was pouring out of me at the same time as my saliva flow was nearly drowning me. I had to keep swallowing to l keep from choking. I was beginning to wonder if perhaps I'd made a miscalculation when the chills started and I became certain of my error. It was ninety degrees and I was shivering with hypothermia, but I was all right; I felt fine, considering what my body was going through, though matters soon became worse.

Then the nausea hit. Not only was I suddenly feeling dreadful, I also felt like I weighed thousands of pounds and could no longer sit up. I vomited quickly and easily, and the last thing I remember before dying is feeling the weight of the entire universe relentlessly pressing me down to the ground.

Existence was black, and blackness was all that existed. Darkness was on the face of the deep, assuming it had a face; it was too dark to tell. In the midst of this great unknowing, this no-thing, a point of awareness arose, and it floated there forever. I no longer existed. There was only a feeble awareness adrift in the depths of the void. If I ever needed help it was at that moment, and it came unbidden. Out of nowhere two words were spoken, softly and clearly: my first and last names. There was a flicker of recognition in the point of awareness when it heard the sounds, but this realization quickly faded to black. Then the two names were spoken again, just as before; no yelling, no urgency, just the names, but this time it registered. This sound was my name, although at first the significance of the fact was entirely lost on me; I was now a name drifting in the void. It wasn't long though before I remembered what and who the name signified and what he had done. I had eaten a single mushroom and passed out; now all I had to do was sit up, which I found was not yet possible. I decided to try for a more attainable goal, that of opening my eyes. Well, at least one eye. It took all the concentration I could gather, but I finally succeeded in forcing an eye open.

Where was I? I had passed out on a beautiful green hill, but now all I could see were giant ropes going up to the sky. They were black, but the fibers that comprised the huge hawsers were iridescent and throwing spectral light all around. I didn't have a clue as to what I was seeing. As I stared with wonder at the colossal ropes my other senses returned and I realized that I was lying on my face. My opened eye was almost touching an embroidered portion of the cloth on which I had been sitting. The embroidery, done in fine black woollen thread, was only a few inches square. The giant ropes at which I had been marveling were tiny embroidery threads.

With great effort I managed to right myself. I was not prepared for the riot of color that greeted me. It wasn't so much the color that surprised me as the lack of definition: I could not focus on anything more than two feet from me, and everything else appeared as shimmering blobs of color with no recognizable form. I looked at my hand and noticed that it came into better focus the closer I moved it to my eyes. I closed one eye and brought my hand up close to my open eye; it was like looking through a microscope. No sooner had I made this observation than another wave of heavy nausea rolled over me. I vomited again and down I went, dead to the world. And this is the way I spent the entire afternoon, vomiting, dying, and coming back to life.

Thinking about this experience a little later I couldn't help but recall the story of Jesus raising Lazarus from the dead. Jesus knew that Lazarus wasn't really going to die, and all Jesus did to revive Lazarus was call his name. If the cult was using the fly agaric it would have been extremely important to weave this motif into the story of their savior, so that if such a thing occurred, as it can, observers would know that the sickness was not "unto death." Like Jesus in the story, the one who "lets you die" is the same one who revives you.

Last Word

AT THE BEGINNING OF THIS BOOK I stated that many of its contentions and suggestions are of a highly speculative nature; the reader, having come this far, will doubtless agree. Whether you agree with the ideas themselves is a different matter. What I hope can be agreed upon at this juncture is that entheogenic drugs, of whatever kind, must have been used at some point by the various people and groups I've discussed. All of that eating and drinking and going to heaven—could it *all* be mere metaphor? I think not, especially when we compare these ancient accounts with the now well-known effects of certain psychedelic drugs. I do understand that accepting this proposition is difficult for those who have not taken any of these drugs, but for those who have the connections are clear and undeniable. I don't know if I am right or wrong in my speculations about *Amanita muscaria*, ergot, and psilocybin, but it seems unlikely that every suggestion is wrong; this statement of course leads to the disturbing likelihood that at least some conclusions are right. And what if they are?

That certain plants and drugs can produce high spiritual or ecstatic states has been established beyond question, whether or not these experiences are accepted as valid by the religions or governments of today. Through the expedient of consciousness-enhancing substances a class of "knowers" has once again arisen in society and it is receiving the same welcome the Gnostics and other "heretics" received in the past: scorn, ridicule, and sometimes active persecution, from both religious groups and governments. These chemically aided spiritual experiences are real; they are psychological facts that meet all the criteria of what is classically deemed a "religious experience." Religion finds this bitter pill impossible to swallow; governments declare it illegal and fill prisons with the "illegally religious" just as surely and irrationally as the Romans filled their jails with early Christians. The religious persecutions of the past have not left us; they have merely changed form.

Entheogenic drugs have the capacity to show us things that we otherwise cannot even imagine; they can reveal our kinship with all life and the universe at large; they can inspire awe, reverence, humility, and great love. Because some of them are also capable of inspiring fear and confusion or loss of body-consciousness, their proper use requires maturity, education, instruction, and guidance, as well as a safe and protected setting. They are not right for everyone and they can also be misused, as we saw with Moses and others, but no one has the right to say they are wrong for everyone or to imprison experimenters and confiscate their possessions. The entire "War on Drugs" mentality is about as wrong-headed and misdirected as it could possibly be, yet governments continue to waste billions of dollars annually trying to force people not to alter their consciousness with anything but the inferior state-sponsored drugs.

While decriminalization of all drugs is probably the first step toward a rational approach to drug policy, I am not going to enter into that debate here. Other books have been and will be written that deal in a much more comprehensive fashion with drug-law reform and the degeneration of society.[116] What I will say is this: psychedelic or entheogenic drugs should not be criminalized. They have played roles in our past of which we are not even aware, as the present work has endeavored to show, and they continue to influence the life of the planet. Never before have so many people known so much about such a wide variety of psychoactive plants. The unprecedented reach and pervasiveness of the electronic and mass media coupled with growing interest in the subject ensures that this trend will continue. Whether we approve of the situation is immaterial: there is no going back to the ignorance of the past. Let us therefore treat the situation with intelligence and compassion.

The informed use of entheogenic, consciousness-enhancing plants and drugs presents a direct and powerful challenge to any system that seeks to spoonfeed the masses with false ideals of nationalism, racism, sexism, or predigested religion, and this is precisely the reason entheogens have been criminalized. We cannot go back to being led around by the nose once the fullness of our humanity is realized, nor to eating pap once the full pleasures of eating are learned; besides, we need roughage or we fill up with our own waste. Expanded consciousness is one genie that can't be put back in the bottle and we're better off for it.

The cat is out of the bag. Pandora's box lies open. The cover has been blown off the Ark of the Covenant. Wisdom cries in the streets and shouts from the rooftops, once again trying to make herself heard above the din. Whoever has ears should listen. Whoever has a voice should consider speaking up, for the time of the end is near, as it always is in this brief life.

Let me testify in no uncertain terms: heaven is much closer, and far easier of access, than we have been led to believe. And it is worth the trip.

Here's the truth on a plate:
you don't have to wait—
nobody is coming
so get a new date

You've just been stood up:
now at last you can sup —
host your own dinner
and fill your own cup

—*cum grano salis*—

APPENDIX

The Legend of Miskwedo

As told by Keewaydinoquay,
an Anishinaubeg medicine woman and storyteller

ATTENTION, I WILL TELL A STORY, a story of The People, a story of Miskwedo, that red-topped mushroom which is the spiritual child of Nokomis Giishik, Grandmother Cedar, and of Nimishomiss Wigwass, our Grandfather Birch. Listen and learn.

Certainly this is true, for it was told by our honored forefathers. Now this happened in the long, long ago times, many uncountable moons gone by and many uncountable trails back, it is thought, at one of the temporary camps during the Great Migration of our people across the continent of *Minissah,* from the Land of the Sun-using toward the Land of the Sun-setting, when they were being led by the Divine Megis to our home, to the promised land of *Keewaydinaukee.*

There were two brothers, so young that they had not yet received their adult names: full brothers they were, both sons of the same woman of the Owl clan and of the same man of the Sturgeon clan. The firstborn was called Elder Brother and the secondborn was called Younger Brother. They lived alone together *(Oh, Wah-ay-eah)* for their parents had died bravely along that Great Migration trail. *Oh, Wah-ay-eah!* They hunted the same quarry, ate the same food, and shared all things in peace and harmony—and that was good. *Ahauw!*

Now one day, at the place about which this story is told, the boys were very hungry, their stomachs empty. Since there were mountains in that place, they climbed up the rocky slopes looking for food. At last they came to a great cave high in the mountainside. It seemed to them that light came out of the cave opening. An amazing sound, a sound like the humming of uncountable bees, was heard. Very carefully and very quietly the brothers approached, curiously peering through the opening. They saw a beautiful meadow in which there grew many tall red and white mushrooms—handsome *wajaskwedeg* they were—turning and revolving, buzzing and murmuring, singing a strange song of happiness under a brilliantly sunny sky.

Quick as a flash of lightning, Younger Brother scrambled through the opening running with joyous abandon into the meadow of murmuring mushrooms.

"Stop! Wait! Stop!" called Elder Brother. "We do not know what Spirits there are in this place. We do not know what they might be."

But Younger Brother did not stop. He was, in fact, already gone!

Younger Brother ran to the tallest, strongest, reddest, most handsome mushroom of them all. White fluffs, like tuft feathers of the forest warbonnet, waved across its shining cap. Streamers of filmy white, like frills of clouds, swirled in rhythm as it revolved. Elder Brother watched aghast as Younger Brother became fused to that giant mushroom's stipe. He beheld Younger Brother begin to grow a bright red cap. At first slowly, then faster and faster, Younger Brother began to spin in the sun. Elder Brother was horrified. Quickly he noted the location of the giant mushroom and the position of the little mushroom which had once been his Younger Brother. Then he ran. He ran as fast as his legs would carry him, away from the bewitching meadow, away from the great cave, away from that awful hole in the mountainside. Back down the winding trails, back down the rocky slopes, he ran, never pausing until at last he came to the village.

"*Awoohee!*"

He gave the emergency call for the elders and the medicine people. Quickly he told them everything that had happened.

"What shall I do?" he begged. "Tell me, Wise Ones, how to save my little brother."

The elders and the medicine people looked at each other. They shook their heads.

"We have never heard of such a thing," they said. "We must ask the Drum."

When they had consulted the Drum, which was a Medicine Drum, they said, "We have an answer, but it is a difficult one. This is what you must do. You must remember every word. You must go to that place called 'The-Place-of-the-Magic-Sands.' It is a high cliff along the lake with a talus slope and great waves pounding the rocks into the sand. There you should collect the magic sands, *Onoman*. Put them in a deerskin bag with sacred tobacco and pull the drawstring tightly. Think a prayer of thanksgiving to the Spirits of that place for their making of *Onoman* (the Magic Sands). Continue running along the trail until you come to 'The-Place-Where-the-High-Trees-Grow-and-the-Eagles-Nest.' Find the highest tree and the nest of the largest eagle. He is a Thunderbird. You must obtain four feathers from his tail. Think to the Thunderbird a prayer of thanksgiving and petition as you keep on running toward the mountain. Follow the same trail to where the light of the great cave shimmers through the opening in the side of the mountain.

"Now face the East with the eagle feathers in your hand, asking Gitchi Manitou's blessing on them. Observe which mushroom is the tallest, strongest, and the handsomest. He is the chief. With utmost speed enter the witching meadow, thrust an eagle feather through the stipe of the chief. He will stop turning. Now locate the wisest Miskwedo among them, the eldest mushroom who is sporulating, the one with the most influence. As fast as you can, put an eagle feather through the stipe of this mushroom. He, too, will stop turning. Now the third eagle feather must be thrust through the stipe of the mushroom which you know to be Younger Brother. Then dump the bag of magic Onoman all over him. Carefully remove every bit of this mushroom, from the shining cap to the bulb at the foot. Do not break off any particle or a part of Younger Brother will be broken too. Carrying the mushroom with you, hurry through the opening in the mountain. Stop just long enough to place the last protective eagle feather across the opening of the cave, then continue down along the trail as fast as you can go. This is what you are supposed to do.

"As you run away from that mountain, the load (your 'Brother' mushroom) will become heavier and heavier, until finally, it will become as it was in the past. There will be your Younger Brother running beside you. But though you recognize him as being there, as he once was, do not speak, do not stop! As you run, it will become more and more as it was in the past, except for one thing—an eagle feather will protrude from Younger Brother's skin. There it must always remain."

All these things occurred then. They happened as it was foretold they would happen. Elder Brother remembered clearly every little thing. He did exactly as he was told, collecting the magic sands and the eagle feathers. He went through the hole in the side of the mountain, placing the protective eagle feathers and dumping the magic sands over Younger Brother. He rescued Younger Brother, who seemed to become as he was in the past—except for one weird thing: an eagle feather stuck out strangely from his skin just as if it had grown there! Together the boys ran swiftly down the trail, back to the camp of The People. There they lived once again, in the same lodge, in peace and harmony. And that was good. *Ahauw!*

Many days and many nights went by. Slowly matters began to change. *Wah-ay-eah.* Elder Brother arose in the mornings, his heart heavy with sadness and foreboding. He worried and he worried and he was unhappy. *Wah-ay-eah.* Younger Brother, on the contrary, arose smiling each day, his heart filled with happiness, his lips singing merriment. *Ahauw, Zahwendahmowin!*

Now Elder Brother noticed that Younger Brother went very frequently behind the wigwam to urinate. He stayed much longer than seemed to be necessary, and particularly, at the full of the moon, he stayed a long, long time. At last Elder Brother, who disliked playing the spy, decided that for his brother's welfare he simply must investigate. So he went out behind the wigwam and discovered, just as he had thought, little Brother was not urinating. He had already gone down the trail further into the woods. Elder Brother followed secretly until he came to a clearing.

What does he behold? There he sees Younger Brother standing in the center of an open space, a large group of people around him. Younger Brother's arms are open wide, spread like the umbrella of a mushroom. His robes are beautiful, glowing red, and tufts of white feathers adorn his head. In a high, humming voice of happiness, like the song of uncountable bees, he sings to The People.

> *"Because of my supernatural experience,*
> *in the Land of the Miskwedo,*
> *I have a cure to alleviate your ills,*
> *To take away all your unhappiness.*
> *If only you will come to my penis*
> *And take the quickening waters flowing from it*
> *You, too, can be forever happy."*

Every time the clouds darken the moon, he urinates. The people catch his urine in *mokukeg,* birch bark containers. They drink this liquid that has been given to them as a great boon by the Miskwedo spirits. All the members of the mushroom cult, all the devotees of Miskwedo, Younger Brother, who is the chief mushroom, the drum chief, the three elders, and three sets of lesser officers, come up in turn and sing their Miskwedo song. Throughout the fullness of time these people sing their happy songs, their hearts are strong, and each one does the work of ten.

Wah-ay-eah, poor Elder Brother! He did not understand the ways of the red-topped mushroom. He did not understand the use of the golden mushroom liquid and the penis elixir. He continued to be filled with foreboding.

"Nothing good can come of it," he lamented. He troubled, he worried, and he was unhappy. *Oh Wah-ay-eah.*

Neither did Younger Brother understand the workings of the Sacred Mushroom. But he went on being happy, and all the people following him continued in a state of bliss.

And so it is and so it continues to this very day, now at this place and at this time, as it was then, "and shall be in the future. All the people who are OLDER BROTHERS, like Elder Brother in our story, because they do not understand, they are unhappy. They trouble, they worry, and they fuss. Neither do the YOUNGER BROTHERS of this world understand, yet still they drink the golden mushroom waters and are happy. They drink the Elixir of the Great Miskwedo, and much is revealed of the supernatural and other knowledge in this way. It is the *Kesuwabo*—the liquid Power of the Sun—*Kesuwabo. Ahauw! Jahwenda-mowining, ahauw!*"[117]

Notes

(P) Author's paraphrase.

Abbreviations used for works frequently cited:

AS Carl Gustav Jung, *Alchemical Studies,* trans. R. F. C. Hull (Princeton, N.J.: Princeton University Press, 1967).

MC Carl Gustav Jung, Mysterium Coniunctionis: *An Inquiry into the Separation and Synthesis of Psychic Opposites in Alchemy,* trans. R. F. C. Hull, 2nd ed. (Princeton, N.J.: Princeton University Press, 1977).

P&A Carl Gustav Jung, *Psychology and Alchemy,* trans. R. F. C. Hull, 2nd ed. (Princeton, N.J.: Princeton University Press, 1968).

P of T Carl Gustav Jung, *The Psychology of the Transference,* trans. R. F. C. Hull (Princeton, N.J.: Princeton University Press, 1969).

1. Rig Veda 4.27.5, from The Rig Veda, trans. Wendy O'Flaherty (New York, NY: Penguin Books, 1981).
2. Ibid. 9.113.4-11.
3. Ibid. 8.48.1-15.
4. Psalms 4.6-7, from The Jerusalem Bible, ed. Alexander Jones (Garden City, N.Y.: Darton, Longman & Todd, 1966).
5. Ibid. 27.1.
6. Ibid. 36.7-9.
7. Ibid. 97.11.
8. Ibid. 104.1-2.
9. Ibid. 112.4.
10. Ibid. 119.130.
11. Isaiah 9.1-2.
12. John 1.4-5.
13. Ephesians 5.8-9.
14. James 1.16-17.
15. Peter 2.9.
16. John 1.5.
17. I think this physical response must be the origin of the belief in yoga theory that there exists a certain *chakra* or subtle organ in the brain which drips a special type of saliva down the back of the throat. This saliva is called *soma,* and so is the chakra. I believe that soma chakra is named after the deity and drink Soma, and not vice versa as yoga theory proposes, because when Soma was drunk four thousand years ago it caused the same clear juices to flow as it does today and was specific to the experience. It is true that higher states of meditation can stimulate this flow as well, but not to the extent that occurs with fly agaric use. This "juice" is completely clear and has a thin consistency and a pleasant, slightly sweet taste. It can flow so much that at times it seems like a cosmic beverage service: one has drunk Soma and because of

doing so one continues to drink, like it or not. If this flow had been stimulated by drinking *sura* (wine) the yogis would have named the region *sura chakra,* not soma chakra.

18. *Rig Veda* 9.74.

19. *Zend Avesta* 48.10. (P)

20. David Flattery and Martin Schwartz, *Haoma and Harmaline* (Berkeley: University of California Press, 1989).

21. Asvamedha Parvan of the *Mahabharata,* 14.54.12-35. (P)

22. Compare the Uttanka story with the Anishinaubeg story. See "The Legend of Miskwedo," in the Appendix.

23. An example: once the guru told my teacher, who was designing a new ashram, to make tunnels from the guru's room to all the other rooms. Secret entrances would then allow him to appear "magically" in the locked room of a given disciple or visitor. Another time the guru asked my teacher questions about a doctor he had never met but was expecting to meet. When he later met the doctor, the guru told him all manner of things about the doctor's life, which utterly amazed the man, who immediately became his disciple.

24. *Rig Veda* 8.48.10.

25. *Rig Veda* 1.154. (P)

26. *Shatapatha Brahmana* 1.2.5.1-9a. (P)

27. See *Mahabharata, Aitareya Brahmana, Shatapatha Brahmana, Ramayana,* etc. (P)

28. *Gita Govinda.* (P)

29. *Shanda Purana* 5.2.14.2-30. (P)

30. *Rig Veda* 2.33. (P)

31. *Brahmanda Purana* 1.2.27; also these *Puranas: Devibhagavata, Kurma, Linga, Padma, Samba,* etc. (P)

32. *Shiva Purana* 2.4.1; 2.4.2. (P)

33. *Saura Purana* 61.64–70. (P)

34. *Skanda Purana* 6.70.24-68; 71.1-20. (P)

35. *Bhagavata Purana* 8.12.12-35; *Agni Purana* 3.17-20. (P)

36. *Bhagavata Purana* 2.40.18-54. (P)

37. *Shiva Purana* 4.12.17-52. (P)

38. *Linga Purana* 1.20.80-6. (P)

39. *Shiva Purana* 3.20.3-7. (P)

40. *Subhasitaratnakosha* no. 35. (P)

41. Some goddess cults have perhaps taken this concept a little far. There is an all-male sect still functioning today in India that worships the goddess Radha, the consort of Krishna. The men are celibate monks, all of whom, if they weren't already, become transvestites when they join the sect. They shave, wear jewelery and make-up, and dress in saris, spending their days in meditation longing for union with Krishna, each one imagining himself to be Radha. Intense desire is needed to enter their ranks; at initiation the testicles of the new member are placed between two stones and crushed, a practice that seems a perverse imitation of earlier Soma-pressings. The sect is dying out.

42. Wendy O'Flaherty Doniger, *Women, Androgynes, and Other Mythical Beasts* (Chicago: University Chicago Press, 1980).

43. If I have exceeded the bounds of propriety or credibility with this last suggestion, or prior suggestions, I apologize, but as Tantric painting and sculpture clearly show, the practitioners were familiar with every conceivable sexual act using any and all available orifices. They also used and still use, drugs of various kinds in their practices. It is then not unreasonable to suggest that their drug-taking may have had a sexual side as well.

44. *Shiva Purana Dharmasamhita* 10.79-215; et al. (P)

45. *Matsya Purana* 155.1-34, 156.1-40, 157.1-24, 158.1-27; *et al.* (P)

46. For some reason quite a large number of men over the centuries have taken this last admonition to heart, as though God had meant it to refer to them personally.

47. Experience has shown that animals, especially cattle and deer, must regard the mushroom in the same way. During mushroom season it is often a race to see who will arrive at a fly agaric first, the ardent forager or

the animals. Cattle and deer like to nip off the young mushrooms in one bite; one often finds round fly agaric bottoms scattered forlornly on the ground, like baby moons with a bite missing.

48. I must note here that I am not singling out the Israelites from among the plethora of peoples or religions that have at some time or other committed similar atrocities, such as the Christian Crusades and the Inquisition. We need only read the newspapers to see that such things are still happening today. I believe that all atrocities past and present, whether religious, political, or otherwise, should be exposed without discrimination. I have obtained my data from the Hebrew scriptures and I can't interpret them any other way. Read, for example, the account in Numbers 31 of Moses' bloodthirsty and sexual attack on the Medianites, his wife's own people. A voice in the head of Abraham, Moses, or anyone else doesn't excuse bad behavior, nor does it reflect on anyone alive today. "God" does not give people such directives, or the right to kill and subjugate others by citing higher authority. No one should be exterminated or mutilated in the name of God.

49. Moses died before he got to the "promised" land and Yahweh wasted no time appointing the fearsome Joshua as his successor. That way, the carnage being perpetrated "in the name of Yahweh" could continue unabated. Some think that Moses was murdered, perhaps after one too many "Yahweh says . . ." comments.

50. Conrad Waldkirch, the printer (not the author) of *Artis auriferae* (1593).

51. Direct biblical quotations in chapters 8 and 9 are all from *The Jerusalem Bible*.

52. Keewaydinoquay, "The Legend of Miskwedo," *Journal of Psychedelic Drugs,* vol. 11 (1–2), Jan.–June 1979.

53. Morton Smith, *The Secret Gospel* (New York: Harper & Row, 1973).

54. Ibid.

55. Cf. the birth of the Angirases, above.

56. All quotations from the Nag Hammadi texts are from *The Nag Hammadi Library,* ed. James M. Robinson, 3rd edition (San Francisco: HarperSanFrancisco, 1988).

57. "Panarium," XXVI, cap. VIII, from Carl Gustav Jung, *Aion* (Zurich: Rascher, 1951), 202, n. 61.

58. *The Other Bible,* ed. Willis Barnstone (San Francisco: Harper & Row, 1984), 263–64.

59. Ibid., 268–85.

60. Jessie Laidlay Weston, *From Ritual to Romance* (Princeton, N.J.: Princeton University Press, 1920).

61. "Toadstool," ancient appellation of the fly agaric, has caused consternation among some researchers who can't figure out how the mushroom received that name. I have thought of several reasons. Toads have an ancient connection with magic and divinity, having attained the status of gods in some cultures, as the fly agaric has. The skin secretions of some frogs is hallucinogenic, as is the skin of the mushroom; the perfect throne for such an intoxicating divinity is the beautiful and entrancing fly agaric. When the mushroom is dried it can take on the appearance of toad skin, wrinkled and warty. After the first extended rains of the season two things appear simultaneously as if by magic: toads and mushrooms, both spawned by the seed of heaven and uniquely connected. When the waters evaporate some toads go into suspended animation, becoming encased in dried mud; like dried mushrooms they revive in water.

62. Hoghelande, *Theatrum chemicum Britannicum, I* (1659), from Jung, *AS,* 322.

63. Arnaldus de Villanova, "Speculum alchimiae," *Theatrum chemicum Britannicum, I* (1659), from Jung, *MC,* 153.

64. "Turba philosophorum," *Artis auriferae, I,* from Jung, *P&A,* 122, n. 33.

65. Hoghelande, *Theatrum chemicum Britannicum, I,* from Jung, *P of T,* 126, n. 14.

66. Senior, *De chemia,* 55, from Jung, *P of T,* 126, n. 14.

67. Jung, *P&A,* 36.

68. Ibid., 324.

69. Maier, *Atalanta fugiens,* 117, from Fabricius, *Alchemy* (Wellingborough, England: Aquarian Press, 1989), 176–77.

70. Norton, "Ordinall," *Theatrum chemicum Britannicum,* from Jung, *P of T,* 125–26.

71. Jung, *MC,* 219.

72. "Tabula smaragdina," *De alchemia,* from Jung, *MC,* 219.

73. Cf. the birth of Hanuman, whose father was the wind-god.

74. *Miscellanea d'alchimia,* (14th-century manuscript,) from Jung, *P&A,* 256, fig. 131.

75. Dorm, "Congeries Paracelsicae chemicae," *Theatrum chemicum Britannicum,* from Jung, *MC,* 216.

76. *Rosarium,* from Jung, *P of T,* 85.

77. *Musaeum hermeticum,* from Fabricius, *Alchemy,* 34, n. 1.

78. Ruska, *Turba philosophorum,* from Jung, *MC,* 20.

79. *Consilium coniugii,* from Jung, *MC,* 220.

80. *Musaeum hermeticum,* from Fabricius, *Alchemy,* 155.

81. *Theatrum chemicum Britannicum, IV* (1659), from Jung, *AS,* 218.

82. *Opera chemica,* from Adam McLean, *The Alchemical Mandala* (Grand Rapids, MI: Phanes Press, 1989), 104–9.

83. *Musaeum hermeticum,* from Fabricius, *Alchemy,* 34.

84. Shiva also sprinkled his "ashes."

85. *Aureum vellus,* from Fabricius, *Alchemy,* 100.

86. Ripley, *Theatrum chemicum Britannicum, II,* from Jung, *AS,* 309.

87. Mylius, *Philosophic reformata,* from Jung, *AS,* 306, n. 19.

88. *Matsya Purana* 154.506-12; *Kumarasambhava Purana* 5.14. (P)

89. *Theatrum chemicum Britannicum, II,* from Jung, *AS,* 307.

90. Ibid., V, 790, from Jung, *AS,* 307.

91. *Theatrum chemicum Britannicum, I,* from Fabricius, *Alchemy,* 87.

92. "De igne et sale," *Theatrum chemicum Britannicum, VI* (1661), from Jung, *AS,* 304.

93. *Sophia,* 10, from Jung, *AS,* 306.

94. *Theatrum chemicum Britannicum, V* (1660), from Jung, *AS,* 307.

95. *Artis auriferae, II,* from Fabricius, *Alchemy,* 170.

96. *Occulta philosophia,* from Fabricius, *Alchemy,* 108.

97. *Musaeum hermeticum,* from Fabricius, *Alchemy,* 126.

98. Ibid., from Fabricius, *Alchemy,* 126.

99. *Atalanta fugiens,* from Fabricius, *Alchemy,* 129.

100. See Integration: *Journal of Mind-Moving Plants and Culture,* number 2/3 (Knetzgau, Germany: Bilwis-Verlag, 1992).

101. *Theatrum chemicum Britannicum,* from Jung, *P&A,* 437.

102. Parzival, Book IX, lines 1494–1501, trans. from Shepard, *The Lore of the Unicorn* (New York: Harper-Collins, 1979), 82.

103. Melchior Szebeni, *Theatrum chemicum Britannicum, III,* from Jung, *P&A,* 398–99.

104. *Atalanta fugiens,* from Fabricius, *Alchemy,* 56.

105. *Symbola aureae,* from Fabricius, *Alchemy,* 18.

106. *Artis auriferae, II,* from Fabricius, *Alchemy,* 18.

107. *Musaeum hermeticum,* from Fabricius, *Alchemy,* 74.

108. Ibid., from Fabricius, *Alchemy,* 68–69.

109. *The Crowne of Nature,* from Fabricius, *Alchemy,* 80.

110. *Uraltes chymisches Werk,* from Fabricius, *Alchemy,* 159.

111. *Musaeum hermeticum,* from Jung, *MC,* 345.

112. Michalspacher, *Cabala, Spiegel der Kunst und Nature* (1616), from McLean, *The Alchemical Mandala,* 53.

113. *Musaeum hermeticum,* from Fabricius, *Alchemy,* 28.

114. "Rosarium," *Artis auriferae,* from Jung, *P of T,* 114.

115. Rosencreutz, *Chymical Wedding,* from Jung, *MC,* 293, n. 136.

116. See Shulgin, PIHKAL; Ott, *Pharmacotheon;* McKenna, *Food of the Gods;* and others.

117. "The Legend of Miskwedo," *Journal of Psychedelic Drugs,* vol. 11 (1–2), Jan.–June 1979.

Illustrations

Illustrations

Abbreviations used for works frequently cited:

P&A Carl Gustav Jung, *Psychology and alchemy,* trans. by R. F. C. Hull, 2nd ed. (Princeton, N.J.: Princeton University Press, 1968).

Figures

1. The god Krishna as a personification of the secret food.
2. Agni drinks from Shiva's penis (Bhuvaneshwara, Orissa. 8th-century).
3. Rama and Hunuman holding mushrooms (photo by Gregory Howard).
4&5. Tracings of Shiva on his pillar, and a fresh mushroom, from Fabricius, *Alchemy* (Wellingborough, England: Aquarian Press, 1989).
6. Tantric initiation (Rajasthan c. 18th century), from Ajit Mookerjee, *Tantra Asana* (Basel: Ravi Kumar, 1971).
7. Adam's Tree of Paradise, from *Miscellanea d'alchimia* (14th-century manuscript).
8. Hand-held baby sun: Vreeswyck, De Groene Leeuw, from Fabricius, *Alchemy,* fig. 110.
09. Tracing of egg (author).
10. Bat-winged rebis: *Rosarium philosophorum,* in *Artis auriferae* (1593), from Fabricius, *Alchemy,* 162, fig. 307.
11. Rebis with five crowns: Mylius, *Philosophia reformata* (1622), from Jung, *P&A,* 244, fig. 125.
12. Rebis with stars: Jamsthaler, *Viatorium spagyricum* (1625), from Jung, *P&A,* 372, fig. 199.
13. Uroboros with birds: Reusner, *Pandora,* from Fabricius, *Alchemy,* 186, fig. 361.
14. Uroboros with flowers: Reusner, *Pandora,* from Jung, *P&A,* 53, fig. 13.
15. The Tree of Life: *Opera chemica,* from Adam McLean, *The Alchemical Mandala* (Grand Rapids, MI: Phanes Press, 1989).
16. Tracing of table (author).
17. Serpent on cross: Eleazar, *Uraltes chymisches Werk* (1760), from Jung, *P&A,* 434, fig. 238.
18. Salamander in fire: *Musaeum hermeticum,* from Fabricius, *Alchemy,* 109, fig. 192.
19. Dried serpent-mushroom (author photo).
20. Spirits leaving serpent: Thomas Aquinas (pseud.), "De alchimia" (16th-century manuscript), from Jung, *P&A,* 251, fig. 129.
21. Hermes with book and birds: Zadith Senior, *De chemia Seniorus,* Strasbourg (1566), verso of frontispiece, from Fabricius, *Alchemy,* 147, fig. 277.
22. Alchemist with eggs and sun: *Speculum veritatis,* 17th century, Biblioteca Apostolica Vaticana, Cod. lat. 7286, E 8, from Klossowski de Rola, *Alchemy, the Secret Art* (London: Thames and Hudson, 1973).

23. Mushroom-shaped tower: Rola, *Alchemy, the Secret Art,* fig. 5.

24. One-legged man with sword hilt: Rola, *Alchemy, the Secret Art,* fig. 2.

25. Stabbed king and snake: Rola, *Alchemy, the Secret Art,* fig. 9.

26. Unicorn with pope: Scalinger, *Explanatio imaginum* (1570), from Jung, *P&A,* 467, fig. 261.

27. Tracing of unicorn (author).

28. Woman with flowing milk: Schwan, *Philosophia reformata,* from Fabricius, *Alchemy,* 79.

29. Earth nursing Sun: Schwan, *Philosophia reformata,* from Fabricius, *Alchemy,* 139.

30. Nursing Mary with priest: Melchior Cibinensis, *Symbolum,* from Maier, *Symbols aureae mensae* (1617), from Jung, *P&A,* 397, fig. 216.

31. Tracing of fig. 23 (author).

32. Naked woman with burning heart: *Symbola aureae,* from Fabricius, *Alchemy,* 22.

33. Slaughter of children: Eleazar, *Uraltes Chymisches Werk,* engraving no. 7, from Fabricius, *Alchemy,* 159.

34. Michelspacher, emblems IV, from Fabricius, *Alchemy,* 201.

35. Tracing of fig. 27 (author).

36. Boy urinating in three streams: *Speculum veritatis,* Cod. lat. 7286, fig.3, from Rola, *Alchemy, the Secret Art,* plate 3.

37. Boy urinating into pot: *Speculum veritatis,* Cod. lat. 7286, fig.4, from Rola, *Alchemy, the Secret Art,* plate 6.

38. The alchemical fountain: Salomon Trismosin, *Splendor Solis* (16th-century manuscript, British Library).

39. Lion urinating: *Musaeum hermeticum,* from Fabricius, *Alchemy,* 175.

40. Pissing boy in mushroom: *Cabala mineralis* (manuscript, British Museum, Add. 5245).

41. Andrea del Verrocchio, *Baptism of Christ,* 1470 (Uffizi Gallery, Florence).

42. Photo of mushroom in cross-section (author).

Photographs

All color photos by the author except plate 9, by Robert Forte.

Index

Abraham, 71–3, 79, 89, 95
Abraham the Jew, 156, 163
Adam and Eve, 77, 64–70, 137, 148, 156, 163
Agape (love-feast), 138
Agaricus muscarius, 186
Agni, 19, 27, 30, 45, 49, 51–2, 61, 83, 104, 140, 149, 171, 180
alchemy, ix, 12, 25, 83, 91, 135, 146, 147, 148, 164, 160–88
Allegro, John, 23–5
Alpert, Richard. *See* Dass, Ram
Amanita muscaria. See fly agaric
amputation, penis, 40–3, 157–8
angels 70, 73, 74, 87–8, 99, 102, 108, 116, 118, 122, 125, 172
Anishinaubeg, 102, 145, 182, 209–12, 213
anointing, 87, 89–90, 116, 127
anorexia, 119, 129, 157
Apocalypse of Adam, 148–9
Apochryphon of James, 141–2
Aquarium sapientum, 193
Ark of God, 76, 85
art, 58, 62, 87, 88, 171, 173–80, 183–6, 188–90, 192, 194–6
Arthur, King, 155
Aryans, 8, 19, 26, 34–5, 39, 50, 73, 96, 116, 126, 142, 186
ascension, 91, 114
Asclepius, 150
Atalanta fugiens, 184, 190
Aurelia occulta, 178
Authoritative Teaching, 149
Ayurveda, 90

baptism, 110, 128, 149, 199
Bible, 4, 7, 10–11, 12, 66–134, 201
birds, 1, 47, 66, 75, 148, 183–5, 188, 193, 199
Blaise de Vigenere, 182
bleeding lance, 155, 159
bliss, 3, 4, 6, 10, 11, 17, 18, 25, 42, 52, 59, 69, 70, 93, 93, 144, 170,

192, 201, 212
Bouts, Diereck, 88–9
Brahmanas, 5, 30, 35
Brahminism, 26, 58, 60, 109
Bruegel, 198
bull, 1, 19, 20, 26, 27, 29, 34, 36, 38, 39, 43, 44, 50, 58, 77, 85, 94, 101, 134, 186
burning bush, 73–4, 78

Cabala mineralis, 196
Cathars, vi, 4, 5, 7, 23–5, 78, 83, 105–34, 135–8, 145
Christus, Petrus: *Nativity,* 198
circumcision 72–3, 79, 80, 89, 108, 116
Claviceps. See ergot
Clement of Alexandria, 106
Concept of Our Great Power, 150
Crowne of Nature, 192
crucifixion, 24, 112, 113, 125

Dass, Ram, 22
Dead Sea scrolls, v, 1, 23, 137, 151
Dionysus, 29, 83
Doniger, Wendy, 62
Dorn, v, 172, 181
dove, 45, 47, 94, 95, 97, 98, 103–4, 108, 117, 155, 157, 183, 184, 199
drug use, vi, 2, 3, 5–9, 25, 26, 43, 49, 53, 58, 59, 81, 90, 123, 126, 127, 144, 145, 160, 161, 169, 206, 207

Eleazar, 192
Eleusis, 115, 119, 128
Elijah, 7, 87–91, 117, 122, 123, 126, 157
Elisha, 7, 87–8, 90–1, 122
elixir, 52, 164, 165, 166, 169–72, 174, 177, 182, 196, 212
Epiphanius, 150
ergot, 81, 82, 115, 119–20, 128, 129,

142, 206
Essenes, 7, 137
Ezekiel, 7, 101–3, 126, 132, 133, 176

Figulus, 181
firebird, 47, 175
fly agaric
  described, 13–14
  effects of, 14–8, 25, 27, 200–5, 210–12
  in alchemy, 170–97
  in art, 51, 57, 58, 62, 171, 173, 175, 176, 177, 178, 179, 183, 184, 185, 186, 188, 189, 190, 192, 194, 195, 196, 198–9
  in Garden of Eden story, 64–70
  in Gnosticism, 135–53
  in Grail legend, 154–64
  in Hanuman myths, 53–8
  in New Testament, 105–134
  in Shiva/Rudra myths, 38–63
  in Vishnu myths, 28–37
  lingas and, 36, 40, 41, 43, 47, 53, 57, 62–3, 80
  Soma and, 6–7, 8–10, 11, 12, 16, 19–22, 24–7, 28–37, 38–40, 42–4, 47–56, 58, 59, 61–2, 68, 70, 73, 79, 83, 96–7, 107, 114, 115–6, 144, 149, 171, 180, 186, 200, 201, 213
  tincture of, 165, 172, 182, 186, 190, 191, 192, 196, 197
  Yahweh and, 7, 11, 71–82, 84–90. 98, 99–101, 103–4, 108, 171, 215

Garden of Eden, 7, 10, 11, 24, 65–70, 79, 146, 163
Garden of Gethsemene, 11, 121–3, 161
Gloria mundi, 195
Gnosticism, 7, 21, 25, 60, 122, 135–53, 155, 165, 203, 206
goddess cults, 59, 214

Gospel of Philip, 145–7
Gospel of Thomas, ix, 143–5, 202
Gospel of Truth, 142–3
Grail legends, 12, 25, 154–64, 166,
        179, 187
Greeks, 6, 29, 50, 107, 115, 130,
        135–6, 148, 176
gurus, 22–3, 60, 62–3, 90, 213

Hanuman, 53–8, 83, 104, 107, 161
Haoma cults, 20, 21, 73, 116
healing, 5, 39, 100, 110, 155, 158, 162,
        165, 176, 180, 197
hermaphrodite, 46, 47, 172, 173, 182,
        187, 196
Hermes Trismegistus, 170
Hermeticism, 50, 135–6, 139, 141,
        170, 171, 181, 183, 197
Hinduism, 4, 6, 28, 31, 58, 59, 60, 144
Hofmann, Albert, 119
Holy Grail. See Grail legends
immortality, 6, 8, 29, 56, 57, 70, 144,
        150, 159
India, viii, 6, 7, 19, 21, 22, 26, 29, 22,
        33, 35, 36, 40, 42, 47, 54, 57,
        60, 63, 73, 80, 83, 85, 90,
        108–9, 115–6, 181, 183, 214
Indra, 9, 21, 27–8, 32–5, 37, 38, 39,
        50, 54–6, 59, 96, 176, 201
initiation 62, 91, 108–9, 117, 122, 141,
        202, 214
Interpretation of Knowledge, 150
Interrogationes maiores Mariae, 150
, Isaiah, 98–9, 101

Jesus, vi, ix, 2, 4, 5, 7, 23–5, 56, 73, 87,
        89–91, 97, 100 105–34, 136–9,
        141–8, 150–1, 154–9, 161, 169,
        171,179, 182, 183, 186, 189,
        190, 193–4, 198–9, 202–3, 205
John the apostle, 7, 24, 73,111, 122,
        124, 130–4, 150, 201
John the Baptizer, 87, 108, 115, 117,
        141, 155, 159, 199
Jonah, 103–4, 110, 118, 120
Joseph of Arimathea, 112, 1214,
        154–5, 157
Judaism, 4, 7, 11, 24, 25, 71–104,
        136–8
Jung, Carl, 167–8, 170

Kesuabo, 145
Khunrath, Heinrich, 172, 187
Krishna, 21, 35–7, 39, 57, 214

Lambspringk,177, 183, 191
Last Supper, 65, 89, 111, 115, 121,
        123–4, 154, 155, 156
Lazarus, 11, 120, 205

light, 3, 9–12, 18, 25, 29, 34, 37, 42,
        43, 65, 66, 69, 92, 93, 98,
        100–1, 102, 106, 108, 115–6,
        117, 127, 129, 136, 137, 139,
        141, 145, 146–9, 152–3, 155,
        159, 161–2, 170, 172, 175, 187,
        189, 197, 201–4, 210
linga, 36, 40, 41, 43, 47, 53, 57, 62–3,
        80
LSD, 17, 22–3, 81, 119–20, 129

Magi, 7, 115, 107–8, 115–6
Mahabharata, 21, 33
Maier, Michael, 168, 178
Manichaeans, 21, 137
manna, 75, 83, 89, 104, 132
Mark the apostle, 106, 112, 122
Mass, 153, 157, 158–9, 161, 189
Mazatec Indians, 8
Melchior Szebeni, 189–90
Mercurius, 171–2, 175, 178, 181–2,
        185–6, 190–1, 193–6
Michalspacher: *Cabala*, 193–4
miracles, 5, 7, 87, 90, 109, 110–1,
        119–21
Miscellanea d'alchimia, 171
Miskwedo, 102, 145, 209–12, 213
Moses, 1–2, 7, 37, 64–5, 73–87, 89, 90,
        92, 94, 98, 102, 120, 122, 124,
        151, 182–3, 196, 207, 214, 215
Museum hermeticum, 173
Mylius, 181

Naasenes, 138
Nag Hammadi texts, vi, 137, 138–53,
        202
Native Americans. *See* Anishinaubeg
near–death experience, 16, 80, 103–4,
        120–1, 203–5

Odes of Solomon, 152–3
On the Origin of the World, 147–8
Opera chemica, 178

panchamrita, 6, 61
Pandora, 207
parables, vi, 105–6, 110, 203
Parsi religion, 21
Paschal candle, 159
Passover, 81, 89, 91,108, 111
Patanjali, 16–7, 203
Paul, 100, 127, 128–30, 161
penis, 1, 20, 24, 37–44, 46–8, 51,
        52–3, 56, 58, 61, 62–3, 72–3,
        75, 80, 83, 90, 134, 145, 151,
        157–9, 162, 171, 212
penis-stones, 62–3
Pentecost, 126–8
Persia, 20, 90, 108, 116

peyote, 9
philosophical tree, 147, 171, 176,
        178–80, 185
philosophers' stone, 154, 164, 166,
        167, 169, 180, 197
phoenix, 47, 148, 156, 163, 175, 176,
        188, 192
pillar gods, 20, 27, 28, 36, 58, 79, 83,
        99, 193
Pine Forest myth, 29, 37, 40–4, 46, 47,
        63, 73, 125
Pordage, 182
propagation, 52, 180–1, 191
prophets, 4, 7, 23, 71–104, 109, 110,
        118, 126, 130
Pseudo-Aristotle, 182
psilocybe mushroom, 8, 17, 19, 34–6,
        206
Puranas, 5, 27, 35, 40, 53, 63, 181

Ramayana, 54–8, 107
rebis, 172–7, 184
resurrection, 57, 113–4, 124–5, 146,
        155, 162
Revelation, Book of 130–4, 136, 142,
        159
Rig Veda, 6, 8–12, 16, 19, 20, 25,
        26–9, 34, 38–9, 48, 96, 97,144
Ripley, 181
Rosarium, 174, 182, 191
Rudra, 29, 38–44, 107, 125, 157, 171

Sabina, Maria, 8
sacrifice, 26, 30, 38, 39, 47–8, 50, 52,
        61, 73, 74, 77, 104, 107, 144
sadhus, 6
samadhi, 5, 6, 16, 17
Scaliger, 187–8
Schwan, 188
secrecy, 5, 84, 90, 99–100, 107, 167
semen, 28, 29, 38, 43–4, 45–9, 51–3,
        56, 61–2, 65–6, 90, 97, 140,
        150–1, 184
Senior, Zadith, 184
serpent, 32–3, 37, 59, 64, 65–9, 74,
        78–80, 83, 86–7, 120, 123, 138,
        151, 172, 174, 175–8, 182–3,
        185, 187, 189, 190, 193, 194–5
sexual act, 2, 40, 42–3, 44–9, 51–3,
        58–63, 67, 80, 131, 150, 174,
        214
Shiva, 27, 32–4, 36, 38, 40, 44–54, 55,
        57, 58–9, 61, 62–3, 73, 78, 79,
        80, 83, 99, 134, 149, 151, 163,
        171, 172, 177, 182, 216
Siberia, 10, 14, 15, 48, 50, 79, 127, 200
Soma, 6–7, 8–10, 11, 12, 16, 19–22,
        24–7, 28–37, 38–40, 42–4,
        47–56, 58, 59, 61–2, 68, 70, 73;

79, 83, 96–7, 107, 114, 115–6, 144, 149, 171, 180, 186, 200, 201, 213
Song of Songs, 91–8, 104, 177
Speculum veritatis, 185, 194
spirits, 90, 100, 145, 210, 212
Splendor Solis, 172, 174, 195
Symbola aurea, 190

Tabula smaragdina, 170
Tantra, 5, 6, 41, 42, 43, 58–63, 97, 214
telepathy, 16–7, 110, 120, 202
Thanksgiving Psalms, 151
Theatrum chemicum, 13, 187
Thomas, ix, 143–5, 202
Titian, 198
toadstool, 29, 58, 83–4, 160, 190, 215
Tree of Knowledge, 10, 68, 147, 156
Tree of Life, 10, 67–8, 70, 131, 134, 146, 147, 171, 178–9 187, 197
Turba philosophorum, 172

unicorn, 154, 186–8
urine, 20–2, 35, 37, 48–50, 61, 79, 119, 122, 140, 145, 151, 169, 176, 190–1, 194–6, 198, 201, 212

Valentine, Basil, 192, 196
van Eyck, Jan, 198
Vedism, 5, 6, 8, 9–11, 12, 16, 19, 20, 25–9, 30, 34, 35, 38–9, 48, 54, 59, 96, 97, 144
Ventura, 181
Verrocchio: *Baptism of Christ,* 199
Vishnu, 28–37, 45, 50, 52–4, 55, 56, 57, 63, 73, 83, 92, 104, 160, 161
Vreeswyck, 173

Wasson, R. G., 8–9, 11, 12, 20–1, 24–5, 27, 50, 62, 94, 200

water
    divine, 84, 169, 181, 190, 191
    from stone, 83–4, 196
    into wine, 49, 110, 119, 127, 201
    living, 97, 111, 120–1, 122, 132, 149, 151, 152, 159
Weston, Jessie, 159
wheels, 1, 39, 91, 101–2, 132, 176
witchcraft, 49, 62, 90, 127, 150
Wolfram von Eschenbach, 154–5, 187

Yahweh, 7, 11, 71–82, 84–90, 98, 99–101, 103–4, 108, 171, 215
Yoga, 5–6, 16–8, 23, 37, 107, 126, 162, 213
Yoga Sutras, 5, 16–7, 162, 203

Zend Avesta, 20–1
Zoroaster, 20–1
Zostrianos, 150

BOOKS OF RELATED INTEREST

PLANTS OF THE GODS
Their Sacred, Healing, and Hallucinogenic Powers
by Richard Evans Schultes, Albert Hofmann, and Christian Rätsch

THE MYSTERY OF MANNA
The Psychedelic Sacrament of the Bible
by Dan Merkur, Ph.D.

THE PSYCHEDELIC SACRAMENT
Manna, Meditations, and Mystical Experience
by Dan Merkur, Ph.D.

SOMA
The Divine Hallucinogen
by David L. Spess

DMT: THE SPIRIT MOLECULE
A Doctor's Revolutionary Research into the Biology of Near-Death
and Mystical Experiences
by Rick Strassman, M.D.

ANIMALS AND PSYCHEDELICS
The Natural World and the Instinct to Alter Consciousness
by Giorgio Samorini

SACRED MIRRORS
The Visionary Art of Alex Grey
by Alex Grey, with Ken Wilber and Carlo McCormick

TRANSFIGURATIONS
by Alex Grey

Inner Traditions • Bear & Company
P.O. Box 388
Rochester, VT 05767
1-800-246-8648
www.InnerTraditions.com

Or contact your local bookseller